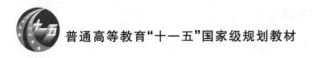
普通高等教育"十一五"国家级规划教材

Selected Articles from American & British Newspapers & Magazines
Volume I

美英报刊文章选读

上册

（第五版）

主　编	周学艺	刘满贵			
副主编	马　兴	艾久红			
编　委	袁宪军	杨小凤	艾久红	陈文玉	丁剑仪
	高天增	葛　红	郭丽萍	李素杰	李　欣
	刘满贵	刘雪燕	罗国华	马　兴	石　芸
	汪学磊	韦毅民	徐　威	杨　博	叶慧瑛
	张慧宇	赵　林	周建萍	周学艺	左　进

北京大学出版社
PEKING UNIVERSITY PRESS

图书在版编目(CIP)数据

美英报刊文章选读.上册/周学艺,刘满贵主编.—5版.—北京:北京大学出版社,2014.5
(大学美英报刊教材系列)
ISBN 978-7-301-24196-7

Ⅰ.美… Ⅱ.①周…②刘… Ⅲ.英语—阅读教学—高等学校—自学参考资料 Ⅳ.①H319.4

中国版本图书馆 CIP 数据核字(2014)第 086750 号

书　　　　名：	美英报刊文章选读(上册)(第五版)
著作责任者：	周学艺　刘满贵　主编
责 任 编 辑：	刘　强
标 准 书 号：	ISBN 978-7-301-24196-7/H・3513
出 版 发 行：	北京大学出版社
地　　　　址：	北京市海淀区成府路 205 号　100871
网　　　　址：	http://www.pup.cn　新浪官方微博:@北京大学出版社
电 子 信 箱：	zpup@pup.cn
电　　　　话：	邮购部 62752015　发行部 62750672　编辑部 62754382
	出版部 62754962
印　　刷　者：	三河市博文印刷有限公司
经　　销　者：	新华书店
	730 毫米×980 毫米　16 开本　18.75 印张　350 千字
	1994 年 12 月第 1 版　2001 年 10 月第 2 版
	2007 年 1 月第 3 版　2010 年 7 月第 4 版
	2014 年 5 月第 5 版　2021 年 6 月第 7 次印刷
定　　　　价：	42.00 元

未经许可,不得以任何方式复制或抄袭本书之部分或全部内容。
版权所有,侵权必究
举报电话：010－62752024　　电子信箱：fd@pup.pku.edu.cn

前　言

　　《美英报刊文章选读》(上、下册)首版于1987年,是迄今在全国所有英语报刊文选课本中唯一曾经教育部高校外语专业教材编审委员会英语编审小组批准的正式教材,并于次年获北京大学科研成果奖。2006年8月,它与《美英报刊导读》和《美英报刊文章阅读》(精选本)一起被列为"普通高等教育'十一五'国家级规划教材",故它为全国许多高校所采用,并受到广大英语自修者的欢迎。

　　现在出版的《美英报刊文章选读》(上、下册)第五版,与前四版一样,是供大专院校英语和新闻专业及其他涉外专业三年级以上学生使用的教材,也可供具有相应程度的从事新闻、外事等工作者及英语爱好者自修之用。此外,本书的课文注释、外加的"新闻写作""语言解说""读报知识""学习方法"及下面提到的《学习辅导》里涵盖的"标题自测""考试样题"等,对大本自考生和考研生等的考试均有重要参考价值。在这两项考试中,尤其是考研试题中报刊内容占的比例较大。

　　《美英报刊文章选读》(上、下册)和《美英报刊文章阅读》(精选本)分别为不同英文水平的高年级学生而编写。《上、下册》课文多,题材更为多样广泛,学生和授课老师对课文有更多的选择余地;《精选本》对课文的注释更为详细,并配有《学习辅导》,学生更易读懂。2009年10月出版的《大学英语报刊文选》为非英语专业用书。这三种书多数课文相同,所以,自修和初次讲授《上、下册》或《大英》者均可将《精选本》(第五版)的《学习辅导》用于参考。

　　《精选本学习辅导》的主要内容有：Summary, Background Information, Language Points, Questions and Answers for Your Reference, Words to Know, Supplementary Reading 等。此外,还有：Self-Test in Comprehension of Headlines, A Brief Iroduction to Tests in Reading Comprehension of English Newspapers & Magazines, and Sample Test.

　　为了加深对词语和课文的理解能力,扩大与课文有关的词汇量和知识面,特选定此书的教材系列之一《美英报刊导读》(第二版)(下简称《导读》)作为学生进一步的助读和学习进修教材。年轻老师可将《导读》用做参考,并可视情况将该书内容充实到课堂教学中,引导学生在阅读报刊文章时发现总结报刊语言特点,认识语言变化规律。

报刊文选有其明显的时效性,第四版出版至今已四载,其间美英国内形势已发生了很大变化,有些课文的内容已过时,为适应教学需要,特选编第五版。第五版全书共40课,更新二分之一以上,内容均配合国策。

读报基本功

阅读美英报刊可以扩大视野,增长知识,学习现代英语,了解世界,获取信息。众所周知,报刊语言具有短、新、奇、活的特点,内容贴近当前实际,不但丰富有趣,且实用性强,所以人们喜欢看报。然而,学习任何知识都必须要有基础,读外刊也不例外。本人认为,学生在中学和大学低年级的阶段首先要打好语言基础,到了大学高年级阶段,要读懂美英报刊,必须夯实两项基本功。

一、拓宽词义面和扩大词汇量

1. 拓宽常用词的词义面

新闻语言与我国学生在中学和大学低年级所学课文的规范语言不完全相同,他们所学大多是关于学习和人生哲理的一些小故事,对报刊语言很陌生,词义面也窄,一见到 run, race, juice, measure, bill, Speaker, chemistry, establishment, community 等就可能只知道是"跑""竞赛""汁""措施""账单""发言人""化学""建立""社区"等这些词的普通单一意义,而不知道从泛指到特指意义变了。如在时政文章中,这些词的意义变窄了,很可能分别为"竞选""竞选""神通""议案""法案""议长""关系""界、当权派或权势集团""共同体或社会"等词义。

1977年8月15日,《泰晤士报》载文称,在现代报纸上,一个词有五六个意思是很平常的。这就增加了读报的难度。不过,此处所谓拓宽词义面,指初学者尤其要注意常见的多义词。不能一见到 culture, interest(s), resources, story 等就想当然认为只是"文化""利益""资源"和"故事"的意思。见在下列例句里的词义:

(1) Indeed, in many regions, "forestry" is synonymous with plantation **culture**. (在许多地区,所谓林业,事实上就是森林**栽培**的同义词。)

(2) Terrorists might hit American **interests** abroad. (VOA)
(恐怖分子可能会袭击在国外的美国**机构**。)

(3) At the root of the problem is money. As a poor nation, China has few **resources** left over for cultural conversation after struggling to

overhaul its command economy, dampen rising unemployment, take care of an aging population, put an infrastructure and modernize its massive military. (*Los Angeles Times*)

(根本的问题是钱,作为一个穷国,中国没有留下多少**钱**用于文物保护……)

(4) Even as Harper was carrying out his espionage tasks, America's Polish mole was discussing the case with Harper's own Polish case officer. Later, he passed on the entire **story** to U.S. agents, including word that the Poles had received congratulations from Yuri Andropov, the late Soviet President and former KGB chief. (*U.S. News & World Report*)

(……后来,Harper 把全部**机密**都传递给了美国特工……)

书里结合课文,通过"语言解说"扩大读者词义面。例如用抽象意义的词来代表具体意义,从抽象到具体,词义有的好理解,有的艰涩难懂,presence 就是一个很好的例证。对 administration 和 establishment 等作了辨析和解说。此外,本书还指出报刊语言主要特点,其中包括修辞格中的借喻法、提喻法、隐语、委婉语等。这些都会扩大学生的词义面,提高他们对报刊语言的认识和理解。

2. 扩大词汇量

美英报刊题材广泛,内容丰富,包括政治、经济、外交、军事、法律、科技、社会、宗教、文教、旅游、时装、美容、广告、漫画等,真是上至天文下至地理,无所不包,堪称是一部活的百科全书。大学生一二年级所掌握的词汇量要读懂上述方面的文章根本不够应付,而且随着时代的快速变化,语言也与时俱进,新词如潮涌,新的表达法也不断产生。例如,围绕 2008 年美国大选,就创造出了"Bush fatigue"(因前总统小布什执政时不得人心而使人们及共和党人都对他极其厌烦)、ABB(Anybody But Bush)等。奥巴马当选前后,更多的词语杜撰出来,如 Generation O(bama)、Obamacan/Obamacon(原本支持共和党候选人的共和党人和保守派选民却把票投给了民主党自由派候选人奥巴马)、on-line Obama(靠网上筹款起家的奥氏)、Obamatum(奥氏竞选势不可挡)、New New Deal(奥政府为救市与 F. 罗斯福的"新政"既有相同也有不同的一面,故又加上一个 New 字)、smart power(美要将软硬实力结合起来运用的"巧实力")。而奥氏能上台执政归功于"It's the economy, Stupid!"此处的 stupid 无贬义,只作"提醒"之用。

所谓新词,多数都是旧词扩展引申出新义,这是读报者的难题之一。如 hardware(计算机硬件)扩大引申为"军事武器或装备",现又引申为"法";而 software 引申为"武器研发计划",五角大楼行话喻战争中的"思想",还喻"创新"及与"法"相配合的"德"和"宗教"等。再如,launch window 这个宇航术语是 20 世纪 60 年代创造的词,window 指"brief period of time",即最佳或最有利的发射时机或时段。

  本书尽可能通过比较法指出相同或类似概念的同义或同义现象的词,以及反义词,扩大学生的词汇量。如"Obama Wins a Second Term as U.S. President"这一课的 Latino 就加上(cf. Hispanic),在别的注释里 Speaker(议长)外加上 Don't get Speaker confused with speaker and spokesman;battlegrounds 加上 tossup/swing/purple states;"The Coming Conflict in the Arctic"课里的 Cold War(cf. cool/hot/shooting war)和 hard-line position(cf. hawk,dove);"Greece as Victim"课词汇和注释里将 arrogance 与 hubris 对比,Medicare 与 Medicaid 作参考,比较词义等等。另外,还通过 presence, establishment, culture 和 generation 等"语言解说",扩大学生们的词义面和增强语言的认知和分析能力。又,根据上下文,在词典和网上却查不到的词义,如 illegals 等,也作了解释(见"间谍行话"。)。

  又,本书除对"新闻写作"中"报刊语言主要特点"作了概括外,还尽可能结合课文内容加以说明。毋庸置疑,关于报刊语言特点,如爱造新词、常用委婉语、提喻法、借喻法、隐语、套语等特点,读报者是必须了解的。不然如见到本书中出现的 entitlements, Brussels, Tallahassee 就会感到茫然。

二、读报知识

  我们认为,凡语言基本功已经过关者,读懂报刊的关键是必备各类用作参考和分析语言的文化知识。也就是说,与掌握语言一样,要读报入门,必须了解美英政府的组成、体制、党派、社会、科普、宗教等重要文化知识。学英语不能仅仅局限于语言本身,还要注意积累各方面的知识。尽管电脑可以帮忙,但代替不了自己的记忆。具有比较广泛的知识,才能收到更好的学习效果。否则,许多问题语焉不详,有的文章读不透,词语理解不深。如为什么美国的政治名言是"All politics is personal"(千选、万选,都是候选人本人在竞选),而英国竞选却主要靠政党(见《导读》第五章第二节"英美政治比较")?为了说明知识的重要性,下面不妨再举四例:

  1. 有的译者不了解美国民主党内自由派是主流,共和党内保守派占多数,将 Demopublican(由 Democrat 和 Republican 拼缀而成)译为美国历史上曾经出现过的"民主共和党人"。其实它现在的词义是"民主党内的保守派"。下面例句中的 Demopublican 指 2000 年美国大选中的民主党副总统候选人利伯曼(Joseph Lieberman),黑人民权运动领袖 Jackson

批评他身为民主党人,可"与共和党人的政见共同点多于民主党人",就是这个道理。

... Jesse Jackson did a number on Lieberman, accusing him of joining with Republicans to dismantle affirmative action programs. Jackson also drew a big laugh from the crowd when he branded Lieberman " a **Demopublican** " who had more in common with Republicans than Democrats. (*The Washington Post*)

(……杰克逊批评了利伯曼,指责他与共和党人一道取消了在就业和教育上照顾黑人和妇女的计划。杰克逊在谴责他是"**民主党内的保守分子**"时,又引起了听众一阵哄堂大笑。论政见,他与共和党人的共同之处要多于民主党人。)

2.《国际先驱论坛报》在 2000 年 12 月 14 日发表的一篇题为"Decision: It's Bush"的文章中有这么一段:

Republicans narrowly retained control of the House in November. The new Senate will be split 50-50, and will include Mr. Lieberman. **But any ties will be broken by the new vice president, Mr. Cheney.**

(在十一月份大选后组成的新一届国会中,共和党仍勉强控制着众议院。在参议院,两党平分秋色,各占 50 席,而且民主党议员中还包括落选的民主党副总统候选人利伯曼。**然而,如果在表决中票数相等,出现相持不下的局面时,新任副总统切尼先生就会打破僵局,而有利于共和党。**)

此处,有的读者一定要问,为什么副总统能打破这种相持不下的局面?他不是参议员,有投票权吗?美国宪法规定,参议院议长(President of the Senate)一职由副总统兼任,在表决出现相持不下的局面时,他才有投票权。这样,问题就迎刃而解了。由此可见,这类问题光凭上下文是解决不了的,初学者必须逐渐积累和丰富读报所需的文化背景知识。

3. 1993 年 10 月 18 日,克林顿任总统不久,《时代》周刊发表了一篇题为"It's All Foreign to Clinton"的文章,开头有这么一段:

Like most people, Bill Clinton is uncomfortable with what he doesn't know and avoids dealing with it. Fortunately for him, the nation he leads usually cares more about **Madonna** than **Mogadishu**; its turn inward following the cold war's end coincides neatly with the President's passion for domestic affairs.

(像许多人一样,比尔·克林顿总统对不熟悉的事处理起来感到为难,所以总是避开。幸运的是,他所领导的国家通常关注**内政**胜过**外交**。随着冷战的结束,重点转向国内,正好与他热衷于内政巧合。)

有的学生曾问道:"怎么将歌星与地名作比较呢?"还有的学生说:

"克林顿是不是对麦当娜感兴趣？真摸不着头脑。"众所周知,"Madonna"是美国曾放荡不羁、父母都觉得有失脸面而不认她为女儿的艳星,"Mogadishu"是索马里首都。克林顿上台时遇上索马里内战,美派兵干涉,结果吃了大亏。了解这一情况后,再联系此段谈到克林顿的"passion for domestic affairs",经验老到的读者就能根据上下文定义此处的 Madonna 指的是 domestic affairs,而 Mogadishu 指 foreign affairs。记者在这里不过是玩了点文字游戏,因为这两个字都是"M"开头,押头韵(alliteration)。从此例可以看出,要学好美英报刊,还得了解"What's going on in the world"才行。

4. 1928 年美国前总统胡佛在竞选总统时提出与家长式管理和国家社会主义相对立的一套经济政策主张,他说:

We are challenged with a peacetime choice between the American system of **rugged individualism** and a European philosophy of diametrically opposed doctrines—doctrines of paternalism and state socialism.

(形势要求我们在和平时期的两种做法之间做出选择,一种是美国对企业的**不干涉**做法,另一种是与美国截然对立的欧洲家长式管理和国家社会主义那一套。)

中西文化概念不同,理解有别。rugged individual 意为具有强烈个性的人,也指住在未开发边疆者。rugged individualism 指美国民族不受拘束、自由放任的特点,与我儒家文化截然不同。用于自由企业,则不容政府干预,让市场去调节。这就是所谓的"Government is best which governs least"(要想管得好,[政府对企业]就得插手少)。此处 rugged individualism 相当于 laissez-faire([法语]：the principle of allowing private business to develop without any state control)。不过,2008 年爆发了金融和经济危机后,美国前总统里根和英国前首相撒切尔夫人所热衷的这种放任自流、无政府监督的极端保守派经济政策已遭诟病。

课　本

鉴于以上所谈的两项基本功,编者在选材时既注意趣味性,又首选具有新闻语言和文化知识两方面的文章。这样的选材原则,既基于本人多年的读报经历和体会,又符合掌握外语的规律。

美英各大报都在头版刊登国内外大事,人们看报也注重时文,学生在这方面知识却较贫乏,可多数外语专业毕业生将从事外事和教学工作。因此,本人从 1987 年至今所编写的教材课文内容,与其他同类教材的一个明显不同之处就是,不但顾及新闻的时效性,还尽量选一些新而信息量大和覆盖面广的文章，并不断地再版更新，这也是其他同类教材所不多见的。然而本人又不赞同盲目选材的做法，即一味追求材料新，今天选这篇，明天选那篇，忽视了学生最急需的是较系统的基本知识。课本，课本，一课之本，课本的优劣与学生能否通过一年半载的学习取得明显的进步关系重大。

课文不宜太浅，否则学生的学习目的会落空，教员也不能通过授课充实自己。记得2002年《21世纪（英文）报》邀请两位美国新闻学教授和我在黄山讲学时，他们中有一位谈到教学感受时说："In teaching newspapers, teachers learn more than students do."意近"教学相长"。

第五版仍保留了第四版中的若干课文。一是新闻有连续性。二是有的课文有值得学习或了解的语言或知识。三是有的文章所描写的有关国家的情况仍未过时。所以初学者切不可因其"旧"而忽视这些课文在打好基本功方面所起的作用。

为了夯实读报基本功，加深对课文的理解，编者结合课文所写的"语言解说""读报知识""学习方法"和"新闻写作"与注释和"前言"相辅相成，对学生具有指导性和启发性，能扩大他们的视野，有助于学习研究新闻语言。"语言解说"重点对媒体理解不当和学生易误解的如 presence, culture, establishment, administration 等加以指明。"读报知识"对美国总统选举、英国人缘何拥护君主制等作了介绍。"学习方法"主要是读懂标题和名师指导词语学习和记忆法等。"新闻写作"指出了报刊若干写作法和语言主要特点。这并非要求学生立即习作，对其而言，要学好报刊，首先要读懂课文，而了解新闻写作特点又有益于读透文章。

众所周知，再新的课文也赶不上时事的发展，不久就会成为明日黄花。为此，在教学过程中如逢"9·11"恐怖袭击、伊拉克战争或全球金融危机这样的大事，授课教师也可酌情选上一二篇作为补充，但不宜多，应坚持以课本为主，让学生打好读报基础。

教 和 学

根据编者的教学经验和我国多数学生的实际英文水平，对一般高校而言，本书的授课既不要将它做精读，也不宜做泛读。做精读会妨碍授课的进度，做泛读恐学生难度太大而不易读懂。凡是到英美国家学习过的人都知道，他们在教学中很注重"量"，一二节课后教员所布置的课外读物和作业一大堆。我国外语教学往往过于注重"质"或"精"。本人主张走中间道路，即质和量并重。为此编者建议，每星期两课时教一篇课文外，根据不同学校学生的英语水平，本科生还要自修一篇。自修的课文应易于课堂上所授课文,授课老师和自修生可以根据不同情况,选择学习本教材中不同难度的课文。

教员授课时应以学生为中心,鼓励他们自己去探索和获取知识。上课时,教师可要求学生先回答 Pre-reading Questions,引导他们对课文的题材感兴趣,进入主题后,再学课文就较容易。同时,这还能促使他们预习和练习口语。接着再逐段或跳跃式选段对学生需要掌握的内容、新闻词语和背景知识进行阅读和问答——启发式讲解。如果备课充分,学生的英语水平又高,教员可采用美英教员教授母语的方法,抛开课本,以《导读》作参考,只讲有关课文的内容、重点词语、背景及写作手法等。这样,学生除预习外,课后还要结合教员在课堂上所讲的内容好好复习课文。这两种授课方式的好处是,使学生通过自学和教师的启发性指导能举一反三,自己主动去掌握知识。与以教员为中心的灌输式教育法相比,学生更能巩固所学,发挥学习潜能。当然,这只是本人的实践和看法。我相信在调动学生主动学习的积极性方面还有更多、更好的教学法。

与中小学阶段不同的是,大学生一定要养成预习或自习的习惯,课前自己先看两遍。第一遍是粗读,快速浏览全文,结合标题,掌握本课的主要内容,并能回答课文前的 Pre-reading Questions。第二遍为细读,通过上下文猜测生词词义,掌握各段内容,并能基本回答习题的 Questions。

读者在学习了这套报刊文选后,借助《导读》和《当代英汉美英报刊词典》,可以先看美英报纸上文字较浅显易懂的报道性文章,然后再看新闻周刊和社评类体裁文章。这样,他们就能独自走上一条读懂报刊之路,这是我们编写此书的最终目的。(详见《导读》"读报经验教训谈")

此外,学生应在平时培养关心时事的兴趣,要听广播和上网,以便随时能学习和积累语言和读报知识。

众所周知,与以往相比,网络使更多人能读懂报刊,对学习起着不可或缺的作用。然而,凡事都有两面,我们不能由此而沉浸在网上阅读文章。须知,那只是 superficial reading,而在纸上能 deep reading,经过思考记忆,获得的知识才牢固。"数字阅读,人变浅薄。"这是以色列一项教学调研得出的结论。

全书课文均取材于美英报刊,编者相信,使用本书的读者和授课教师对其内容能够作出正确的判断,这是不言而喻的。

本书定会有错误或不妥之处,衷心希望读者不吝赐教。

周学艺
2013 年秋于北大燕北园
E-mail:zhou_xueyi@sina.com

Contents

美英主要新闻报刊简介 …………………………………………… 1

Unit One
China（Ⅰ）

Lesson One
Text　China Opens Doors of State-run Companies to World's Top Talent
　　　（中国国企为世界高端人才敞开大门）
　　　(*The Washington Post*, November 16, 2011) …………… 1
新闻写作　何谓 News ………………………………………… 8

Lesson Two
Text　A Race We Can All Win
　　　（中国发展：美中双赢的竞赛）
　　　(*Newsweek*, December 31, 2007) …………………… 11
新闻写作　导语 ……………………………………………… 16

Lesson Three
Text　An American in Beijing
　　　（中国经济迅猛发展，留学生蜂拥而至）
　　　(*Time*, April 4, 2008) ……………………………… 19
语言解说　Presence ………………………………………… 27

Unit Two
China（Ⅱ）

Lesson Four
Text　Tiger Mom ... Meet Panda Dad
　　　（熊猫爸爸挑战虎妈育儿经）
　　　(*The Wall Street Journal*, March 29, 2011) ………… 30
新闻写作　新闻体裁 ………………………………………… 39

Lesson Five
    Text Home at Last
         （海外学子回国创业）
         (*Newsweek*, July 31, 2000) ·················· 41
    语言解说 名词定语及理解上的陷阱 ············ 48

Lesson Six
    Text China Finds Western Ways Bring New Woes
         （西方生活方式给国人带来新的苦恼）
         (*USA Today*, May 19, 2004) ··············· 50
    新闻写作 报刊文体 ···························· 58

Unit Three
United States(Ⅰ)

Lesson Seven
    Text Debt Burden Alters Outlook for US Graduates
         （求学负债：美国毕业生前景堪忧）
         (*The Financial Times*, June 1, 2012) ········ 60
    语言解说 金融危机催生新词 ··················· 68

Lesson Eight
    Text Is an Ivy League Diploma Worth It?
         （上常春藤名校，值吗？）
         (*The Wall Street Journal*, November 8, 2011) ········ 72
    读报知识 Ivy League, Seven Sisters &
               Russel Group ······················ 78

Lesson Nine
    Text Five Myths about the American Dream
         （关于美国梦的五种误读）
         (*The Washington Post*, January 6, 2012) ······· 79
    新闻写作 报刊语言主要特点 ··················· 86

Unit Four
United States(Ⅱ)

Lesson Ten
    Text Pentagon Digs In on Cyberwar Front

（五角大楼构筑网络战争攻防体系）
(*The Wall Street Journal*, July 9, 2012) ·············· 89
读报知识　美英等国情治机构简介 ······················ 96

Lesson Eleven

　　Text　Spies Among US: Modern-Day Espionage
　　　　（现代间谍就在我们身边活动）
　　　　(*The Daily Beast*, July 21, 2010) ·············· 99
　　语言解说　间谍行话 ······································ 108

Lesson Twelve

　　Text　Terrorized by "War on Terror"
　　　　（反恐,反恐,越反越恐）
　　　　(*The Washington Post*, March 25, 2007) ·············· 111
　　语言解说　Culture/Cultural ······························ 124

Unit Five
United States（Ⅲ）

Lesson Thirteen

　　Text　Obama Wins a Second Term as U.S. President
　　　　（奥巴马连任总统：任重道险）
　　　　(*The Washington Post*, November 7, 2012) ·············· 126
　　读报知识　美国总统选举 ································ 136

Lesson Fourteen

　　Text　The Economy Sucks. But Is It '92 Redux?
　　　　（经济不振,难道08年大选是92年的翻版吗?）
　　　　(*Newsweek*, January 21, 2008) ·············· 139
　　语言解说　Stupid 和 Technical(ly) ·············· 155

Lesson Fifteen

　　Text　Is America's New Declinism for Real?
　　　　（美国现在真的衰落了吗?）
　　　　(*The Financial Times*, November 24, 2008) ·············· 157
　　语言解说　Establishment ································ 165

Lesson Sixteen

　　Text　Iraq: Who Won the War?

（伊拉克战争：谁是赢家？）
(*The Independent*, March 16, 2008) ……………… 168
语言解说　Political Donation/Contribution ……………… 182

Unit Six
Britain

Lesson Seventeen

  Text Little Sympathy for Margaret Thatcher among Former Opponents
    （铁娘子离世，反对派欢呼）
    (*The Guardian*, April 8, 2013) ……………… 184
 读报知识　英国政党简介 ……………… 192

Lesson Eighteen

  Text Britain's Embattled Newspapers Are Leading the World in Innovation
    （英国报纸引领全球改革潮流）
    (*The Economist*, Jan 6, 2011) ……………… 194
 学习方法　读懂标题（Ⅰ）……………… 201

Lesson Nineteen

  Text Mrs. Windsor, Anyone?
    （君主制废留之争）
    (*The Financial Times*, June 2, 2012) ……………… 203
 读报知识　英国人缘何拥护君主制 ……………… 220

Lesson Twenty

  Text Stealing a Nation
    （英美狼狈为奸，霸占他国，撵走百姓）
    (*New African*, November, 2006) ……………… 223
 读报知识　英国政府部门及官职 ……………… 234

Unit Seven
Prominent Figures of the U.S. and Britain

Lesson Twenty-one

  Text He's Back All Right, Now with a Memoir
    （施瓦辛格回忆录：令人难以置信的传奇故事）

    (*The New York Times*, September 30, 2012) ············ 237
 学习方法 读懂标题(Ⅱ) ·· 248

Lesson Twenty-two
 Text Bill Gates is retiring, sort of
    (世界首富盖茨退休了吗?)
    (*International Herald Tribune*, June 27, 2008) ········ 251
 学习方法 读懂标题(Ⅲ) ··· 261

Lesson Twenty-three
 Text He's Just Like You and Me, Except for the £31bn Fortune
    (股神巴菲特的成功之道)
    (*The Sunday Times*, March 9, 2008) ···················· 263
 语言解说 Mentor 和 Guru 等 ··· 275

美英主要新闻报刊简介

美国和英国的日报总数约两三千家，其中绝大多数是地方性报纸，全国性大报极少。美英各种期刊多达一万余种，其中多数是专业性和商务消费类刊物。下面分别简要介绍若干在美英国内外有影响的新闻报刊。

美 国 报 刊

美国报纸大体上可分为两种类型：通俗小报（tabloid）面向一般市民；大报讲究质量，力求吸引知识界。小报为了迎合读者兴趣、追求轰动效应，对天灾人祸、罢工等新闻，挖空心思配上煽情的标题，对性、暴力、明星私生活则尽情渲染，配以大量图片，以招引读者，忽视了社会责任，结果降低了质量。发行量虽大，对重大问题却缺乏深远的影响力。严肃而高质量的大报，销量不及小报，影响力却大。

1. The New York Times《纽约时报》，1851 年创刊。属苏兹贝格（Sulzberger）家族所有。同《华盛顿邮报》和《洛杉矶时报》一起被列为美国最有影响的三家大报。它内容充实，资料齐全，拥有一批名记者，因而有"博大精深，当之无愧为美国第一大报"之说。在评选优秀报纸的民意测验中，曾多次夺冠，同时，也是获美国最高新闻奖"普利策奖"（the Pulitzer Prize）最多的一家美国报纸，订户遍及国内外。为了招徕更多的客户，2001 年发行网络版。

《纽约时报》一贯标榜客观和公正，其报铭是，"刊登一切适合刊登的新闻"（All the News That's Fit to Print），但现在政府以爱国为名不让其自由行事。该报常用较大篇幅刊登政府重要文件和领导人讲话，不时发表一些批评政府政策的报道和评论，并在政府默许下披露一些内幕和机密。它与东部权势集团渊源较深，所报道和评述的国际新闻基本上反映美国政府的外交政策及其动向。它虽有"执美国舆论之牛耳"之说，然而这家有着 160 余年历史的报纸，2003 年却因报道两条假新闻出丑，信誉受损。后来又东山再起，2009 和 2010 年获多项普奖。

其主要读者是美国政界、工商界和知识界等上层人士。日发行量约一百多万份，在美国日报排行榜上名列第三。

2. The Washington Post《华盛顿邮报》，1877 年创刊。注重报道国会

消息，号称"国会议员和政府官员早餐桌上少不了的一份报纸"。与《纽约时报》一样，曾多次揭发政府丑闻。如导致尼克松下台的水门事件(Watergate)和副总统阿格纽(Spiro Agnew)丢官的索贿案。2013年它又首先在美刊载斯诺顿(Edward Snowden)揭发情报机构的窃听事件。

该报原属格雷厄姆(Graham)家族所有，因在网络时代处境艰难，已于2013年8月卖给了亚马逊创始人贝索斯(Jeff Bezos)。

邮报还出版小开张的全国性周末版(The Washington Post National Weekly Edition)。发行量名列第五。

3. Los Angeles Times《洛杉矶时报》，1881年创刊。号称美国最有影响的三大报之一，是西部老大。在20世纪50年代，曾因竭力支持尼克松竞选总统而引起美国政界重视，随后一跃成为全国有影响的大报。自由派色彩较浓。先前属洛克菲勒家族所有，后被芝加哥论坛报集团收购。该报销量排名第四。

4. USA Today《今日美国报》，由甘内特报业集团(Gannet Co., Inc)创办于1983年，是美国唯一的全国性日报，因为其他报纸都冠以New York, Washington和Los Angles等地方色彩的字眼。它利用通信卫星在全美各地同时印刷和发行，彩色技术的运用使美国其他报纸纷纷效仿。

该报报道翔实而不浮夸。原以国内新闻为主，较少刊载国际新闻，为迎合大众化趣味，一味模仿电视。为此而付出了巨大的经济代价，后来改变了这一倾向。在2009年，发行量退居第二。

5. The Wall Street Journal《华尔街日报》，创刊于1889年。社址在美国金融中心纽约市华尔街附近，几年前由美籍澳大利亚媒体大亨默多克(Rupert Murdoch)买下该报及其母公司"道-琼斯公司"(Dow Jones & Company Inc.)，以报道经济方面动态为主，是金融企业家必读的报纸。2009年，发行量夺回排名第一的位置。次年即叫板《纽约时报》。

"道-琼斯公司"与香港《南华早报》(South China Morning Post)、日本《经济新闻》和新加坡及马来西亚的《海峡时报》(Straits Times)合股，于1976年在香港出版《亚洲华尔街日报》(The Asian Wall Street Journal)，行销亚洲各地。

6. International New York Times《国际纽约时报》，2013年10月15日由《国际先驱论坛报》改为现名，旨在提高《纽约时报》在全球的吸引力。早在1963年，由《华盛顿邮报》与《纽约时报》及原来的《纽约先驱论坛报》(The New York Herald Tribune)联手在巴黎出版，行销欧亚各地。后来由前两家合办，并发行亚洲版。2002年变为《纽约时报》一家独办。主要读者群是在海外工作的美国人和讲英语的移民，影响力远大于发行量。

美英主要新闻报刊简介

7. *The Christian Science Monitor*《基督教科学箴言报》,1908年在美国波士顿创刊,由美国基督教教会创始人艾娣(Mary Eddy)(1821—1910)任社长。旨在抑制当时黄色报刊耸人听闻的新闻浪潮。历来少登犯罪及灾祸等消息,一贯拒绝刊登烟酒广告,以示忠于教义。以精心处理新闻报道、对国际问题分析透彻和具有独到之处而著称,以往常入选美国十大名报。因资金不足,1989年缩减版面,削减栏目,影响力大不如前。2009年后仅出网络版。

8. *Time*《时代》周刊,1923年创刊于纽约,由时代—华纳出版公司(Time-Warner Inc.)出版(近年来时代已兼并CNN和AOL[美国在线],后来又与AOL分离)。它是美国三大新闻周刊中最成功的一家,影响和发行量也最大。除发行国内版、军队版、大学生版外,还发行国外版。国外版又分欧洲版、亚洲版和拉丁美洲版。

《时代》以报道精彩、及时,分析问题深刻和文字新颖取胜,自称是"现代英文的代表"。每期除综述一周国内外重大时事外,还对经济、科技、音乐、文教、宗教、艺术、人物、书刊、体育等方面的新闻精选整理,综合分析和评述,并配以插图和背景材料分类刊出,使之较一般报纸报道更具有深度,但又不是这些方面专业性杂志,旨在让没有时间天天读报的"忙人"了解世事。政治上较保守,倾向于共和党。

9. *Newsweek*《新闻周刊》,创刊于1933年,新闻周刊公司原属华盛顿邮报公司。2010年8月,被美国一位亿万富翁买下,并在2013年只出电子版。同年8月又被IBT媒体集团收购,并于次年重启纸质版。在订阅等方面以《经济学家》为榜样,不再与原来的竞争对手《时代》周刊相仿。

《新闻周刊》除了有名记者综述重大事件和报道、评论白宫新闻外,原来还聘请国外的名记者撰写专栏评论。

10. *U.S. News & World Report*《美国新闻与世界报道》,周刊,1948年由 *The United States News*,*World Report* 和 *U.S. Weekly* 三家刊物合并而成。与《时代》周刊和《新闻周刊》并称为美国三大新闻周刊。

该刊着重登载美国政治、经济、军事和国防问题等综合性报道与评论。专题报道美国国内问题和对官方人物的访问是其一大特色。文字较上述两份周刊浅显易懂。

11. *Reader's Digest*《读者文摘》,创刊于1922年。号称资本主义世界发行量最大的月刊。用英、德、法、西、意、日、中、阿拉伯等17种语言在几十个国家和地方出版。在国内发行量为1,800万份,居国内各杂志之首。在国外发行量为1,200万份。

该杂志原以摘取书刊的报道为主,现在文摘只占60%,其余为本刊或特邀记者所写文章。编辑方针是"每月从一流杂志选出文章,去粗取精,力求紧凑,兴味永存"。每期内容广泛,从国内外政治、社会、科学到生活琐事,无所不包。体裁活泼,有小说、散文、日记、小品、游记等。另一特色是利用文末到处补白,插以警语、箴言、座右铭、笑话等。此外,为帮助读者扩大词汇量,还辟有"Word Power"栏,独具一格。

12. *Fortune* 前译《幸福》,现译《财富》杂志,创刊于 1930 年,由时代—华纳公司在芝加哥出版。原为月刊,1978 年改为双周刊。以丰富专业知识为背景,对各行各业的经营,做深入研究报道,极具权威性。尤其是每年 5 月第一周刊登的美国企业 500 强排行榜(The Fortune 500)、8 月第二周刊登的外国企业 500 强排行榜(The Fortune 500 Outside the U.S.)、外国 50 家最大的银行排行榜(The Largest Banks Outside the U.S.)及全球 50 家最大的工业公司排行榜(The Largest Industrial Companies in the World)最具权威性。此外,有时还发表一些有分量的外交及军事方面的文章。

13. *Business Week*《商业周刊》,创刊于 1929 年。向全世界发行,每期约 95 万份。总部设在纽约,是美国著名财政企业杂志。国内版主要报道和评论美国的商业、经济、金融、贸易、企业经营和管理等方面,同时也报道一些世界经济和商业动态以及美国公司海外活动。1980 年创办国际版,栏目与国内版类似,以海外经济为主。

14. *Far Eastern Economic Review*《远东经济评论》,创办于 1946 年,周刊,在香港出版。1997 年香港回归中国后,业主易人,由道-琼斯公司出版。主要报道和评论远东国家和地区的经济,但也发表政治、军事等方面文章。语言较《时代》周刊等浅显些。订户主要是该地区的公司,其次是投资和关注该地区的美欧公司。

英 国 报 刊

英国报刊发行与美国不尽相同,国内外财团控制的大报业集团的报纸占全英发行量的 90%,这些大集团以往又都集中在伦敦市中心的"舰队街"(Fleet Street)。因此,Fleet Street 原本常用来借喻伦敦或英国"报界"或"新闻界",今天已风光不再。为了改善发行和促进海外销售,有的已迁往伦敦其他地区或外地城市,甚至到了海外,如《卫报》在德国发行国际版,《金融时报》直接在德国、美国和日本等国印刷发行。现在英国各报已纷纷缩小开张,但这与大报和小报无关,是两个概念。

英报按风格和内容分为 quality/popular/mid-market papers,"质量类"报纸是严肃性的全国性日报,编辑水平高,读者对象是受过较高教育的上层和中产阶级人士。星期日各大报都单独出版,报名加上 Sunday,以示区别。*Daily Express*《每日快报》、*Daily Mail*《每日邮报》、*Daily Mirror*《每日镜报》、*Daily Star*《每日明星报》和 *The Sun*《太阳报》都是"通俗类"小报,消息不如 quality papers 那样严肃可靠,往往追求轰动效应。如《太阳报》就以登载英国王室成员和政界人士的桃色新闻和美女照片而"著称",发行量居首位,读者基本是工人阶级和中产阶级。"中间市场类"指介于这两者之间的报纸。下面介绍英国国内外有影响的几家质量类报刊和三份杂志。

1. The Times《泰晤士报》,创刊于1785年,是英国一家历史最悠久的报纸,也是一家西方最有影响的大报。读者为统治阶级、高级知识分子和工商、金融界人士。虽标榜"独立",其实政治观点中间偏右,支持保守党的政策或主张多些。英国有所谓"掌权者读《泰晤士报》"一说。该报的"读者来信"栏(Letters to the Editor)办得特别出色,许多知名人士在这个非正式论坛高谈阔论,对舆论有很大影响,大都代表当权派观点。

《泰晤士报》在世界各地派有记者,以较大篇幅报道和评论国际、国内重大新闻。过去曾由于内容过分严肃,不符合一般读者的趣味,因而发行量下降,利润锐减。1978年底曾因劳资纠纷和经济问题停刊一年之久。1981年,英国九大报业集团之一的国际新闻社(News International)老板、美籍澳大利亚媒体大王默多克从加拿大财阀汤姆森(Kenneth Thomson)手中买下该报。

《泰晤士报》有几种以周刊形式出版的副刊,其中《泰晤士报文学副刊》(Times Literary Supplement)认为是英国最有影响的一家文学周刊,刊载的文章和书评具有权威性。

《泰晤士报》发行量平日近30万份,在英国质量类报纸中排名第五。星期日无报,由《星期日泰晤士报》(The Sunday Times)补缺,俗称"The London Times"和"The Thunderer"。在美国,该报又称 The London Times 或 The Times of London,以区别于 The New York Times 和 Los Angles Times 的简称"The Times"。

2. Financial Times《金融时报》,1888年创刊,是皮尔逊上市公司(Pearson plc)(培生集团)旗下一份国际性大报,也是世界上有代表性的一家金融商情报纸。在英国有"大老板们读《金融时报》"一说。各国政府、大企业家、银行和大学、研究机构均重视该报的报道与评论。政治上中间偏右。

《金融时报》着重报道财政、金融和工商等方面的消息、问题研究和动向。有时攻击英国政府的金融政策,因而往往影响官员的金融思想。它是英国每天提供伦敦股票市场的金融指教的唯一日报,因此闻名遐迩,在政治、文化等方面也发表文章与评论。重视国际消息,派驻海外的记者多,日发行量多年来一直称雄英国质量类报纸。

3. *The Guardian*《卫报》，创刊于1821年，原名《曼彻斯特卫报》(*The Manchester Guardian*)。20世纪50年代末，迁至伦敦，去掉"Manchester"带地方色彩的字眼，同《泰晤士报》、《每日电讯报》和《金融时报》构成英国质量类报纸的"四巨头"。英国有"有掌权欲者读《卫报》"一说。政治上中间偏左，倾向工党。主要读者群是中产阶级。

2013年6月，美国前情报机构雇员斯诺登(Edward Snowden)首先在香港将美国对全球的监控事件透露给《卫报》，该报登载后名声大振。

4. *The Daily Telegraphy*《每日电讯报》，创刊于1855年，原为一家"通俗类(popular)"报纸，20世纪70年代后期成为"质量类"报纸。在英国有"怀念昔日大英帝国时代者读《每日电讯报》"一说。该报常反映中间偏左的政治观点。

5. *The Independent*《独立报》，1986年创办，是英国资历最浅的日报，属于Tony O'Reilly 的 Independent News & Media 集团。与中间偏右的《泰晤士报》和中间偏左的《卫报》相比，《独立报》政治上较中立。

6. *The Economist*《经济学家》，创刊于1843年，是英国大型综合性周刊，与《金融时报》同属皮尔逊父子公司(S. Pearson & Son, Ltd)，是《金融时报》报业集团的台柱，名气很大。每期一半篇幅刊载国际政治及时事文章，社论深受广泛重视。另一半专刊工商、金融、科学及书评。通常支持保守党观点，只是偶尔支持工党。

该刊撰稿不署名，不搞"文责自负"，以示刊物对每篇文章负责。也不搞花哨的版面，以精彩的文章及准确的统计数字和图表来吸引高知读者，国际信誉卓著，是英国十大重要而畅销杂志中的佼佼者。

7. *The Spectator*《旁观者》，1828年创刊，全国性周刊中历史最悠久的杂志，面向高级知识分子。公开支持保守党，反对工党的政策。对英国亲美疏欧的外交政策，常提出批评。在英国十大重要而畅销的杂志中名列第三。

8. *New Statesman*《新政治家》周刊，1913年创办，公开支持、宣传工党的政策和主张，是其喉舌。

Unit One
China（Ⅰ）

Lesson One

课文导读

针对科研和技术人才缺口持续扩大的弊端,中国政府提出了人才优先发展的战略布局,旨在努力提升劳动人口的教育水平,发展创新经济,实现从"中国制造"型向"中国创造"型经济转变。"千人计划"就是一个人才发展项目,旨在吸纳外国专家和中国的海外学子来华工作,引导技术创新,以提升中国工业领域的竞争力。同样,中国为他们提供优厚的薪资待遇和永久居住签证。作者呼吁美国重视中国这一人才战略,但也客观地分析了中国现存的不尽如人意的科研环境以及引进人才战略面临的挑战。作者在提出质疑的同时,也引导我们思考一个问题:显然,单凭引进外智和吸引回国人员解决不了创新问题,那么中国创新的出路又在哪里?

Pre-reading Questions

1. How do you see the prospect of China's development?
2. What is mostly needed for China's innovation?

Text

China Opens Doors of State-run Companies[1] to World's Top Talent
By Vivek Wadhwa[2]

1   The top talent in countries around the world have a new suitor: the Chinese government.

2   China has a severe shortage of skilled talent and, in a policy reversal[3], has decided to open its doors to talent from around the world. This could mean that the brilliant NASA[4] scientists the U.S. laid off, could find new employment—and a new home—in Shanghai or Beijing.

3   Chinese research labs have long had difficulty recruiting qualified workers to perform necessary research and development, and its corporations struggle to find competent managers. The situation will likely get worse as China's high-tech industries grow and it increases its national R&D[5] spending from the present 1.62 percent of GDP, according to the Chinese government, to the planned 2.5 percent by 2020. China's President Hu Jintao, in May 2010, declared talent development a national priority in order to fill the void. The goal is to dramatically increase the education level of China's workforce and to build an innovation economy[6].

4   China has launched several high-priority programs to encourage skilled Chinese to return home—all in an effort to meet the country's pressing talent demands. One of these programs is the "Thousand Foreign Talents Program[7]." The program's goal is to bring 2,000 experienced engineers, scientists, and other experts of Chinese origin back from the West. The government also announced that it aims to cultivate 100 "strategic entrepreneurs"[8] who can lead Chinese firms getting into the ranks of the world's top 500 countries.

5   Both efforts are running ahead of target according to Dr. Huiyao Wang[9], the Director General of the Center for China and Globalization[10] and an advisor to the Chinese government. China had recruited more than 1,500 "high quality talents," according to Wang, and 300 returnees had been enrolled in management training courses by August 2011. The courses were conducted by senior ministers. These individuals, while re-learning how to operate successfully within the Chinese system, are expected to serve as a critical catalyst in transforming China's innovation environment in ways that will enhance the country's competitive edge[11] across a range of key, strategic industries.

6   China is getting more ambitious, based on the initial recruitment

successes of the returnee program.

7   The Chinese government invited me to attend the International Conference on the "Exchange of Talent" held in Shenzhen on Nov. 5. Vice Premier, Zhang Dejiang launched China's "Thousand Foreign Talents Program," which, for the first time, opens China's doors to skilled foreigners to secure long-term employment in China. The Chinese government announced that it will allow foreign nationals to take senior roles in science and technology sectors and state-owned enterprises. They will also pay foreigners salaries equal to what they can earn at top paying jobs in America. And the government announced that it intends to offer permanent resident-type visas to foreign entrepreneurs.

8   This announcement was front-page news in China, and its importance should not be underestimated in the U.S. where these developments were not widely covered. These programs, which were announced with amazing fanfare, represent a significant break from the traditional "use Chinese" policies and a greater openness to the outside world. Chinese governors and senior officials from across the country participated in the ceremonies, and the Chinese government claimed the conference had 100,000 attendees. The festivities that accompanied this were nothing short of dazzling, with cultural entertainers and acrobats brought in from all over China.

9   Denis Fred Simon, author and Vice-Provost for International Affairs at the University of Oregon was one of the nine foreign experts at the Shenzhen conference. China, said Simon, sees talent as the next big global race for driving competitiveness and innovation. The country is determined to win this race if only to ensure it can complete the goal of transforming its economy. Wang also explained that the Chinese see this new talent pool as the key to moving from a "made in China" orientation to a "created in China" capability[12]. China's future growth, continued Wang, will rely more on the new talent strategy, even as its past successes were built mainly on its population dividend and investment.

10   But sometimes things aren't as rosy as they seem.

11   Some of the returnees have found themselves victims of discrimination and petty jealousy from those who stayed behind. Moreover, they have struggled to re-adapt to China's relationship-oriented culture[13], which stands in sharp contrast to the performance-oriented culture[14] of the West. Compared

to the generally transparent set of rules and decision-making processes that are commonplace in U.S. and European research and university settings, returnees are frequently confounded by the "personalized" ways research proposals are evaluated and research grants are distributed. The reality is that despite the good intentions of the program, the Chinese research environment remains plagued by plagiarism, fraud, and other scandals.

12　　There is an even greater challenge, however. Returnees are refusing to make full-time commitments to their new Chinese employers. Many have returned only sporadically, often not meeting the stated residency requirements of the Thousand Talents Program.

13　　The best of the Chinese talent pool abroad has not yet chosen to return to China, especially in the science and technology fields, said Simon. Some who were considering returning home, he said, are still watching and waiting as their peers cope with the challenges of returning. Family considerations also pose an important barrier, said Simon, as many Chinese expatriates based overseas would prefer their children to complete their education abroad and not have to suffer through China's "examination hell" prior to college.

14　　Discussions with Chinese government leaders in Shenzhen made it clear that Chinese leaders are not satisfied with the level of innovation in the country. I told them that I didn't believe that China could fix this problem merely through returnees. China would need to learn some of the techniques that Indian industry has employed to upgrade its workforce. China's most critical challenge will be to create a more conducive environment for entrepreneurship. Innovation requires risk-taking, breaking existing systems and challenging the norms. Within Hu Jintao's model of a "harmonious" society (what he calls "hexie shehui"), this presents some real challenges.

15　　Until China allows and encourages more "out of the box[15]" thinking and behavior, it simply won't innovate, nor will it produce the types of breakthrough products top Chinese leaders wish to see coming out of China's research labs and key enterprises. (From *The Washington Post*, November 16, 2011)

New Words

acrobat /'ækrəbæt/ *n.* one that performs gymnastic feats requiring skillful control of the body 杂技演员

attendee /ˌæten'diː/ *n.* a person who is present on a given occasion or at a given place 出席人

catalyst /'kætəlɪst/ *n.* sth that causes an important event to happen 催化剂；刺激因素

commonplace /'kɒmənpleɪs/ *adj.* ordinary; unremarkable 司空见惯的

conducive /kən'djuːsɪv/ *adj.* tending to promote or assist 有益的，有助于的

confound /kən'faʊnd/ *v.* to confuse and surprise by being unexpected 感到震惊

dazzling /'dæzlɪŋ/ *adj.* amazingly impressive 炫目的，非凡的

dividend /'dɪvɪdend/ *n.* a sum of money paid to shareholders of a corporation out of earnings; advantage 股息；利益；好处

enhance /ɪn'hɑːns/ *v.* to increase or improve in value, quality, desirability or attractiveness 增强，使强化

entertainer /ˌentə'teɪnə(r)/ *n.* one who tries to please or amuse 娱乐人士，使他人快活的人

entrepreneur /ˌɒntrəprə'nɜː(r)/ *n.* one who organizes, manages, and assumes the risks of a business or enterprise 企业家

expatriate /ˌeks'pætrɪət/ *n.* one who lives in a foreign land 身处异国他乡的人

fanfare /'fænfeə(r)/ *n.* a lot of publicity or advertising 炫耀，大张旗鼓的宣传

fraud /frɔːd/ *n.* deceit; trickery, or intentional deception 欺骗

norm /nɔːm/ *n.* a standard or model or pattern regarded as typical 规范

orientation /ˌɔːriən'teɪʃn/ *n.* a usually general or lasting direction of thought, inclination, or interest 方向；定位

peer /pɪə(r)/ *n.* one that is of equal standing with another 同等的人，同龄人

petty /'petɪ/ *adj.* marked by or reflective of narrow interests and sympathies; narrow-minded 小气的

plagiarism /'pleɪdʒərɪzəm/ *n.* an act or instance of plagiarizing 剽窃

plague /pleɪg/ *v.* to cause continual discomfort, suffering, or trouble to 使人痛苦，受罪

pool /puːl/ *n.* a supply of money, goods, workers or other resources, which is shared between and may be used by a number of people 共用的资源(钱、物品、人力等)
priority /praɪˈprətɪ/ *n.* sth that needs attention, consideration, service etc, before others 优先考虑的事
Provost /ˈprəʊvəʊst/ *n.* the head of certain colleges (某些学院的)院长
reversal /rɪˈvɜːsəl/ *n.* an act of changing from one state to the opposite state 逆转
recruit /rɪˈkruːt/ *v.* to fill up the number of (as an army) with new members 招募
returnee /rɪtəˈniː/ *n.* a person who returns 海归,还乡者
rosy /ˈrəʊzɪ/ *adj.* characterized by or tending to promote optimism 乐观的
scandal /ˈskændl/ *n.* loss of or damage to reputation caused by actual or apparent violation of morality or propriety 丑闻 (*cf.* affair; -gate)
sector /ˈsektə(r)/ *n.* a part of a field of activity, esp. of business, trade etc (尤指商业、贸易等的)部门;界;领域,行业
sporadically /spəˈrædɪklɪ/ *adv.* appearing or happening at irregular intervals; occasionally 零星地,偶尔地
suitor /ˈsuːtə(r)/ *n.* one who courts a woman or seeks to marry her 追求女性欲与其结婚者
transparent /trænsˈpærənt/ *adj.* easily detected or seen through 透明的
vice-provost *n.* (大学)副校长
void /vɔɪd/ *n.* the empty area or space 空白
workforce /ˈwɜːkˌfɔːs/ *n.* the force of workers available 劳动力

Notes

1. state-run company—国营企业
2. Vivek Wadhwa—美国杜克大学普拉特工程学院主任、哈佛大学法学院访问学者,商业创新领域的著名学者,曾经创立过两家科技公司,同时他还是美国商业周刊(*Business Week*)的专栏作家。
3. policy reversal—政策转型 Here, it refers to a change of policy from encouraging Chinese students to study abroad to opening the door to talent from around the world.
4. NASA—*abbrev.* National Aeronautics and Space Administration—美国国家航空和宇宙航行局 Started in 1958, it is the agency of the

United States government that is responsible for the nation's civilian space program and for aeronautics and aerospace research. Since February 2006, NASA's mission statement has been to "pioneer the future in space exploration, scientific discovery and aeronautics research."

5. R&D——研究与发展 abbrev. research and development
6. innovation economy——创新经济,是指以信息革命和经济全球化为背景,以知识和人才为依托,以创新为主要推动力,保持快速、健康发展的经济。
7. "Thousand Foreign Talents Program."——海外高层次人才引进计划,简称"千人计划"。该计划主要是围绕国家发展战略目标,从2008年开始,在国家重点创新项目、学科、实验室以及中央企业和国有商业金融机构、以高新技术产业开发区为主的各类园区等,引进2000名左右人才并有重点地支持一批能够突破关键技术、发展高新产业、带动新兴学科的战略科学家和领军人才来华创新创业。
8. "strategic entrepreneurs"——战略企业家。中国在2010年提出中央企业人才工作的重点是要培养100名左右战略企业家,即拥有大局观念和战略思维、忠实维护国有资产权益、引领企业做强做大的出资人代表队伍。
9. Dr. Huiyao Wang——王辉耀博士,中国与全球化研究中心主任。
10. Center for China and Globalization——CCG,中国与全球化研究中心 an independent, non-profit think tank based in Beijing. CCG conducts research in a range of social science areas including world affairs, international talent issues, sustainable development, entrepreneurship and globalization. It was founded by a number of returned scholars from the west together with the Policy Advisory Committee(政策顾问委员会)of the China Western Returned Scholars Association(WRSA,欧美同学会). Its aim is to utilise its "pool of first-class scholars, business leaders and experts in government, to address issues on how best to position China in a globalized world".
11. competitive edge——优势,领先 the strategic advantage one business entity has over its rival entities within its competitive industry. Achieving competitive advantage strengthens and positions a business better within the business environment.(竞争优势)

  edge——advantage(新闻常用小词)

12. moving from a "made in China" orientation to a "created in China" capability—从"中国制造"向"中国创造"能力的转型
13. relationship-oriented culture—以人际关系或人情为主的现象、风气或环境。这样的氛围,一团和气,缺乏批评,难以创新。(见第12课语言解说 Culture)
    -oriented—designed for, directed towards, motivated by, or concerned with(形容词性后缀)
14. performance-oriented culture—以绩效为主的气氛或氛围
15. out of the box—remarkable or exceptional; extraordinary—出格的,摆脱常规

Questions

1. What is the main reason for China to open its door to talents from other parts of the world?
2. What is the "Thousand Foreign Talents Program"?
3. So far, what has China been doing in welcoming the returnees?
4. What are the favorable conditions offered to attract those overseas talents?
5. What problems have some of the returnees found after coming back to China?
6. Why is there hesitation among those overseas Chinese?

新闻写作

何谓 News

对新闻的定义众说纷纭,连英英词典的词源意义也只是用 probably 这样不确定词:"Middle English *newes*, probably plural of *newe* (literally) that which is new, noun use of adjective; perhaps patterned on French *nouvelles*."(*World Book Dictionary*)这就是说,news 是 new 的复数。无论是报刊报道的新人、新事、新思想和新情况都突出一个"新"字,这是 news 的关键。否则,就不是新闻了。

一般而言,新闻(news)的定义有广义和狭义两种。广义的新闻泛指在媒体上出现的所有文章。狭义的新闻即"消息",单指对最新发生的事件的客观报道,而不表达报道者的意见。世界各国对广义新闻的功能的解释各异,不存在被全球媒体普遍接受的定义或规定。在我国,政府要求

新闻界起宣传、教育和激励群众的作用。在西方国家,没有任何机构或个人指定它应担任哪种角色。尽管如此,其特性是共同的,即都是向公众报道新的事实,传递各种消息。这样,美英等国媒体就自我选择担任起提供信息、教育、改革、娱乐、激励等部分或所有角色。

美国报刊新闻尤其强调猎奇,将之奉为天条,正如俗话所说:"狗咬人不是新闻,人咬狗才是新闻"(It is not news when a dog bites a man, but absolutely news when you find a man bites a dog)。为了加深对这句话的理解,不妨看看下面这幅美国政治讽刺漫画:

瞧,媒体是如何剧烈争抢这种庸俗的猎奇式"人咬狗"新闻的。
图中英文为"LOCAL NEWS"(当地新闻)

从西方新闻理论来看,表扬好人好事的正面新闻不是新闻,只有"坏"消息才是"好"新闻,是"乌鸦嘴"。如天灾人祸、社会丑恶现象、突发的悲剧性事件等,尤其战争是最典型的"坏"新闻。这样,我们在看西方媒体的报道,总是看到"好"的新闻少,"坏"的新闻多,包括对中国的报道也是负面内容多,正面内容少。新闻学的一个原则是:"好事不出门,坏事传千里。"每天在媒体上所见所闻尽是"坏事",不管是杀人放火,天灾人祸,无不即刻传播遐迩。在这种情况下,No news is good news. 得不到什么消息才是最好的消息。这与西方新闻的理念是分不开的,可这与我国新闻界要求报道正面消息为主、负面消息为辅的原则是不同的。所以我国的媒体在西方有"报喜鸟"之称。

还有人认为,所谓新闻,无非是天南海北之事,你看 NEWS 不就是 north, east, west 和 south 的首字母缩略词吗!此说是否有道理,也只能"见仁见智"了。(详见《导读》*第一章第二节)

---

* 《导读》指《美英报刊导读》(第二版)(周学艺编著,北京:北京大学出版社,2010年出版)。

Lesson Two

课文导读

中国 30 年的经济改革引起世人注目,但却常被西方误解。一些美国政界人士每当大选年为迎合选民在经济方面缺乏安全感的心理,就把中国当替罪羊,将美国很多问题如失业率上升、经济不振等问题都归罪于中方的贸易顺差,而不究美方的过度消费和政策不当。本文写于 2007 年,2008 年大选却没有纠缠这类问题,这或许是个例外,也或许与此年爆发的全球金融危机有关。威胁论根源是西方政界人士通过世界史得出结论,新崛起的强国终会挑战旧的强权,殊不知中国实行的是和平共处的对外政策。

该篇文章的作者身为美国高官和媒体大亨,却能结合自己的工作经历和所见所闻,较客观地得出结论,认为中美两国的发展是互利互惠的,中国对美国不是威胁,而是机会。美国要做的不是阻碍中国发展的脚步,而是要通过克服自身的弱点防止自己落后。与部分人所持的"中国威胁论"相比,作者将中美两国的竞争看做是"一场能双赢的比赛"。他认为双方应该抓住机遇,相互依存。在中国快速发展的今天,我们既要肯定成绩,也应正确地认识到我们自身的问题,防止脑子膨胀。同时要善于学习借鉴国外的经验教训,在这场双赢的竞赛中更好地壮大自己。

值得注意的是,该篇文章在 *Newsweek* 刊出时,编辑在国内版和亚洲版"Top of the Week"(本周要闻)目录里使用的标题与作者的不同,分别为:"Why America Shouldn't Fear China" 和 "China Isn't a Threat But an Opportunity"。这两个标题似乎更能点出本文的主题。这可能是期刊编辑与作者或记者常意见不同的一个原因。

Pre-reading Questions

1. What place does China rank in the world economics?
2. Are your parents and uncles better off than they were thirty years ago?

Text

A Race We Can All Win

The American system still has inherent advantages, but we can't slow down.

By Michael Bloomberg[1]

1   China's economic transformation over the past two decades is a fascinating, but still poorly understood, story. Many American politicians have played to voters' economic insecurities by scapegoating China[2], suggesting that the Chinese are the source of our problems and a threat to our prosperity. But based on my 35 years of experience in the private sector[3], and six years running the nation's largest city, I believe that China is not a threat to America, but an opportunity. An incredible opportunity.

2   While we should recognize that China and the United States are competitors, we should also understand that geopolitics and global economics are not zero-sum games[4]. Just as a growing American economy is good for China, a growing Chinese economy is good for America. That means we have a stake in working together[5] to solve common problems, rather than trying to browbeat or intimidate the other into action. And it means we should seize on[6] opportunities to learn from one another.

3   In early December I met with business and government leaders in Beijing and Shanghai. It was not my first trip to those cities: the company I founded 25 years ago has built offices in 130 cities, including Beijing, Shanghai and Hong Kong. Over the years I've watched China emerge as an economic dynamo, but I've also seen the frailties underpinning its system. From a distance of 7,000 miles, it's easy to think that China is overflowing with success. But the picture on the ground[7] is far more complicated.

Forging the Future: At a hip new sushi bar in Beijing

4　　When I landed at the Pudong airport near Shanghai on my recent visit, I rode the high-speed magnetic-levitation train[8] that runs between the airport and the city: with a top speed of 268 miles per hour, it's far faster than any train in the United States. This high-tech train of the future symbolizes how Shanghai, with its rising skyscrapers and booming financial markets, is working to rival New York as the city of the future.

5　　But one of the chief reasons China built the maglev train—and why other countries like Japan are also developing maglev networks—was to help relieve their increasingly congested roads and increasingly polluted air. When you are in Shanghai or Beijing, it is impossible to escape either, and together, they threaten to choke the Chinese economy and its people[9]. The growth of Chinese cities is also exposing other fundamental long-term economic challenges for China. For instance, China's education system is simply not producing enough skilled workers—engineers, doctors, scientists and managers—to meet the demands of its economy. At the same time, health-care costs are skyrocketing, which is causing rising financial anxiety among Chinese families.

6　　Congestion. Pollution. Education concerns. Rising health-care costs. If this all sounds familiar, it should.[10] In New York and across America, we face similar problems in all of these areas, but with all the hyperbole about China, it's easy to forget that we remain substantially ahead. We also have a system of government that is far less corrupt and far more stable, owing to our democratic politics, free press and open, transparent markets.[11]

7　　The challenge that we face is not preventing China from catching up with where we are today, but preventing ourselves from slowing down. That means overcoming the political inertia that has stopped us from investing in the 21st-century infrastructure that we need—not just high-speed rail lines but bigger ports, more mass-transit systems[12], more clean-energy capacity[13] and more extensive broadband systems.

8　　It also means overcoming widespread inertia in our efforts to improve the affordability of health care and the quality of education. In New York, we're proving that raising standards and holding schools and students accountable for[14] results can lead to dramatic improvements in student achievement. America has the most advanced, cutting-edge universities in the world, driving innovation in every field. But to maintain that edge, we need a public-school system that is just as good, and that prepares our students to succeed in the new economy.

9   This summer's Olympic Games will give China a chance to showcase its impressive economic progress. But it will also remind the world that much work remains to be done in building a healthy society where differences of opinion—on politics, philosophy and faith—are respected as fundamental human rights. We live that lesson[15] every day in New York, and as China may yet come to see[16], it is our greatest competitive advantage in the global economy. (From *Newsweek*, December 31, 2007)

New Words

afford /əˈfɔːd/ *v.* to be able to do sth without causing serious problems for oneself   **affordable** /əˈfɔːdəbl/ *adj.*   **affordability** /əˌfɔːdəˈbiliti/ *n.*

boom /buːm/ *v.* to increase or develop rapidly   **booming** /ˈbuːmɪŋ/ *adj.*

broadband /ˈbrɔːdˈbænd/ *n.* a system of sending radio signals which allows several messages to be sent at the same time (宽频带；宽波段)

browbeat /ˈbraʊbiːt/ *v.* to make sb do sth by continuously asking them to, esp. in an unpleasant threatening way (威逼，恫吓)

congested /kənˈdʒestɪd/ *adj.* traffic-crowded (交通拥挤的)   **congestion** /kənˈdʒestʃən/ *n.*

choke /tʃəʊk/ *v.* to cause to have great difficulty in breathing; to restrain the growth, development, or activity of (使窒息；堵塞)

cutting-edge /ˈkʌtɪŋ-edʒ/ *adj.* the most advanced (最先进的，一流的)

dramatic /drəˈmætɪk/ *adj.* impressive, sudden, and often surprising

dynamo /ˈdaɪnəməʊ/ *n.* a machine by which mechanical energy is converted into electrical energy (发动机)

edge /edʒ/ *n.* advantage

emerge /ɪˈmɜːdʒ/ *v.* to begin to be known or noticed

expose /ɪkˈspəʊz/ *v.* to lay open to view

frailty /ˈfreɪltɪ/ *n.* lacking in strength or health (脆弱，弱点)

geopolitics /ˌdʒiːəʊˈpɒlɪtɪks/ *n.* the study of the effects of a country's position, population etc on its political character and development

（地理/地缘政治学）（由 geography 和 politics 拼缀而成）

hyperbole /haɪˈpɜːbəlɪ/ *n.* a way of describing sth by saying it is much bigger, smaller, worse etc than it actually is（夸张）

inertia /ɪnˈɜːʃɪə/ *n.* a tendency for a situation to stay unchanged for a long time［(长期)维持现状,停滞不前］

infrastructure /ˈɪnfrəˌstrʌktʃə/ *n.* the basic systems and structures that a country or organization needs in order to work properly, for example, transport, communications, and banking systems（基础设施）

inherent /ɪnˈhɪərənt/ *adj.* intrinsic to the essence or constitution of sth; innate（固有的；内在的）

intimidate /ɪnˈtɪmɪdeɪt/ *v.* to frighten sb by behaving in a threatening way, esp. in order to make him do what one wants（威吓）

overflow /ˌəʊvəˈfləʊ/ *v.* to flow over or beyond a brim, edge, or limit

prosperity /prɒsˈperɪtɪ/ *n.* a condition of having money and everything that is needed for a good life

relieve /rɪˈliːv/ *v.* to lessen; to make become less

rival /ˈraɪvəl/ *v.* to be as good or important as sb or sth else

scapegoat /ˈskeɪpgəʊt/ *n.* sb who is blamed for sth bad that happens, even if it is not his fault（替罪羊）*v.* to make a scapegoat of（代人受过）

showcase /ˈʃəʊkeɪs/ *n.* an event or situation that is designed to show the good qualities of a person, organization, product etc

skyrocket /ˈskaɪˌrɒkɪt/ *v.* to increase suddenly and greatly

substantially /səbˈstænʃəlɪ/ *adv.* essentially; very much

transformation /ˌtrænsfəˈmeɪʃən/ *n.* a complete change in sb or sth

underpin /ˌʌndəˈpɪn/ *v.* to underlie; to be hidden beneath; to be at the basis of（潜伏在……之下；支撑）

Notes

1. Michael Bloomberg —1942— , New York City's mayor since 2002, founder of the financial news and information company（金融新闻和信息公司）. After attending Johns Hopkins University to study electrical engineering, where he was a self-financed student, he obtained his MBA from Harvard Business School in 1966. He was then hired by Salomon Brothers to work on Wall Street.

2. Many American politicians have played to voters' economic

insecurities by scapegoating China—许多美国政界人物迎合选民在经济方面的不安全感,把中国当替罪羊。(此处 scapegoating 为名词动词化用法,专有名称名词也能作动词,这一特点在报刊语言中尤其突出。)

  play to—to behave so as to win the favor of(sb)

3. private sector—those industries and services in a country that are owned by private companies, not by the state 私营部门
4. we should also understand that geopolitics and global economics are not zero-sum games—我们还应该明白,地理政治学和全球经济学并不是一方赢必然导致另一方输的赌博。

  zero-sum game—a game in which a gain for one side entails a corresponding loss for the other 零和游戏,指在一项游戏中,参加者有输有赢,赢家所得正好是输家所失,总合永远为零。现在广泛用于指有赢家必有输家的竞争与对抗。与之对应的是"双赢"概念,也是本文作者所强调的要点。

5. we have a stake in working together—we are concerned about working together

  stake—a personal or emotional concern, interest, involvement, or share

6. seize on—to make use of
7. on the ground—at the actual place where sth, esp. a war, is happening, rather than in another place where the situation is being watched or discussed 在现场
8. magnetic-levitation train—maglev train 磁浮列车
9. it is impossible to escape either... to choke the Chinese economy and its people—you can escape neither increasingly congested roads nor increasingly polluted air, and these two things together threaten to prevent the Chinese economy from developing and do harm to Chinese people's health.
10. If this all sounds familiar, it should.—如果这些听起来很熟悉,那毫不奇怪。(In the sentence, "this" refers to what has been mentioned previously with respect to each individual entry rather than as a whole. "It" stands for "this".)
11. We also have a system of government... free press and open, transparent markets.—我们有一个比较廉洁和更加稳定的政府系统,这都归功于我们的民主政治、言论自由和开放透明的市场。[The

author of the article, being an American, cannot completely avoid showing his ideological bias [意识形态的倾向] though what he says about China is true. An American would generally believe that the political system in the United States is the most democratic in the world, and thus the least corrupt and the most transparent.]
12. mass-transit systems—transport systems that serve members of the general public, usually charging set fares. While this term is generally taken to include rail and bus services, wider definitions might include scheduled airline services, ferries, taxicab services etc. 大众运输系统
13. clean-energy capacity—清洁能源的生产量
14. hold sb accountable for sth—to make sb take the responsibility for sth
15. live that lesson—to put that belief into practice in our everyday life
16. China may yet come to see—China may still need to understand it gradually in the future.

Questions

1. What are the different views between the author and some other American politicians on China? Why does he think so?
2. What does the author see behind the growing Chinese economy?
3. What common problems do both China and America meet? Give an example to illustrate how China is solving these problems.
4. Compared with China, what are the advantages for America to solve these problems? Do you agree with the author?
5. In the author's opinion, how can America face the challenge?
6. Do you agree with the author's opinions about China and the US? Please illustrate your own views with some examples.

新 闻 写 作

导语(Lead)

消息报道中的导语十分重要,一般在消息的第一个自然段,有时也由前两个自然段组成。迅速点出新闻的主题,这是消息区别于其他体裁的一个重要特征。导语用三言两语写出消息中最主要的、最新鲜的事实,使

读者先获得一个总的概念,再吸引读者继续看下去。可以说,导语是消息的概括,而标题又是导语的概括。

导语的作用是什么?美国新闻学家威廉·梅茨在《怎样写新闻》一书中认为有三点:(1)告诉读者这条消息的内容。(2)使读者愿意看下去。(3)必要时制造适当的气氛。还有人认为导语的作用可以概括为:(1)用简洁的文字反映消息要点,让读者大体了解消息的主要事实和主题思想。(2)引出主题以及阐述、解释这个主题的新闻主体。(3)唤起读者注意,吸引读者往下看。

一百多年来,导语产生了"两代"。什么是第一代新闻导语?如前所述,在导语里必须具备五个 W 和一个 H 要素(When, Where, Who, What, Why, and How),即何时、何地、何人、何事、何故、如何。具体地讲,就是在什么时候发生的?在什么地方发生的?事情牵涉到什么人?发生了什么事?事情为什么会发生?事情是怎样发生和发展的?西方新闻学鼻祖之一戴纳提出,新闻导语必须回答五个 W 和一个 H。这个观点,曾经在相当长的时间里被认为是导语写作的金科玉律。这样的导语具有具体、完整的长处,看了导语,对消息的主要内容大体上都知道了。短处是内容太多,主次不清,重点不突出。再则,文字和重点易重复,展开难以顺畅。不适用于特写这样的软新闻体裁,缺乏悬念感。于是一些新闻工作者对导语进行改革。1954 年,《纽约时报》总编辑在采访部里贴出这样一个布告:"我们认为把传统五个 W 写在一个句子或一个段落里没有必要,也许永远没有必要。"这时顺便提醒一下读者,凡教过"托福"者无不知道,它的问答题往往都是这类问题。

通过改革,许多消息导语里只突出一两个新闻要素,其余新闻要素放在后面的主体或结尾,这样就可以更突出重点。这种出现在上世纪 50 年代至 70 年代的新闻导语,称为第二代导语。从导语的形式来分,有叙述式、设问式、评论式、结论式、描写式和对比式等等。有的新闻专家列出 10 多种形式的导语,但不管多少种,都可归结为"direct lead"和"indirect lead"两种形式。不过这里要着重阐明倒金字塔式导语,五个 W 和一个 H 是构成一则完整的消息不可缺少的要素。以往直接的消息报道或纯消息一般采取"倒金字塔形式",其特点是将新闻报道最重要的五个 W 和一个 H 按重要性的顺序头重脚轻地安排,把新闻的高潮和结论放在最前面的导语里,然后按事实的重要性递减的顺序来安排(in the order of descending importance),由此突出最重要、最新的事实。

应该说明,新闻报道现在仍采用倒金字塔式结构形式为主,但不一定在导语里全部都包括五个 W 和一个 H,或许只有三个或四个 W,另一个或两个 W 出现在下面段落里,这是后来改革的结果。

由于导语形式多样,报道手法跟着翻新。如"时间顺序式"(Chronological Order Form)、"悬念式"(Suspended Interest Form)和"解释性报道式"(Interpretative Reporting Form)等。时间顺序式,有如香肠,一根接一根,所以又称为"香肠式"(Wiener Form)。时间顺序式多用于体育比赛,作案过程,厂家发展或名人讣告之类的消息报道。"悬念式"多用于特写。"解释性报道式"与纯新闻的客观报道不同,着重探讨理念,事情成败原因,寻求答案等。这种形式尤其在刊物中数量居多。(详见《导读》一章二节)

Lesson Three

课文导读

　　随着全球化的进一步推进,国际交往和交流的广度和深度日增。留学生作为各国文化交流的重要组成部分,其数量也在不断增长。本文报道了一名美国大学生在中国的留学生活,介绍了他来华学习的背景和目的,例如他本人和政府都认为留学回国后易找工作。通过这一个体,可以管窥不同国家文化交流的目的、益处及前景。越来越多的美国学生选择来华学习,他们已将亚洲作为重点。随着中国经济力量日益增强,中文也必将成为全球交流用得较多的一种语言。

　　现在国人中有人早已脱贫致富,不少学生也纷纷出国学习。这样既可以将国外的先进技术和优秀文化知识学到手,回国后进行应用和传播,同时又把我国悠久的历史文化传播到全球,使各国更了解中国。这样,世界各国的留学生都成了民间交流的大使。

Pre-reading Questions

1. Do you have a plan to study abroad? Why do you intend to do so?
2. If you are going to study abroad, which country do you want to go? Explain your reasons.

Text

An American in Beijing

By Lauren Konopacz

1　　Each year, thousands of U. S. students choose to spend a semester abroad in all sorts of places, from England to Spain to Australia to India. After spending a semester at a university in Beijing, The Globalist's Lauren Konopacz explores the myriad benefits of studying abroad—particularly in China.

2　　In the 2005—2006 academic year, the most recent period for which data are available, 223,534 U. S. students studied abroad. That number equals only 1% of enrolled U. S. students. Of that 1%, only 9.3% chose to study abroad in Asia. That means that just 20,788 U. S. students went abroad to the Asian region.

3 In other words, the number of U. S. students who spent time in Asia during that academic year couldn't even sell out a Red Sox game.[1] Fenway Park—one of the smallest ballparks in the United States—has a capacity of 36,108. Taking that point further, only about 6,000 students chose to study in China.

4 They could not even sell out a Portland Sea Dogs[2] game—the Red Sox' minor league team. Of all my friends, only the ones who I know through Chinese classes went to China, and the eight of us couldn't even fill a dugout.

■ So why did they go?

5 There are a number of reasons to study abroad. In fact, according to the American Council on Education, 79% of the U. S. population agrees that students ought to study abroad, in contrast to the fact that only 1% go.

6 Many students who go abroad have the goal of learning a language. There is no better way to improve language skills than by being immersed in a language other than your own. Studying abroad also offers students an opportunity to travel, to expand one's worldview, to enhance the value of a college degree—and to make international connections.

7 Studying abroad can have excellent benefits for future employment opportunities by providing students with international skills and experiences. Connections made while abroad could easily lead to future opportunities.[3]

■ Uncle Sam wants YOU to go abroad[4]

8 Even the U. S. Senate recognizes the importance of a study abroad experience to future employment. Senate Resolution 308, passed on November 11, 2005, lists several reasons why such an experience is important for both the student and for the United States as a whole.

9 Several of these points address the fact that "federal agencies, educational institutions and corporations in the United States are suffering from a shortage of professionals with international knowledge

and foreign skills."

■ Understanding self

10   Perhaps most importantly, study abroad offers a chance to understand another culture, and to better understand your own culture. Resolution 308 agrees that study abroad programs "empower students to better understand themselves and others through a comparison of cultural values and ways of life."

11   Much of what people consider to be "self" is simply a set of beliefs and assumptions about life that are the products of factors such as social group, economic class, family background and national culture. Foreign experience allows students to recognize these assumptions in both their host culture and their own.

12   Aside from a foreign cultural experience, students are able to re-examine the assumptions of their own lives and the assumptions of the societies they belong to.

■ So why Asia?

13   Asia has played a huge role in shaping U.S. history and foreign policy. Korea, Vietnam, the World Wars—even the Spanish-American war was concerned with U.S. presence in Asia.[5] The U.S. Open Door policy was officially introduced as far back as 1899[6], and unofficially introduced with Commodore Perry's visits to Japan in 1853.[7]

14   Despite extensive U.S.-Asian involvement, the educational system in the United States is heavily U.S.-European focused.[8] Throughout my education prior to college, I took several courses on U.S. and European history, but only one course on Asia—and that was a high school elective.

15   Asia continues to affect the United States. Three of the six world regions listed as trade partners on the United States Trade Representative's website are in Asia (North, South and South East Asia). Two of the top five import and export partners of the United States are located in Asia.

■ Why China matters

16   China receives 5.3% of U.S. exports and contributes 15.9% of its total imports, placing it in the top five in both categories (the other

Asian nation in that top five is Japan). Twenty-one percent of China's exports go to the United States, making it China's top export partner. The nation has a relatively steady average yearly GDP growth of 10—11%. Thus, there are clear economic reasons to understand China.

17 Though 69% of U. S. students are able to find China on a map, only 18% are aware that Mandarin Chinese is the most spoken language in the world (74% think it is English), and 50% think that the Chinese population is only twice that of the United States (when it is really four times that).

18 So while the average American student is aware of China's geographical presence, they are not quite as aware of its cultural presence. [9] This is grossly unfair. China has a population of 1.3 billion and 5,000 years of uninterrupted history. Both of these numbers dwarf their U. S. counterparts. There is a clear need to raise cultural awareness of China in the United States.

■ **Choosing China**

19 Why did I become one of the 6,000 students who go to China?

20 Like most of those 6,000 students, I made my decision based on any combination of the reasons listed above. One of my majors is Asian Studies. I chose to pursue a degree in that field because it is so incredibly underrepresented, but still so important. [10] In high school, I had the opportunity to take a history course on Asia. The fact that I knew so little about it both appalled and intrigued me. It was so refreshing to go beyond the boundaries of U. S. and European history.

■ **Practical interests**

21 When I arrived at college, I was told that the Asian Studies degree required—quite rightly—study of an Asian language. I chose Chinese—hard though it may be—because of the economic and cultural factors I previously mentioned. Given China's growing economic importance and

global predominance, learning Mandarin was simply practical. Plus, my interest in the region made it appealing.

22　　As a university student, I knew I would go abroad, and as a student of the Chinese language, I knew I would go to China.

23　　I am definitely part of the 79% of the U.S. population who feels emphatically that the study abroad experience is unequaled. Globalization has rendered today's world absolutely in need of people with cultural experience other than their own.[11]

■ Travel and language

24　　I also had a desire to travel and a great curiosity about new places, and, like most students, new ideas. As a Chinese student, China was an easy choice. I was thrilled about the chance to apply the skills I had spent so much time and energy cultivating.[12]

25　　I also knew that immersing myself in Chinese could only improve my language level. Finally, being in a foreign country whose language I could speak, gave me so many opportunities to learn about the culture directly from the people who lived there.

■ Making textbooks a reality

26　　My study abroad experience really served to bring my classroom experience to life. Everything that I had learned and read about was right there for me to physically experience.

27　　Just as an art history student must forgo their textbook to go to the museum in order to best experience a work of art, a student of culture or language must forgo their textbook to go abroad in order to best experience that culture or language.

28　　For me, China both reinforced things I had already learned and taught me new things, while at the same time it inspired new interests and curiosities. I am confident that any student willing to push his or her boundaries and go somewhere new will have a similar experience. (From *Time*, April 4, 2008)

New Words

academic /ˌækəˈdemɪk/ *adj.* relating to education, esp. at college or university level 学院的，学术的

address /ə'dres/ v. to try to solve a problem

appall /ə'pɔːl/ v. to cause sb to have strong feeling of shock or of disapproval 使惊骇

ballpark /'bɔːlpɑːk/ n. a field for playing baseball with seats for watching the game 棒球场

counterpart /'kaʊntəpɑːt/ n. sb or sth that has the same job or purpose as sb or sth else in a different place 对等的人或物，对手，同行

cultivate /'kʌltɪveɪt/ v. to work hard to develop a particular skill, attitude, or quality 培养

dugout /'dʌɡˌaʊt/ n. a low shelter at the side of a sports field, where players and team officials sit 棒球场边供球员休息的地方

dwarf /dwɔːf/ v. to be so big that other things are made to seem very small 使变矮小

elective /ɪ'lektɪv/ n. a course that students can choose to take, but they do not have to take it in order to graduate 选修课程

empower /ɪm'paʊə/ v. to give sb more control over their own life or situation; to give a person or organization the legal right to do sth 使能够；授权于

enroll /ɪn'rəʊl/ v. to officially arrange to join a school, university, or course 入学（或入会等）；登记；成为成员

forgo /fɔː'ɡəʊ/ v. to give up; not do or have sth pleasant or enjoyable 作罢，放弃

globalist /'ɡləʊbəlɪst/ n. a person who supports the idea of globalization 支持全球主义者

immerse /ɪ'mɜːs/ v. to put sb or sth deep into a liquid so that they are completely covered; become completely involved in an activity 沉浸，使陷入

intrigue /ɪn'triːɡ/ v. to interest sb a lot, esp. by being strange, unusual or mysterious 激起兴趣

Mandarin /'mændərɪn/ n. the official language of China 汉语普通话

myriad /'mɪrɪəd/ n. & adj. a very large number of things; very many 无数（的），种种（的）

prior /'praɪə/ adj. existing or arranged before sth else or before the present situation; before 优先的，在先的

reinforce /ˌriːɪn'fɔːs/ v. to give support to an opinion, idea, or feeling, and make it stronger 加强，加固

render /'rendə/ v. to cause sb or sth to be in a particular condition

致使

resolution /ˌrezəˈluːʃən/ n. a formal decision or statement agreed on by a group of people, esp. after a vote; strong belief and determination 决议;决心

semester /sɪˈmestə/ n. a term, esp. at universities 学期

underrepresented /ˌʌndərepriˈzentɪd/ adj. being not fully represented, shown or described 未被充分代表的;没有充分表现的

worldview /ˈwɜːldˌvjuː/ n. someone's opinions and attitudes relating to the world and things in general 世界观

Notes

1. In other words... a Red Sox game. —That is to say, there are fewer U. S. students who are willing to study in Asia for a year than the tickets sold out for a Red Sox (红袜队) match. The Red Sox, or the Boston Red Sox, is the name of a popular baseball team in America. Baseball is known as America's national pastime. But the International Olympic Committee announced last year that it was dropping baseball from its list of sports after the 2008 Summer Games.
2. Portland Sea Dogs—From the context, we can infer that the Portland Seas Dogs (海狗队) is also the name of a sports team, which is junior to the Red Sox in size, reputation or achievement. Here the writer uses an analogy to explain the fact that only a small fraction of U. S. students go to China to study.
3. Connections made while abroad could easily lead to future opportunities. —Relationships that the students have developed while they are studying abroad could easily lead to future employment opportunities or success.
4. Uncle Sam wants YOU to go abroad—This sentence is an imitation of the very famous army recruiting poster: "I Want You for U. S. Army." Uncle Sam is a national personification of the United States, often portrayed as a tall, white-haired man with a goatee. He is often dressed in red, white, and blue, and wears a top hat.
5. Korea, Vietnam... U. S. presence in Asia. —朝鲜战争、越南战争、两次世界大战、甚至美西战争都与美国在亚洲的势力范围有关。(此处的 Korea 和 Vietnam 分别指 the Korean War 和 the Vietnam War,是报刊常见的借代用法。另外,说 Spanish-American War 与亚洲有关,

是因为这场战争是 1898 年美国为夺取西班牙属地古巴、波多黎各和菲律宾而发动的战争。美西战争是列强重新瓜分殖民地的第一次帝国主义战争。)

6. The U. S. Open Door policy was officially introduced as far back as 1899—By the late 19th century, Japan and the European powers had carved much of China into separate spheres of influence, inside of which each held economic dominance. The U. S., coming late to imperialism, held no sphere of influence in China. In 1899 U. S. Secretary of State John Hay proposed an "Open Door" policy (门户开放政策) in China in which all nations would have equal trading and development rights throughout all of China. It reflects American political and economic self-interest.

7. Commodore Perry's visits to Japan in 1853—In 1853, Commodore Matthew C. Perry sailed a small American steam-powered naval squadron(中队) into Yedo (later Tokyo) Bay. The mission entrusted (委托/任) to him by the President was to persuade Japan to open ports for trade and to cease cruel treatment of ship-wrecked American seamen.

8. Despite extensive U. S.-Asian involvement, the educational system in the United States is heavily U. S.-European focused. —Though the U. S. and Asia have a close connection or relation, for business or political purposes, the educational system in the United States is mainly focused on European history and the correlation between U. S. and Europe because the early settlers in the country were from Europe.

9. So while the average American student is aware of China's geographical presence, they are not quite as aware of its cultural presence.—理解此句子中的抽象名词 presence 要看第 17 段和此段以下的段落(见"语言解说")。

10. I chose to pursue a degree in that field because it is so incredibly underrepresented, but still so important. —I decided to get a degree in Asian studies for this is a very important field, yet the number of students enrolling in this field is surprisingly inadequate.

11. I am definitely part of the 79% of the U. S. population... people with cultural experience other than their own. —Surely I am among those 79% of the population who strongly agrees that the

experience of studying abroad is better than any other ways of studying. Globalization has made the world of today definitely in need of people with different cultural experiences apart from their own.
12. I was thrilled about the chance to apply the skills I had spent so much time and energy cultivating. —I was extremely excited and happy that I had a chance to communicate in Chinese. The skills are developed at the cost of much of my time and energy.

Questions

1. According to the American Council on Education, why is it necessary for students to study abroad?
2. As to the importance of studying abroad, what were listed by Senate Resolution 308?
3. Why is China the worthy place for U. S. students?
4. What benefits has the author gained from studying in China?

语 言 解 说

Presence

presence 的词义有时难以捉摸,只有先弄懂上下文,再作判断。在现代英语中,presence 并非只有"存在"一义,而是在不同的场合具有种种不同的含义。它是现代报刊用语中一个典型的舍具体求抽象的实例,这与西方人擅抽象思维和国人长于形象思维有关。本文第 18 段在一个句子里有两个"presence",均为"存在"之义,意为"……地理上有中国这个国家,但对其文化知之甚少",第二个 presence 结合下句也可理解为"历史",即"中国的文化历史或文明史"。但在本文第 13 段的"... even the Spanish-American war was concerned with U. S. presence in Asia"可理解为"势力"或"影响"。下面见该词用于外交作"显示(军事)实力"(showing the flag)讲引申出的种种意义的例句:

1. 影响;实力,势力
   a. Grassroots leaders are trying to step into the vacuum. Last fall former city councilman Ron Leeper founded Save the Seed, an organization that provides adult male mentors to African-American children. Fighting Back, a fledgling drug-and-alcohol-counseling group

funded by a private grant, hopes to expand its **presence** in troubled west Charlotte. (*Newsweek*)

b. His price for a coalition arrangement would have been political autonomy for Scotland and Wales, with which Labour agreed, as well as electoral reform to make proportional representation the basis for future elections, which would give the Liberal Democrats a larger **presence** in Parliament. (*Time*)

2. 外交使团或机构

Britain is committed to maintaining a worldwide diplomatic **presence**. Diplomatic or consular relations are maintained with 183 countries and there are missions at nine international organisations or conferences. (*Britain*)

3. 联合国"维和部队"

Indonesians opposed to **the UN presence** in East Timor protesting Friday outside UN offices in Jakarta. The UN said 20 more people died at the hands of militias in West Timor, but Indonesia denied the claim. (*International Herald Tribune*)

4. 驻扎,留驻

a. The Pentagon confirmed the **presence** of American troops in northern Afghanistan for the first time Tuesday and credited them with improving the effectiveness of U.S. bombing raids. (AP)

b. Despite the problems with civilian reconstruction and pressures from European governments to consider leaving a force behind after IFOR leaves, the White House—with an eye on the presidential election campaign—will not even discuss for now any possibility of an American troop **presence** in Bosnia past President Clinton's December deadline. (*U.S. News & World Report*)

5. (外来的)军事力量;军队;警察

The key decisions must still be made by and with Israel. The problem is how to give the Palestinians a homeland that would not pose a threat to Israeli security. Mr. Begin seems to think that this can be achieved only if Israel retains responsibility for security in the West Bank. This is not necessarily the case. An Israeli **presence** might exacerbate tension and provoke insecurity, whereas the Palestinians living on the spot, who have as great an interest in peace as the Israelis, might be able to police themselves more effectively. (The *Times*)

presence 作为抽象意义的词可用来代表具体意义。这种虚实的转化会产生词义艰涩、含糊的新义,所以有时词义难以确定。还有的出于政治上的策略,如前联合国秘书长哈马舍尔德(Dag Hammarskjöld,1905—1961)就喜欢此词的含糊其辞。他曾说:"There is **a UN presence** wherever the UN is present."此处"a UN presence"指什么?"维和部队"、"外交官"、"外交使团"或"军事观察团"? 此语妙在便于灵活掌握,使对手或政敌抓不住话柄。

以上可见,"a presence"可指"出访的外交官"、在海外的"航空母舰"、"永久性军事基地"、"军队"或"警察"等。(详见《导读》二章一节)

Unit Two
China (Ⅱ)

Lesson Four

课文导读

2011年,一位华裔美国妈妈出版了一本名为《虎妈战歌》的书(书名又译为:《我在美国做妈妈:耶鲁法学院教授的育儿经》)(*Battle Hymn of the Tiger Mother*),在中美两国引起了轰动,并引发了一场关于中美教育方式差异的大讨论。究竟什么才是教育孩子的终极目的?有人说她是尽心尽力的好妈妈,帮助孩子最大限度地发挥了潜能;也有人说她太过分了。这其中有一位自称是熊猫爸爸的美国父亲在《华尔街日报》上公开挑战"虎妈"的育儿方式。想到熊猫憨态可掬的外形就能够猜出几分,熊猫爸爸崇尚的是宽松的教育理念,并且怀着一份坚持到底的信心,到底他有什么勇气和理由向虎妈宣战?有着中国生活背景的他是否对于教育方式的差异有着更深刻的理解?

现在我国创造力当然比不上美国,但也在不断进步。这是否都归结为中国的死板或应试教育?值得我们研讨。

Pre-reading Questions

1. How were you raised when you were young?
2. When you've skimmed the article, have you benefited from it or not?

Text

Tiger Mom[1]... Meet Panda Dad[2]

By Alan Paul

1   I have watched the uproar over the Tiger Mom debate with growing annoyance that one simple question remains unasked: Where are the dads?

2   I am a father of three who has been on the frontline of parenting for years, thanks to my wife's demanding career and my own freelance

lifestyle. I refuse to cede the entire discussion about proper child-rearing to mothers, Tiger or otherwise[3]. When my kids were 2, 4 and 7, our family of five moved from suburban New Jersey to Beijing.

3   Our 3½ years in China give me an unusual insight into what author Amy Chua claims is not only the best way of parenting but also the Chinese way.

4   During our first weeks in Beijing, we attended a talent show[4] at our children's British school and watched Chinese students ascend the stage and play Chopin etudes and Beethoven symphonies, while their Western counterparts ambled up and proudly played the ABCs under their flapping arms[5]. It was enough to make anyone pause and ponder the way we are raising our kids.

5   But time in China also taught me that while some here view a Chinese education as the gold standard, many there are questioning the system, noting that it stifles creativity and innovation, two things the nation sorely needs. Further, having seen it in action, I have a strong aversion to hard-driving "Tiger" parenting, certain that is not a superior method if your goals are my goals: to raise independent, competent, confident adults.

6   Call me the Panda Dad; I am happy to parent with cuddliness, but not afraid to show some claw.[6]

7   Though I have had primary child care duties since our eldest son was born 13 years ago, I too have always worked, sometimes juggling a variety of demanding deadlines with an increasingly complex family schedule[7]. As a result, controlled chaos reigns in our house—and it works for us, even if this has befuddled some friends and family members and sent weak-kneed babysitters scurrying for the door.

8   It has also been a plus for our children, giving them space to take on responsibilities, be independent and see their parents pursuing their own interests and careers while also being very involved in one another's lives. And it introduced them to a simple fact early: Life itself is controlled chaos and success depends on navigating it, rather than waiting for things to be perfect.

9   This is largely a male perspective. To make a sweeping generalization, moms tend to be more detail oriented, and order driven. Dads often care less about the mess, can live with a bit more chaos and more easily adopt a big

picture view. If my wife and I swapped positions, life would certainly be more orderly. But she cedes to my style of parenting because I am in charge of the day-to-day stuff. Her ability to do this is a key to us having a strong, thriving relationship; you can't backseat drive how your children are being raised[8].

10   This only works if you share the same basic values and the differences are small bore rather than big picture. She would not tolerate me calling the kids garbage or chaining them to a piano bench[9]; we would both view this as barbaric and counterproductive.

11   Kids raised in this fashion have more of an opportunity to develop their own personalities and interests. Our home is like a state university, where you can get a great education but you have to do your own legwork. A typical night: one kid has a big project due, another has a school play, the third has soccer practice; mom is working late because there is an international crisis brewing but she will barrel home to be sitting in the auditorium when the curtain rises[10]; and I am trying to help everyone while fielding calls on a story[11] I have to finish writing that night after the kids go to bed.

12   It's not the hyper-orderly household that Amy Chua portrays, but the kids are constantly learning to take responsibility for their own homework, play time and everything else. Doing so allows them to take genuine pride in their accomplishments. They need to succeed for their own benefit, not to prove that their parents are successful. It's sheer narcissism to believe that your child's every success and failure is a reflection of your worth[12]. Get over yourself[13].

13   Living in a Beijing housing compound, I watched Western and African kids running through the streets in roving packs of fun-seekers[14] while their Chinese friends looked dolefully out the window in the midst of long hours spent practicing violin, piano or character-writing. When they were done, they unwound by picking up video game consoles. It looked like a sad, lonesome way to grow up and nothing I would ever prescribe to my children. And of course it's not the only style of Chinese parenting. I saw plenty of kids smashing these same stereotypes.

14   It also seems insane to cast an eye around the upper-middle-class American milieu Ms. Chua is discussing and conclude that the problem

is that our child-rearing is too laid back. The shallowness of this concept will be obvious to anyone who has ever stalked a suburban soccer sideline or listened to New York parents prep their 18-month-old for nursery school interviews. God help us all if Ms. Chua's books convinces these same people that they simply have not been trying hard enough.

15 It's easy to understand a traditional Chinese drive for perfection in children: it is a huge nation with a long history of people thriving at the top and scraping by at the bottom without much in between. The appeal in contemporary America stems from a sense that our nation is becoming stratified in similar ways and is about to get steamrolled by China[15]. If you can't beat them, join them[16].

16 It's an understandable impulse but it's wrong. Forcing a child to constantly bend to your will can lead to docile mama's boys or girls seeking approval for everything they do—or lead to constant rebellion and head-butting. Banning playing and sleeping at friends' houses furthers a dangerous sense of isolation, denying them the ability to make the very social connections and interactions that they will need throughout life. These are the very skills that kids should be honing for success as a functioning adult, far more important than being able to play piano. Kids need more unstructured play[17], not less.

17 Aside from being a much cheaper option than babysitters, sleepovers also help children learn to sleep anywhere, in any bed, with any pillow. This is not an ability to be scoffed at. It is, in fact, one of three goals everyone should realistically set for raising their kids: get them to adulthood with no sleeping, eating or sexual hang-ups. Do that and you will have done your job, launching them off with the foundation needed to thrive.

18 Drop the hubris of thinking you can pick your children's friends, interests and musical passions. Instead, help them grow up to be highly functioning, non-neurotic contributors[18] with a strong sense of self. They will thank you.

19 And so will society. (From *The Wall Street Journal*, March 29, 2011)

New Words

amble /ˈæmbl/ v. walk slowly and in a relaxed manner 从容地走，漫步
ascend /əˈsend/ v. leads up to a higher position 上升；爬坡
aversion /əˈvɜːʒən, -ʃən/ n. a feeling of strong dislike or unwillingness 厌恶，反感
barbaric /bɑːˈbærɪk/ adj. extremely cruel or uncivilized 野蛮的；半开化的；粗俗的
barrel /ˈbærəl/ v. infml to move very quickly, esp. unsafely
befuddle /bɪˈfʌdl/ v. cause to be unable to think clearly 使迷惑不解
brew /bruː/ v. (esp. of sth bad) to be in preparation or ready to happen; develop 酝酿，孕育（尤指坏事）
cede /siːd/ v. give over 让给，放弃
compound /ˈkɒmpaʊnd/ n. an area enclosed by a wall, fence etc., containing a group of buildings （有围墙等的）场地（大院，楼群）
console /kənˈsəʊl/ n. a flat surface containing the controls for a machine, piece of electrical equipment, organ, etc. （机器，仪器等的）控制台，仪表盘
counterproductive /ˌkaʊntəprəˈdʌktɪv/ adj. achieving the opposite result from the one that you want to achieve 产生相反效果的；事与愿违的；适得其反的
cuddliness /ˈkʌdlɪnɪs/ n. state of being lovable, suitable for cuddling 可爱，值得拥抱
docile /ˈdəʊsaɪl/ adj. quiet and easily controlled, managed, or influenced 温顺的，驯良的
dolefully /ˈdəʊlfəlɪ/ adv. with sadness; in a sorrowful manner 寂寞地
demanding /dɪˈmɑːndɪŋ/ a. needing a lot of time, attention and effort 需要技能的，费力的
etude /eɪˈtjuːd/ n. a piece composed for the development of a specific point of technique 练习曲
flap /flæp/ v. to wave or move slowly up and down or backwards and forwards, usu. making a noise 摆动，拍动
freelance /ˈfriːlɑːns/ n. a writer or artist who sells services to different employers without a long-term contract with any of them 自由作家，自由记者
hang-up /ˈhæŋʌp/ n. difficulty, inhibition, obsession 困难，障碍
hard-driving adj. 要求过高的，过于苛责的
head-butt /ˈhedbʌt/ v. hit you with the top of their head 用头顶撞（某人的下巴或身体）；顶撞

hone /həʊn/ v. to yearn or pine 渴望；渴慕
hubris /ˈhjuːbrɪs/ n. overbearing pride or presumption. 傲慢；狂妄自大
juggle /ˈdʒʌgl/ v. to give enough time or attention to your work and your family 尽力同时应付；尽量兼顾
legwork /ˈlegwɜːk/ n. infml work that needs much walking about or tiring effort 跑腿活，跑外工作
milieu /miːˈljɜː/ n. (pl. milieus 或 milieux) the environmental condition 环境；周围
narcissism /ˈnɑːsɪsɪzəm/ n. an exceptional interest in and admiration for yourself 自我陶醉，自恋
navigate /ˈnævɪgeɪt/ v. to direct carefully and safely 驾驶
parent /ˈpeərənt/ v. to act as a parent 抚育，养育
parenting /ˈpeərəntɪŋ/ n. the activity of bringing up and looking after your child
plus /plʌs/ n. a welcome or favorable condition 有利的附加物，有利条件
roving /ˈrəʊvɪŋ/ a. (of groups of people) tending to travel and change settlements frequently （人群）流动的，徘徊的
scoff /skɒf/ v. infml to speak or act disrespectfully; laugh(at) 嘲弄，嘲笑
scrape /skreɪp/ v. to live, keep a business etc. with no more than the necessary money 勉强维持，艰难经营
scurry /ˈskʌrɪ/ v. to move about or proceed hurriedly 急匆匆；赶忙
sheer /ʃɪə(r)/ adj. pure; unmixed with anything else; nothing but
sleepover /ˈsliːpəʊvə(r)/ n. an occasion of spending a night away from home or having a guest spend the night in your home (esp. as a party for children)（尤指小孩）在朋友家过夜的晚会
smash /smæʃ/ v. to defeat, destroy, or put an end to
sorely /ˈsɔːliː , ˈsəʊr-/ adv. fml very much, greatly
stalk /stɔːk/ v. to hunt by following closely and quietly and staying hidden 潜步跟踪；潜进
steamroll /ˈstiːmrəʊl/ v. to crush or force using very great power or pressure 推进；压倒
stereotype /ˈsterɪətaɪp/ n. a fixed set of idea about what a particular type of person or thing is like, which is (wrongly) believed to be true in all cases 模式化的见解，老套，旧框框
stratify /ˈstrætɪfaɪ/ v. usu. pass to arrage in separate levels or strata （一般用被动语态）使分层，使成层

stifle /'staɪfl/ *v.* to prevent from happening or developing 压制,阻止
symphony /'sɪmfəni/ *n.* 交响乐,交响曲
swap /swɒp/ *v.* to exchange or give (something) in exchange for
unwind /ˌʌn'waɪnd/ *v. infml* to stop being nervous; relax, esp. after a period of great effort and pressure 放松,松弛一下
uproar /'ʌprɔː(r)/ *n.* loud confused noise from many sources 喧闹;吵闹
weak-kneed /ˌwiːk'niːd/ *adj.* lacking strength of character or purpose 易屈服的;软弱的

Notes

1. Tiger Mom—Amy Chua(1962—), Yale law professor who raised her two daughters in Chinese parenting way. She got the name from her book *Battle Hymn of the Tiger Mother* published in 2011 in which Chua describes her efforts to give her children what she describes as a traditional, strict "Chinese" upbringing. Chua uses the term "Tiger Mother" to mean a mother who is a strict disciplinarian. Her article in the *Wall Street Journal* (WSJ) titled "Why Chinese Mothers Are Superior" on January 8, 2011 which is an excerpt from her book has generated widespread debate on what constitutes good parenting and Chua received ample criticism after the WSJ essay. (耶鲁大学华裔教授蔡美儿在《虎妈战歌》一书中描绘了自己教育两个女儿的严苛的中国方式,引爆了世界对东西方教育方式的大讨论。)

2. Panda Dad—The author calls himself Panda Dad as a scream of rage and frustration against the Tiger Mom hoopla (喧嚣). He weighs in on raising kids, unwilling to defer to the Tiger Mom way of child-rearing. This report as a Panda Dad manifesto for the WSJ quickly caught fire and caused a stir that led to him being interviewed on the NBC *Today* show.

3. I refuse to cede the entire discussion about proper child-rearing to mothers, Tiger or otherwise (Par. 2)—As for proper child-rearing, I don't want to just leave the discussion among mothers, no matter they are tiger mother or not. (就正确的育儿方式而言,我不能坐看只有妈妈参与的讨论,不管她们是不是虎妈。)

   cede to—to give to another person, esp. after losing a war 割让,放弃

4. talent show—an event where participants perform talents of singing,

dancing, acrobatics, acting, drumming, martial arts, playing a unicorn instrument, or other activities to showcase skills, sometimes for a reward, trophy or prize. Many talent shows, like school talent shows, are performances rather than contests, but some are actual contests, awarding prizes to their participants.

5. Chinese students ascend the stage ... under their flapping arms—Chinese students get on the stage playing difficult piece of music very skillfully, but their Western schoolmates walk leisurely up the stage and proudly play the simple song of ABCs with their arms waving up and down.

    a. Chopin—F. F. Chopin(1810 — 1849) was a Polish composer and virtuoso pianist. He is widely considered one of the greatest Romantic piano composers. 肖邦，波兰作曲家、钢琴家，19 世纪欧洲浪漫主义音乐代表人物

    b. Beethoven—Ludwig van Beethoven (1770 — 1827) was a German composer and pianist. A crucial figure in the transition between the Classical and Romantic eras in Western art music, he remains one of the most famous and influential of all composers. 贝多芬，德国作曲家、钢琴家、指挥家，维也纳古典乐派代表人物之一

6. I am happy to parent with cuddliness, but not afraid to show some claw—I am happy to be a mild and amiable dad but I would show my authority and dignity if necessary. 我很满足于这种亲切可爱但有时也不怕显露威仪的父亲形象。

7. juggling a variety of demanding deadlines with an increasingly complex family schedule—dealing with different writing tasks before the tight deadlines and at the same time arranging more complex family affairs.

8. you can't backseat drive how your children are being raised—you can't just give unwanted advice about how to raise your children; you have to take the responsibility and get involved in parenting on your own.

    backseat drive—to give unwanted advice to the driver about how to drive

9. calling the kids garbage or chaining them to a piano bench—calling the kids "garbage" or forcing them to practice piano for hours. (This is what the Tiger Mom did to her daughter.)

10. mom is working late because ... when the curtain rises—No matter how busy mom is with her work related to the international crisis looming large, she will make time to attend in time the school play performed by our kids. 作者的妻子也供职于财经报道的《华尔街日报》，因此世界经济危机使得报道任务加重，工作繁忙。……
11. while fielding calls on a story—while answering phone calls about a report
　　　field—to answer questions, telephone calls etc 回答，应对
12. It's sheer narcissism ... a reflection of your worth. —If you believe your child's very success and failure is a sign of your worth, you are totally overestimating yourself.
13. Get over yourself—Make clear the fact; don't think so much of yourself.
14. ... running through the streets in roving packs of fun-seekers...—running through the street wandering in crowds to seek fun. 走街串巷，自由地结伴玩耍
15. The appeal in contemporary America ... get steamrolled by China. —在当代美国出现这种呼声是源于这样一种感觉：我们的国家正在被按照类似的方式划分阶层，而且很快就要被中国所赶超。
　　　stem from—to exist or happen as a result of
16. If you can't beat/lick them, join them. 赢不了，早入伙（以便从中获利）；胜不了，成朋友；败下阵，快归顺。这是吹得天花乱坠的商战策略，美国人的阿Q精神，政界、商界时髦语，倒不失为保住面子的好办法。此处的意思是既然美国教育孩子的方法不如中国，就跟中国学好了。因为在一次世界中学生学习能力评估计划赛上，上海队名列第一，这震撼了美国。
17. unstructured play—play that is organized or regulated; free play
18. non-neurotic contributors—people who can contribute to the society without much anxiety or sensitivity

Questions

1. What role should a father play in child-rearing according to the author's experience?
2. What insight is given to the author by his several years in China?
3. Why does the author call himself Panda Dad?
4. How does the author think about order and chaos at home?

5. According to the article, is the American child-rearing too laid back?
6. What are the three final goals that everyone should realistically set for raising their kids in the author's view?
7. What is Mr. Alan Paul's attitude towards sleepovers?

新闻写作

新闻体裁

新闻体裁(forms of news writing)指报道形式,如何划分众说纷纭,不但中外不同,中国也不统一。例如中国有的主张分为五类:(1)消息,包括动态、综合、经验、述评等消息四类。(2)通讯,可分为人物、事件、概貌和工作等通讯及小故事五类。(3)新闻特写,有人物、事件、旅行等特写及速写。(4)调查报告。(5)报告文学,一种介于新闻与文学之间的边缘体裁。有的主张分消息、特写、通讯、专访和述评五类。美英等国有人认为除消息报道体裁外,专稿、述评、采访、杂文、传记等等都是特写体裁。然而,人们较多倾向于将它分为消息、特写和社评三类。

消息(News)

消息报道分两类:一类是通讯社的电讯或报道,短小精悍,内容最真实,被称之为"纯硬性新闻"(pure hard news),有的报纸将之辟为"Brief(ly)"栏。另一类报刊的报道比通讯社的要详细得多,但有的由于夹杂着记者的推测和描绘,往往不如前者真实和经得起推敲。

特写(Feature)

新闻特写常指再现新闻事件、人物或场景的形象化报道,吸取了一般新闻报道和文艺作品的长处,其结构则取两者之长。消息在导语部分就往往把最重要、最新鲜、最吸引人的内容突出在最前面,而特写虽然也是一种新闻报道,但不少则常采取引人入胜的悬念式(suspended interest form)写作手法,逐渐娓娓道来。

社论和评论(Editorial & Commentary)

社论是一家报纸或杂志的编辑部发表的权威性评论,所代表的是编辑部的观点,是一家报纸的灵魂,要了解其对某事的倾向,需要从社论看起。它常以第三者口吻说话,或对人对事直接发表意见,表明立场、观点和倾向,或提出问题,或号召人们采取行动。评论是署名文章,往往在报道文章后就报道中提及的人和事发表评述,启示读者。这是社论和评论所不同的。社评类文章也报道事实,但以评论表明立场为最终目的,这与新闻报道只叙事而不评论大有区别。在文字上,报道类文章一般较简明,社论则较严肃正规,评论或言论(Opinion)则较活泼。评论可以嬉笑怒骂、讽刺影射,尤其常用借古讽今的手法。因此后两类文章较难读懂。读社论要了解有关人和事的背景,而读评论则还要有较深的语言功底和较广的知识,因为专栏作家在文章中常引经据典。

　　社论和评论往往都开门见山,在第一段点出论题,类似引子,引导读者往下读。接着就逐段逐点展开分析评说。末段则为结论。当然,有的写法并非如此,如将事实和结论都置于首段或前两段。这与特写采用的倒叙手法有别。

　　以上有关消息、特写和社评的写作手法和用语不同,《导读》均以文章为例进行解析。

Lesson Five

课文导读

随着知识经济时代的到来,全世界出现了高科技人才紧缺的危机。发达国家除了大力加强人才培养外,还以"沙漠风暴"的方式发动了一场人才争夺战,锋芒直指那些在全球性人才大战中明显处于劣势的发展中国家。截至2012年底,改革开放以来我国出国留学人员达到264万人,回国人员达到109万人。回归率为41%。千金何足惜,一士固难求。从全球经济发展的视角来看,我们最需要的是人才,最缺乏的也是人才。面对知识经济和全球人才危机的挑战,我国滞后的用人环境和机制,已成为阻碍生产力发展的重要因素。如何以凿石索玉、剖蚌求珠之精神,创造培养、吸引和招揽人才的良好环境和机制,值得我们思考和努力。

当然,正如本文所言,那些暂时留在国外继续从事研究或工作者,亦同样能为中国做出巨大的贡献。

Pre-reading Questions

1. Do you know anyone who has come back to China after studying abroad?
2. Some of the students who have studied abroad choose not to come back. What do you think are the reasons?

Text

Home at Last

For a group of Harvard M. B. A. s,
returning to China means a chance to
serve the country—and get rich.

By Brook Larmer

It was one of those all-night gabfests when graduating students, in boozy camaraderie, bare their deepest feelings. Only this was more serious: the 11 classmates who gathered at an apartment on the Harvard Business School campus in May 1999 were wrestling with the fate of China. Surrounded by empty beer bottles and bags of potato chips, the friends—all from China—were discussing whether to go home or not. Each of them had received lucrative offers from America's top companies. Still, China had changed dramatically in the decade since most of them had left. The nation now offered more personal freedoms and economic opportunities than ever before. And it desperately needed elite managers like them. Zhang Wei, a buoyant 29-year-old woman whose dream was to become China's answer to[1] American talk-show host Oprah Winfrey[2], implored her classmates to follow their hearts back home. "We can't sacrifice the present for the sake of tomorrow," she said. "We should start doing right now what we really want to do."

2 The words were pure Oprah, but they proved prophetic. In a matter of weeks, the youngest man in the room—a 26-year-old former national math champion named Shao Yibo—scribbled down a business proposal, sold his belongings and left for Shanghai, where he launched a Chinese version of the Internet auction giant, eBay. On the way, he stopped off for a day in Silicon Valley[3] and persuaded investors to give him $400,000. Weeks later classmate Tan Haiying returned to Shanghai to visit friends before starting an investment-banking job in New York. She never used her return ticket to the United States: Shao persuaded her to join his firm as chief operating officer[4]. Within a year three other members of the clique—Huan Yiming, Renee Chen and Herbert Wang—also returned to launch start-up companies. And Zhang? She landed a business-development job at Rupert Murdoch's[5] News Corp. in Beijing. She also works overtime pursuing her Oprah dream. Once a week she hosts a popular talk show on Beijing TV that takes on such daring topics as AIDS, drug abuse and—yes—Internet dating.

3 By the time the Chinese students converged on HBS, they were not looking for an escape, but an edge for their eventual return to China. After years of working for consulting firms, multinationals or start-ups, all of them felt the need to deepen their understanding of Western business culture. At HBS, the Chinese students quickly gravitated together. The old hands helped the newcomers learn how to drive, shop for food, ride the subway. Three of them shared a flat, and because

they cooked Chinese food, it soon became a hangout. The group vacationed together, snorkeling in Puerto Rico, skiing in Vermont, relaxing on Cape Cod. They bonded so well that they even wrote a book, in Chinese, about their HBS experience.

4 But the dilemma about the future always loomed large[6]. When Chinese Prime Minister Zhu Rongji spoke at nearby Massachusetts Institute of Technology in April 1999, shortly after graduation, he invited business-school graduates to return home, stressing that China's greatest need was management expertise. "We were all struggling with the choices," says Eric Xin, a 30-year-old management consultant who has decided, for the moment, to stay and work for McKinsey & Co. "We have deep roots in China, but we're also flying high in the Western world." Now with a 1-year-old son and another on the way— "I can have more than one child here," Xin says, only half-joking—Xin and his lawyer wife plan to stay in Washington a few more years, gaining experience abroad before going back to China. "I want to test myself to see if I can survive in a pure American environment," he says. Still, he admits, "sometimes I stop in the street and wonder, 'What am I doing here?'"

5 For some of the Harvard grads, China is still too underdeveloped, especially in the financial sector, to lure them back. "There's a lot of thunder, but not much rain," says Peter Chen, a debt specialist[7] with GE Capital[8] in Tokyo. But for others, it is simply that family comes first. Huang Jingsheng, who at 43 is the oldest of the group, is worried about subjecting his wife and two young boys to Beijing's pollution. For the time being, Huang is living in clear-aired Sacramento, California, where he works as a venture capitalist for Intel Capital, handling occasional China deals. "There are different ways of helping China," he says. "My classmates have found one way. I'm still figuring out how to do the same thing—and making the right choice for my family."

6 The Class of '99 grads[9] are a new breed of returnee. Except for Zhang, they are not working for law firms or multinationals, but building their own companies. And that makes their impact on China even greater. It's not just the millions of dollars in foreign capital they are bringing in. (Shao and Tan have raised more than $25 million for their online auction house, Eachnet.) They are shaping a whole new

industry. After graduation, Herbert Wang worked for six months at Nortel in Toronto, but he quickly returned to Beijing to found Prient, a start-up that helps old-line companies go online[10]. "I felt that I could add more value to my country by running my own company," he says. "I couldn't do that in the U.S."

7   But returnees are forced to adjust to local practice, too. In China, business is not simply about profits, but relationships. Huan Yiming came back to China earlier this year after working at Sun Microsystems. In Shanghai, where she set up her wireless-applications company, Etonenet, she says she "had to relearn China. I tried to structure this like a Silicon Valley company, but I quickly realized this wasn't the U.S." Her employees didn't know what stock options were, and she didn't know how to navigate the local bureaucracy. So she hired an old friend to be her local partner. "We have to be modest to learn how local business works," Huan says.

8   That cultural understanding is precisely what Zhang is trying to promote on her TV show, "Common Ground." The program's slogan: "Building a bridge between China and the world." Each week the show takes advantage of her experience in the United States to look at sensitive issues from local and foreign perspectives, in English and Mandarin. This month, in a segment on Internet dating, Zhang presided over a marriage proposal between an American man and the Chinese girlfriend he met on the Internet. Oprah, indeed! Back in her office at News Corp., under a poster for her favorite TV show, "Friends," Zhang fiddles with[11] the Snoopy chain[12] on her cellular phone. "Things are changing so fast here," she says. "The whole point is to show that people have different values, that not everybody thinks the same about every issue. And that may be new for China."

9   Still, change is not always comfortable. Zhang left behind a group of close friends in the United States and returned to a world that was virtually foreign to her. She has few friends in Beijing, and she still feels a need to tread lightly on the set[13]. "The producers are taking a real risk to have me host the show," she says. "I've gotten a lot of my values from abroad, and the show has no script[14]." When she chose to do her first program on AIDs, the producers seemed more concerned about her young, casual appearance than the delicate subject matter[15].

They dressed her up in a prim gray suit. "I told them: 'Please let me be me!'" says Zhang. "Now they realize that the host needs to have his or her own personality."

10 It's been more than a year since the Chinese members of the class of '99 gathered for their soul-searching discussion over beer and potato chips. Today they are too busy—and live too far apart—to get together much. In August the U. S. contingent[16] will have a mini-reunion at Zhang's wedding, which is being held in Los Angeles because "more of our friends are there," she says. When Zhang and Peter Chen visited Shanghai a few months ago, they managed to meet Shao, Tan and Huan for a cup of coffee. But the group couldn't meet until after midnight. And even then, they were just taking a break from the hardest—and most exhilarating—work of their lives. (From *Newsweek*, July 31, 2000)

New Words

boozy /ˈbuːzɪ/ *adj.* intoxicated; addicted to drink （酩酊的，嗜酒的）

Cape Cod a peninsula of SE Massachusetts, extending 65 miles E and N into the Atlantic （位于美国马萨诸塞州南部的"科德角"）

camaraderie /ˌkæməˈrɑːdərɪ/ *n.* friendliness between people who like each other or work together as part of a group （同志之爱，友情）

converge /kənˈvɜːdʒ/ *v.* to come together from different directions; meet

edge *n.* keenness, as of desire or enjoyment; zest （渴望）

exhilarate /ɪɡˈzɪləreɪt/ *v.* to make lively or glad

gabfest /ˈɡæbfest/ *n.* an informal gathering or session for the exchange of news, opinions, and gossip （非正式的聚会）

gravitate /ˈɡrævɪteɪt/ *v.* to feel attracted to sth or sb

hangout /ˈhæŋaut/ *n.* a place where people gather informally to talk, drink, and eat

lucrative /ˈluːkrətɪv/ *adj.* (esp. of a business, job or activity) producing a lot of money; making a large profit

perspective /pəˈspektɪv/ *n.* 角度；观点，看法

prim /prɪm/ *adj.* formal

prophetic /prəˈfetɪk/ *adj.* accurately describing or predicting what will happen in the future

segment /ˈseɡmənt/ *n.* division or section

Snoopy *n.* a TV cartoon character: Snoopy chain (key chain "史努比锁链")

snorkel /'snɔːkəl/ *v.* to swim using a snorkel (戴呼吸管潜泳)

version /'vɜːʃən/ *n.* a copy of sth that has been changed slightly

wrestle /'resəl/ *v.* to try very hard to deal with (sth) which is difficult, such as trying to solve a problem or make a decision

Notes

1. sb's answer to—sb or sth that is considered to be just as good as a more famous person or thing
2. Oprah Winfrey —1954— , American television talk-show host(名人访谈节目黑人女主持人) and actress, whose nationally syndicated talk show became one of the most popular programs on television. Born in Kosciusko, Mississippi, to unmarried parents who separated after her birth, Winfrey had a troubled childhood, experiencing neglect and sexual abuse. At the age of 13 she went to live with her father in Nashville, Tennessee. There she became an excellent student, winning a full scholarship to Tennessee State University. While in college Winfrey became the first black woman to anchor the news on the local Nashville television station. After graduating in 1976, she worked as a television newscaster and later as a television talk-show host in Baltimore, Maryland. In 1984 she became the host of the television talk show "A. M. Chicago." In 1985 the show was renamed "The Oprah Winfrey Show." Dealing openly with controversial subjects, it achieved national syndication in 1986. A major factor in the show's popularity was Winfrey's ability to connect emotionally with her guests. In 1986 she formed HARPO Productions to produce her show and other projects. Winfrey's role as Sofia in the film *The Color Purple* (1985) won her a 1986 Academy Award(美国电影艺术科学院颁发的年奖,即奥斯卡金像奖) nomination as best supporting actress. She also appeared in *Native Son* (1986) and produced and costarred in the television miniseries *The Women of Brewster Place* (1989). Her exclusive interview with the reclusive American pop music superstar Michael Jackson was aired on television in 1993 and highly publicized. 奥普拉·温弗里是美国家喻户晓的名人,有的新词语就与其名 Oprah 有关。

3. Silicon Valley—in west-central California, U. S. It occupies the San Jose and Santa Clara valleys and also includes the communities of Sunnyvale, Santa Clara, Los Altos, and also Mountain View. It derived its name from the dense concentration of electronics and computer corporations and their factories that sprang up there in the 1970s and '80s (silicon is the basic material of the semiconductor elements in computer circuits). By the early 1990s the economic emphasis in Silicon Valley had partly switched from computer manufacturing to research, development, and marketing of computer products and software. (硅谷)
4. chief operating officer—运营主管，负责运营的行政副总管(*cf.* CEO，行政总管；不宜译成"官"，因为他既非官员，也非军人)
5. Murdoch, Rupert—1931— , Australian-born media magnate whose business holdings include newspapers, magazines, television stations, and news services. Current holdings include the Fox Broadcasting Company, *TV Guide* magazine and the *London Times*. He boosted the circulation of many of his newspapers by creating a tabloid mix of sex, crime, and sports stories topped with giant sensationalized headlines. He was born in Melbourne, Australia, and educated at the University of Oxford. He became a United States citizen in 1985.
6. loom large—to be important, have great influence
7. a debt specialist—见"语言解说"
8. GE Capital—*abbrev.* General Electric (Capital)通用电气公司投资部门：通用是美国和全球最大的工业公司。本课还有 Intel Capital，指英特尔公司的投资部门。
9. The Class of '99 grads—指(19)99届毕业班
10. help old-line companies go online—to help traditional companies advertise or do business through the Internet
11. fiddle with—to keep moving or touching sth with one's fingers, esp. when you are bored or nervous
12. Snoopy chain—the chain which holds keys together, with the figure of snoopy on it
13. tread lightly on the set—to take care in the place or setting while TV programs and films are directed and produced
14. the show has no script—指这个节目没写好或没有现成的稿子

15. the delicate subject matter——很微妙的题材，即前面提到的 sensitive issue(敏感的问题)
16. the U. S. contingent——here the U. S. graduates from Harvard Business School

Questions

1. Why did some of the HBS grads choose to come back to China although they had received lucrative offers from America's top companies?
2. What profession do they usually like to go in for?
3. Why did most of them choose to take up IT industry?
4. Why did some of them decide to stay in the U. S. while some chose to come back?
5. What do you think is the biggest obstacle preventing the elite from coming back home?
6. What does the title of this article "Home at Last" mean?

语言解说

名词定语及理解上的陷阱

在现代英语中，以名词定语替代形容词的现象，在报刊语言中尤其普遍，并成为一种时髦。如本课的 debt specialist 就是一例。再如 1950 年发生的朝鲜战争，朝鲜还是用的形容词，为 Korean War，可是到了 1957 年发生的越南战争和后来发生的海湾战争、波黑战争和科索沃战争则均以名词作定语了，分别为 Vietnam/Gulf/Bosnia/Kosovo War。又如由已故美国著名经济学家和外交家 John K. Galbraith 在 1958 年出版的《富裕社会》一书还是用的 affluent，为 *The Affluent Society*，而现在则被 affluence society 所代替。又如前用 Silent Generation，现用 Silence Generation。

当然，我们不能以此类推，认为所有的名词定语即可与相应的形容词互相置换，如本文中出现的 Peter Chen, a debt specialist 就不能理解为他是一个"负了债的专家"，而是"处理债务的专家"。有些名词定语在意义和功能上与用相应的形容词有很大的差别，试看以下两类词组：

bankruptcy lawyer	bankrupt businessman
处理破产诉讼的律师	破了产的商人
economy measure	economic measure
节约措施	经济措施
efficiency expert	efficient worker
研究提高工作效率的专家	工作效率高的工人
obesity specialist	obese specialist
肥胖症专家	胖专家
riot police	riotous police
防暴警察	闹事的警察
capacity audience	capacious room
满座的听众或观众	宽敞的房间

对比以上两类词组，名词 bankruptcy 等和形容词 bankrupt 等在意义上的差异一目了然；此外，还可以看出，名词及其相应的形容词虽然都用了定语，但前者侧重于职能方面修饰或限制另一名词，而后者则在属性方面起修饰作用。①

然而，以上有的名词定语是否用得妥当还值得研究探讨。如 riot police，是否用 anti-riot police 更好呢？事实上这两种用法都有（至于"中国模式"，外刊上既有用 Chinese model，也有用 China model 的）。一个国家领导人如果遭众人恨，万人骂，当他处于风雨飘摇之中，警方或全体警察起来造反闹事也不是不可能，只是根据常识少见罢了。再如 fire department（"消防署"或"消防队"），也只能根据常识，政府不能成立一个 department 专门去放火。又如对于 drug ring（毒品或贩毒集团）和 drug team（缉毒队）不会理解错误是因为这个政治贬义词 ring 与 team 不同，所以不易产生误解。但有的两种释义都可以，如 drug tsar 的意思既可指"缉毒大王"，也可作"大毒枭"讲。

以上可见，如无上下文，单凭孤零零一两个词是易产生不同理解的。"词本无义，义随人生"（Words do not have meanings; people have meanings for words）这句英语中的名言讲的就是这个道理。此外，同样一句话也须视对象和情况，不然会闹出笑话。

---

① 参见陆国强编著：《现代英语构词》，上海译文出版社，1981，p. 27。

Lesson Six

课文导读

"西方生活方式给国人带来新的苦恼"一文说明,随着改革开放政策的不断深入,中国的经济飞速发展,中国在世界政治、经济及文化领域的地位日益提高,同时中国也成了国外消费品的大市场。由于生活的富足,许多人逐渐放弃了传统的简朴和节制的生活方式。结果各种原本只在西方流行的疾病在中国也大行其道,使一些人苦不堪言;同时,国民经济也受到影响。这不能不引起我们的高度关注和警惕。

Pre-reading Questions

1. Describe your own lifestyle?
2. Do you like Western or Chieses lifestyle, or their combination?

Text

China Finds Western Ways Bring New Woes

Battles with the bulge and the bottle[1]
are one downside of spreading prosperity
By David J. Lynch

1   China is the fastest-growing market for American goods, an ally in the war on terror and, at the same time, an emerging rival to U.S. pre-eminence in Asia. In coming years, its major cities will host the Olympic Games and a World's Fair while its movie, fashion and sports stars attract growing numbers of fans. China in the 21st century appears poised to reclaim the greatness it enjoyed for thousands of years before it slid into the eclipse in the late 1840s.[2] Yet Beijing's leaders face daunting challenges. An authoritarian political system demands reform. Economic vitality and growing regional clout coexist with woes that bedevil all developing countries: environmental degradation, poverty

and preventable illnesses. Understanding the world's most populous nation has never been more vital. So throughout this year, *USA TODAY* will offer an occasional story on contemporary China to illustrate how much has changed and how much remains to be done if this is truly to be "The Chinese Century".

BEIJING

2   In cities across China, signs of the better life spawned by 25 years of economic growth abound. Gleaming glass towers form proud, modern skylines. Private sedans throng roads once navigated only by bicyclists. Well-dressed men and women stride briskly past ads for foreign brands such as McDonald's and Microsoft.

3   China today little resembles the impoverished, hermetic land that existed before its leaders began freeing the economy in 1978. But these visible improvements mask the dangers of moving too swiftly from its scarcity to abundance. Today's spreading prosperity is redrawing traditional Chinese living patterns to mimic Western habits—for good and ill[3].

4   There is perhaps no better way to appreciate how much has changed in China than by examining the people themselves. Consider what today's Chinese eat and drink. In a country where a famine killed 30 million people as recently as the early 1960s, more than one-fifth of adults are now dangerously overweight or obese. The proportion is expected to approach 40% in two decades.

5   Washing down[4] all that food, the average Chinese person now drinks more than four times as much alcohol per year as in 1978, the beginning of China's economic opening. Alcoholism—though still low by Western standards—appears to be surging in more prosperous urban areas.

Affluence's effects showing up

6   As China strives toward its goal of a *xiaokang* or moderately well-off society, many Chinese are trading a venerable lifestyle that emphasized restraint for something closer to Western indulgence. The public health consequences are as predictable as they are deadly. From 1995 to 2025, deaths from diet-related illnesses such as heart disease, high blood pressure, strokes and adult-onset diabetes[5] are expected to

increase 10 times faster than population growth, according to Barry Popkin, a University of North Carolina economist who studies dietary changes in developing countries.

7   "The increase in life expectancy they've seen could slow down or turn around.[6] Certainly, the burden of health care costs is going to go up immensely," he says. "With China so important economically, this is one of those things that could drag it (down)[7] if they don't deal with it."

Sedentary lifestyles

8   China today is an emerging economic power, eagerly anticipating a national coming-out party at the 2008 Beijing Olympics[8]. In 1978, when Deng Xiaoping launched market-oriented reforms, the typical city-dweller earned less than $200 annually. There were no private restaurants; many everyday goods were in chronic short supply; most people could consume little more than what they needed to survive.

9   From a beachhead in four special economic zones along China's coast, Deng gradually expanded permissible free-market activities. Starting in the 1980s, consumer luxuries such as televisions and stereos as well as labor-saving products such as washing machines and refrigerators became commonplace.

10   At the same time, hundreds of millions of people swapped the rigors of farm life for more sedentary jobs on assembly lines or in offices. People who once walked or bicycled long distances to work increasingly began driving. In 1985, there were fewer than 1,100 private cars in Beijing. Today, there are more than 2 million. As people grew wealthier—and less active—they ate fewer vitamin-and fiber-rich cereals and more meat, chicken and eggs. And they began using pricey, and fattening, vegetable oil to stir-fry more elaborate meals. "In the past, we had meat, but not as much as now. For instance, if we had four dishes, three would be vegetables and one would be meat. Today, it's the opposite," says Zhang Shuying, 56, a Beijing homemaker.

11   Over the past 20 years, the amount of fat in the diet has more than doubled. In cities like Beijing, where fast-food restaurants such as KFC have proliferated, one-third of the calories in the typical diet now comes from fat—an amount equal to the USA's unhealthy levels. Even

vegetables have been corrupted. One popular dish that makes doctors cringe is *zha qiehe*, eggplant stuffed with pork and then fried.

12   From 1989 through 1997, the percentage of overweight males in China almost tripled. By 2025, more than 38% of Chinese adults will be fighting the battle of the bulge, according to Popkin.

13   Those figures pale in comparison with the United States, where an estimated 60% of all adults are overweight. But for China, the emergence of a weight problem represents a change without precedent in the country's modern history. Dietary and lifestyle changes that emerged in the United States over several generations of industrialization have swept urban China in just one.

14   His countrymen's swelling waistlines are no mystery to Liang Yong, 25, who still hopes to lose another 50 pounds. "Life is getting better," he says. "That's why they're getting fat."

Imported beers, breweries

15   Seated at a table in the rear of Nashville, an intimate, Western-themed bar[9], four friends enjoy a drink and quiet conversation. In the next room, a guitarist reprises old Sting[10] songs. The shelves behind the bar hold bottles of Budweiser, Heineken and about a dozen other imported beers and liquors such as Glenfiddich scotch and Grand Marnier cognac.[11]

16   Hao Jun, 30, one of the patrons, used to come to this same spot in the late 1980s, when it was home to a neighborhood market. For 1 kuai (a little more than 12 cents), he could buy enough vegetables to last all day. "Now, one glass of this Boddington's (ale)[12] that we're drinking costs 50 kuai," Hao says.

17   Before Deng's economic reforms, alcohol supplies were limited. But as the economy welcomed foreign investment, breweries sprang up in almost every Chinese province. By 1981, beer output was 91 times what it had been when the communists seized control in 1949, according to the World Health Organization.

18   Increased supplies of alcohol, together with rising disposable income, have spurred drinking. The WHO—measuring consumption by the amount of the intoxicating agent ethyl alcohol people ingest—found the typical Chinese person consumed 176 ounces of ethyl alcohol in

2000. That was a 320% jump since 1978. Actual consumption likely is about one-third higher, since the WHO's figure doesn't include homemade brews produced in rural stills.

19　　"I'm convinced China is on track for major alcohol problems[13]," says Ian Newman, professor of health education at the University of Nebraska-Lincoln. "Per-capita consumption of alcohol is going up as fast as anywhere in the world."

20　　At the end of the 1970s, alcoholism care like that offered here by Anding Hospital was virtually unknown. But demand for such services has risen sharply during China's decade-long boom. Last year, the program treated roughly 300 people, almost three times the figure from two years earlier. The vast majority are men. But in 2000, for the first time, the center began seeing female alcoholics.

A problem of the future

21　　If nothing is done to halt the spread of unhealthy eating and drinking, China will face substantial financial costs. In 1995, China spent almost $12 billion to treat diet-related diseases. Popkin says that by 2025, that figure is likely to increase by at least 25%. Heart disease, strokes and adult-onset diabetes, linked to unhealthy diet and inactivity, already are on the rise.

22　　If China achieves its goal of quadrupling the size of the economy by 2020, its people will enjoy a standard of living roughly comparable to that of the West in 1990. But as it rushes to duplicate the comfort and convenience of life in the developed world, China risks copying the Western lifestyle's worst attributes, some Chinese health professionals are warning.

23　　In January, officials began training doctors throughout China to apply new national guidelines aimed at achieving a healthier diet. And Beijing newspapers are full of ads promoting quick-acting diet plans that use a "secret formula" to strip away excess fat[14].

24　　"This is the right time to do something," says Chen Chunming of the Chinese Center for Disease Control and Prevention. "If we take action now, we're not going to repeat the experience of the Western world." (From *USA Today*, May 19, 2004)

New Words

acupuncture /ˈækjʊˌpʌŋktʃə/ *n.* the treatment of illness or pain by sticking the ends of needles into a person's body at particular places（针刺疗法）

affluence /ˈæfluəns/ *n.* a plentiful supply of material goods; wealth

alcoholic /ˌælkəˈhɒlɪk/ *n.* a person who drinks alcoholic substances habitually and to excess or who suffers from alcoholism（酗酒者；酒鬼）

alcoholism /ˈælkəhɒlɪzəm/ *n.* the condition of being addicted to alcohol; the diseased condition caused by alcohol dependency（酗酒；酒精中毒）

attribute /ˈætrɪbjuːt/ *n.* a quality or characteristic inherent in or ascribed to sb or sth（特征）

beachhead /ˈbiːtʃhed/ *n.* a first achievement that opens the way for further developments; a foothold（立足点）

bedevil /bɪˈdevl/ *v.* to worry, annoy, or frustrate; to plague

brewery /ˈbruːərɪ/ *n.* an establishment for the manufacture of malt liquors, such as beer and ale（酿酒厂）

bulge /bʌldʒ/ *n.* swelling; a sudden, usually temporary increase in number or quantity

chapter /ˈtʃæptə/ *n.* a local branch of an organization, such as a club or fraternity

clout /klaʊt/ *n.* influence and power to get things done

cognac /ˈkɒnjæk/ *n.* 干邑白兰地酒（产于法国的科纳克）

cringe /krɪndʒ/ *v.* to be embarrassed about sth（畏缩；局促不安）

daunting /ˈdɔːntɪŋ/ *adj.* worrying because sth is difficult or frightening

dietary /ˈdaɪətərɪ/ *adj.* of or relating to diet

disposable /dɪˈspəʊsəbl/ *adj.* remaining to a person after taxes have been deducted; free for use; available（税后的；可自由支配的）

doctrinaire /ˌdɒktrɪˈneə/ *adj.* of a person inflexibly attached to a practice or theory（教条主义的）

downside /ˈdaʊnsaɪd/ *n.* a disadvantageous aspect

eclipse /ɪˈklɪps/ *n.* a fall into obscurity or disuse; a decline

ethyl /ˈeθɪl/ *n.* 乙基

hermetic /hɜːˈmetɪk/ *adj.* impervious to outside interference or influence（密封的；与外界隔绝的）

heyday /ˈheɪdeɪ/ *n.* the period of greatest popularity, success, or power; prime

impoverish /ɪmˈpɒvərɪʃ/ *v.* to reduce to poverty; make poor

ingest /ɪnˈdʒest/ *v.* to take into the body by the mouth for digestion or absorption(摄取;咽下)

inpatient /ˈɪnpeɪʃənt/ *n.* a patient who is admitted to a hospital or clinic for treatment that requires at least one overnight stay

intoxicating /ɪnˈtɒksɪkeɪtɪŋ/ *adj.* (of drink) containing alcohol and making sb drunk(醉人的)

mimic /ˈmɪmɪk/ *v.* to copy or imitate closely, especially in speech, expression, and gesture

navigate /ˈnævɪgeɪt/ *v.* to travel or find your way through a difficult or dangerous place

obese /əʊˈbiːs/ *adj.* very fat in a way that is unhealthy

per-capita /pəˈkæpɪtə/ each person (人均)

pre-eminence /priːˈemɪnəns/ *n.* the quality of being more important, powerful, or capable than other people or things in a group

pricey /ˈpraɪsɪ/ *adj.* expensive

proliferate /prəˈlɪfəreɪt/ *v.* to increase or spread at a rapid rate

proof /pruːf/ *adj.* used after a number to show the alcoholic strength of a drink (标准酒精度数的)

pudgy /ˈpʌdʒɪ/ *adj.* short and fat

quadruple /ˈkwɒdrʊpl/ *v.* to multiply or be multiplied by four

quick-acting *a.* functioning or producing results quickly

reclaim /rɪˈkleɪm/ *v.* to bring back sth that you have lost or sth that has been taken away from you, or ask it back (要求收回;恢复)

redraw /riːˈdrɔː/ *v.* to draw again and change

reprise /rɪˈpraɪz/ *v.* to repeat or resume an action

rigor /ˈrɪgə/ *n.* a harsh or trying circumstance; hardship

sedentary /ˈsedəntərɪ/ *adj.* characterized by or requiring much sitting (久坐的)

solace /ˈsɒləs/ *n.* comfort in sorrow, misfortune, or distress; consolation

spawn /spɔːn/ *v.* to produce in large numbers; to give rise to; engender

spotty /ˈspɒtɪ/ *adj.* lacking consistency; uneven(缺乏连续性的;不稳定的)

spur /spɜː/ *v.* to incite or stimulate

still /stɪl/ *n.* an apparatus used for distilling alcoholic drinks(蒸馏器;酒厂)

stir-fry *v.* to cook small pieces of vegetables, meat, etc. quickly by stirring them in a small quantity of very hot oil. (用旺火炒)

surge /sɛːdʒ/ *v.* to increase suddenly
swap /swɒp/ *v.* to exchange or trade one thing for another
upheaval /ʌpˈhiːvəl/ *n.* a sudden, violent disruption or upset(动乱;剧变)
vendor /ˈvendə/ *n.* one that sells or vends
venerable /ˈvenərəbl/ *adj.* worthy of respect, especially by religious or historical association
woe /wəʊ/ *n.* sadness; deep distress or misery; misfortune; calamity

Notes

1. the bulge and the bottle—the rapid increase in people's weight and in the amount of alcohol they drink
2. China in the 21st century ... in the late 1840s. —看来中国在 21 世纪已做好一切准备,恢复它在 19 世纪 40 年代后期的衰落前所享有的几千年的伟大强盛。
    a. be poised to—to be completely ready to take action at any moment
    b. slide into—to change to a particular state, attitude, or kind of behavior gradually and smoothly 不知不觉地陷入,逐渐陷入
3. for good and ill—whether it may tend to good or evil
4. wash down—to swallow (food) with the help of liquid
5. adult-onset diabetes—diabetes that begins after one has grown up or has entered adulthood
6. The increase in life expectancy they've seen could slow down or turn around. —It is possible that life expectancy(预期寿命) will increase more slowly or begin to decrease.
7. drag it (down)—to make it weak; prevent its development
8. eagerly anticipating a national coming-out party at the 2008 Beijing Olympics 一热切期待着全民出动,支持 2008 年奥运会。
    national coming-out party—It is expected that all the people in the country will become active in a movement to support the 2008 Beijing Olympics.
9. Western-themed bar—a bar that has been decorated and furnished in Western style
10. Sting—a rock singer born in 1951 in England
11. The shelves behind the bar ... Grand Marnier cognac. — 吧台后面

的货架上摆放着一瓶瓶百威啤酒、喜力啤酒和十余种其他进口啤酒和酒精饮料,例如格兰非帝兹纯麦威士忌和大马尼尔法国白兰地。
12. Boddington's (ale)—(伯丁顿麦芽酒) Boddington's was first produced in Manchester about 200 years ago. Now it is available almost everywhere in the world.
13. I'm convinced China is on track for major alcohol problems. —I'm sure China is going to have major alcohol problems.
    on track for—heading for; on the way to
14. strip away excess fat—to remove or get rid of the fat that is more than needed; lose weight

Questions

1. According to the writer, what is the best way to understand the change that has taken place in China?
2. What did the traditional Chinese lifestyle emphasize? What about the Western lifestyle? How can this change of lifestyle affect people's health? How can it influence China's economic development?
3. What are the two main factors that lead people to gain weight? What have caused the changes in people's lifestyle and diet?
4. According to the writer, is people's drinking habit influenced by alcohol supplies?
5. Will unhealthy eating and drinking lead to substantial financial costs? Why?

新 闻 写 作

报刊文体

　　根据《现代汉语词典》的定义,文体是文章的体裁;体裁指的是文学作品的表现形式。中外对 style 历来争议不断,如文体即形式或修辞、解说技巧等,约有二三十个定义,真是众说纷纭,莫衷一是。报刊文体大致有如下几种定义或说法:

1. 新闻体

　　journalese(新闻体),尤指 type of news reporting,是最常见的含有贬义的定义,即指报道性文章多陈词滥调,行文仓促,思想性或说理性肤浅,还不时夹着口语(Webster's Dictionary)。这个定论是以往受传统偏见的约束,瞧不起报刊英语,把它跟粗俗低级语言划等号。现在报刊质量早已大大提高,语言简明实用,富有创意,这是不争的事实。所谓行文仓促是不得已而为之,日报得天天出,与期刊有别。但现在罕见 Alan Warner 写的 Short Guide to English Style 一书中举例文章"Zoo Mountain Goat Leaps Lions' Enclouse Rescued by Keepers"那样,充斥着如 lions and elephants 比作"monarches of the wilds"(与"King of beast"一样)、"brute creation"(无理性之动物)、"sawdust Caesar"(喻马戏团训狮员)等夸张或陈腐之词。至于夹着口语,这与为了表明"客观公正",记者以第三者口气论述有关(见"报刊语言主要特点""常用套语")。只要读了本节"体裁"所举三篇文章,便知一二。

改革开放后,由于以前众所周知的原因,国内不少人因跟不上时代和语言的发展,一时看不懂外国报刊,又视之为当代必读之物,才逐渐认识到其重要性。

2. 综合体

报刊是由消息、特写、社评、采访、杂文、传记等多种体裁组成的,甚至还有散文、日记、游记和小说连载等等,无所不包,集多种体裁与题材英语之大成,所以说它是综合体。还有人无奈地称之为特殊文体。

3. 实用文体

报刊题材多样,语言紧贴当今现实而又简明,学了就能用。

4. 文学文体

四川大学曹明伦教授在《中国翻译》一文里,根据 19 世纪英国诗人、社会评论家马修·阿诺德(Matthew Arnold)所说的"Journalism is literature in a hurry"(报刊新闻是匆匆写出的文学作品)这句话,将报刊新闻定义为文学作品。还有的学者也将这种新闻急就章归类为文学,既然是文学,那又是何种文学文体?值得探讨。

以上说明,要给报刊文体下一个众所接受的定义并非易事,这与人们从不同角度审视报刊和文体有关。

Unit Three
United States（Ⅰ）

Lesson Seven

课文导读

这是一篇在若干调研报告基础上撰写的专题报道。由2007—2008年的次贷危机引发了2008年10月的美国金融危机和全球危机及经济衰退或危机，对美国的经济造成了严重影响，就业机会减少，税收收入锐减，预算计划和项目不得不进行削减，教育预算当然也不能幸免。这样，给学生提供的资助和贷款势必减少。与此同时，学生面临两个问题：一是学费上涨，要想完成学业，中低收入家庭的学生不得不举债或兼职工作。二是莘莘学子在完成了学业，获得了学位后，能否苦尽甘来，找到工作，而该工作的薪酬是否与文凭相符，使他们能逐渐偿还助学贷款，开始自己职业生涯的春天？读完本文，便可见一斑。

现在我国的大学毕业生也面临着在大城市找工作的难题，只要拓展视野，到真正缺人才的西部和广大农村去，他们不是找不到用武之地，而是人才远远供不应求！这是与美国学生处境的不同之处。

Pre-reading Questions

1) Do you think college education can ensure one a bright future? Why or why not?
2) What are the factors that influence one's decision about choosing majors in college?

Text

Debt Burden Alters Outlook for US Graduates

By Shannon Bond and Jason Abbruzzese in New York
and Robin Harding in Washington

1　　At universities across the US, the class of 2012[1] is celebrating the end of college. But, for the estimated 1.8m students receiving bachelor's degrees this spring, the financial crisis[2] that unfolded during their first year on campus in 2008 is still casting a long shadow over their futures.

2   Almost five years after the crisis began, the overall unemployment rate is still mired above 8 per cent while that for recent university graduates is stuck at 6.8 per cent.

3   For many young Americans, the promise of a degree has turned to disappointment as they find themselves struggling to find their first job, still burdened by student debt.

4   What is worse, studies show that graduating at a time of high unemployment can blight a young person's earning power for the rest of their career—and have an impact on the broader economy as well.

5   In a widely-cited paper, Lisa Kahn[3] of the Yale School of Management[4] looked at data from the early 1980s recession[5], and found a one-percentage-point increase in the unemployment rate for college graduates led to a 6—7 per cent drop in initial wages[6]. Even 15 years later, their wage loss was a statistically significant 2.5 per cent.

6   Seventeen-year-old Chelsea Katz, who plans to attend the University of Maryland[7] in the autumn, said she took into account the economy and possible debt when picking a school and choosing her degree.

7   "For a long time I have wanted to study business but definitely a major factor in that is the more promising outlook for a business major coming out of college," Ms. Katz said. "The idea of post-college debt definitely scares me but I try and focus on the present, not the future, while keeping in mind coming out of college with the minimum amount of debt possible."

8   A survey from Rutgers University[8] found two-thirds of graduates who finished college between 2006 and 2011 would have made different choices, such as majoring in another field, taking on more internships or part-time jobs, started looking for work sooner, choosing a different institution or even skipped higher education altogether.

9   "There's a lot of 'I wish I had known' thinking we see from the students encountering the harsh realities of the labour market," [9] said Carl Van Horn, director of Rutgers' Heldrich Center for Workforce Development[10], which conducted the study.

10 Half of the students surveyed were working full-time, with another 12 per cent working part-time and 20 per cent pursuing graduate or professional degrees[11].

11 About a quarter of the employed graduates said their position was below their level of education, a quarter said they were earning less than they expected, and a quarter said they had to accept a job outside their field in order to find work.

12 The median starting salary for those who finished school between 2009 and 2011 fell to $27,000 from $30,000 in 2006 and 2007.

13 These conditions are squeezing young people's ability to repay the student loans that have become a standard part of higher education as soaring tuition fees outpace income growth[12].

14 In the past decade, published prices for tuition fees have risen 29 per cent at private schools and 72 per cent at public institutions, according to the College Board[13]. The public universities, once seen as a ticket to higher earnings for middle and low-income students, have been hard hit by deep cuts to state budgets that have transferred more of the cost burden on to students and their families[14].

15 "We as a nation have been disinvesting in postsecondary education," said Mark Kantrowitz, publisher of FinAid. org[15], a website on financial aid. "When grants don't keep pace with college costs, you have three main outcomes: students graduate with thousands of dollars of additional debt, students shift to lower cost schools, such as community colleges[16], which have a negative impact on graduation rates, or they just don't go to college."

16 As expenses have gone up and grants have gone down, students are left with one choice: borrowing more.

17 Two-thirds of students who graduated with a bachelor's degree in 2008 took on debt to finance their education, according to the Pew Research Center[17], compared with 59 per cent in 1996. The average amount of debt rose to $23,287 from $17,075 in the same period.

18 The US Senate[18] is wrangling over how to extend a modest subsidy for student loans that is due to expire at the end of June but, in a sign of growing political sensitivity over student debt, both Barack Obama[19] and his Republican challenger Mitt Romney[20] are calling for action.

19 In an address to graduates of New York's Barnard College[21] in May, Mr. Obama, a 1983 graduate, struck a sombre note[22]: "Just as

you were starting out finding your way around this campus, an economic crisis struck that would claim more than 5m jobs before the end of your freshman year.... And you may be looking toward the future with that same sense of concern that my generation did when we were sitting where you are now."[23] (From *Financial Times*, June 1, 2012)

New Words

alter /'ɔːltə(r)/ v. to make or become different, but without changing into sth else
blight /blaɪt/ v. to have a deleterious effect on; ruin. 使产生恶果，毁坏
cast /kɑːst/ v. to turn or direct
disinvest /ˌdɪsɪn'vest/ v. take one's money out of a place or business in which one invested in 减资，投资缩减
expire /ɪk'spaɪə(r)/ v. (of sth which lasts for a period of time) to come to an end; run out
grant /grɑːnt/ n. money given esp. by the state for a particular purpose, such as to a university or to a student during a period of study 补助金，助学金
harsh /hɑːʃ/ adj. unpleasant or painful; severe
intern /'ɪntɜːn/ n. a person who has nearly finished professional training, esp. in medicine or teaching, and is gaining controlled practical experience, esp. in a hospital or classroom 实习医师；实习教师；实习生
median /'miːdɪən/ adj. in or passing through the middle
mire /'maɪə(r)/ v. to cause(a person) to be caught up in difficulties 使……陷入困境
outlook /'aʊtlʊk/ n. future, probabilities
outpace /ˌaʊt'peɪs/ v. to perform a particular action faster or better than they can
promise /'prɒmɪs/ n. expectation or signs of future success, good results, etc.
promising /'prɒmɪsɪŋ/ adj. showing signs of likely future success; full of promise 有希望的，有前途的
recession /rɪ'seʃn/ n. a period of reduced trade and business activity
repay /rɪ'peɪ/ v. to return (what is owed) to (sb.); pay back 偿还，报

答

scare /skeə(r)/ *v.* to cause sudden fear to; frighten

sensitivity /ˌsensəˈtɪvəti/ *n.* the condition or quality of being strongly or easily influenced or changed by sth. 敏感

skip /skɪp/ *v.* to pass over or leave out; not do or deal with the next thing; fail to attend or take part in(an activity); intentionally miss 跳过,略过;故意错过

soar /sɔː(r)/ *v.* to rise rapidly or to a very high level

sombre /ˈsɒmbə(r)/ *adj.* sadly serious, grave, dark

squeeze /skwiːz/ *v.* to cause money difficulties to, esp. by means of tight controls or severe demands 给……造成财务困难

stuck /stʌk/ *adj.* fixed in a position; impossible to move

subsidy /ˈsʌbsədi/ *n.* money paid, esp. by the government or an organization, to make prices lower, make it cheaper to produce goods, etc. 补助金,津贴

unfold /ʌnˈfəʊld/ *v.* to (cause to) become clear, more fully known, etc.

wrangle /ˈræŋgl/ *v.* to argue, esp. angrily, noisily, and over a long period 争吵,争论

Notes

1. the class of 2012 —美国指2012届毕业班,非2012级,而我国指的是2012级入学的新生。

2. the financial crisis—also known as the 2008 financial crisis. It is considered to be the worst financial crisis since the Great Depression of the 1930s, and resulted in the failure of key businesses, declines in consumer wealth, and a downturn in economic activity leading to the 2008—2012 global recession(世界经济衰退) and contributing to the European sovereign-debt crisis(欧洲主权债务危机). The financial crisis was triggered by the subprime crisis(次贷危机) which was caused by a complex interplay(相互作用或影响) of policies adopted by American government to encourage people to buy houses and provide easier access to loans for subprime borrowers(次级借款人). 金融危机由次贷危机(2007—2008)引起。见《导读》"经济用语"之详解。

3. Lisa Kahn—a labor economist with interests in organizations and education. From 2010 to 2011 she served on President Obama's Council of Economic Advisers(经济顾问委员会) as the senior

economist for labor and education policy. She has examined the consequences of graduating from college in a bad economy, finding surprisingly long-lasting, negative wage effects.

4. the Yale School of Management—the graduate business school of Yale University 耶鲁管理学院
5. the 1980s recession—A recession in the United States from 1980 to 1982. The US entered a recession in January 1980 and returned to growth six months later. Although recovery took hold, the unemployment rate remained unchanged through the start of a second recession in July 1981. The downturn ended in November 1982. The principal cause of the 1980 recession included contractionary monetary policy(紧缩货币政策) adopted by the Federal Reserve(美国联邦储备委员会) to combat double digit inflation and residual effects of the energy crisis(即 oil crisis。因阿拉伯国家和以色列打的"十月战争"而使中东国家对美国和其他西方国家进行石油禁运[Arab oil boycott]所致), and the second downturn was caused by the fact that manufacturing and construction failed to recover before more aggressive inflation reducing policy was adopted by the Federal Reserve in 1981.
6. a one-percentage-point increase … a 6－7 per cent drop in initial wages—the graduates' wages from their first job decreased by 6－7% once the unemployment rate increased by one percentage. 大学毕业生的失业率每增加一个百分点,他们的起薪就会减少 6－7%。
7. University of Maryland—a public(公立的) research university, located in the city of College Park in Prince George's County, Maryland. founded in 1856,the flagship institution(顶尖大学) of the University System of Maryland and the largest university in the state and in the Washington Metropolitan Area.
8. Rutgers University—a State(州立) University in of New Jersey, an American public research university and the largest institution for higher education in New Jersey. 罗格斯大学
9. There's a lot of 'I wish I had known' thinking we see from the students encountering the harsh realities of the labour market.—From the students who are faced with severe realities of labour market, we find many of them feel regretful for their previous choice, and wish they would have made a different decision. I wish I

had known 是虚拟语气。这里是说,美国大学生面对劳动力市场低迷,就业困难的严酷现实,就有了"我早知道就好了"这种想法。意指他们早知道会是现在的情况,他们当初会有不同的选择,可能选择不同的专业,不同的学校,甚至选择不接受高等教育等等。

10. Rutgers' Heldrich Center for Workforce Development—a research and policy organization, founded in 1997, dedicated to applying research to address the core challenges of New Jersey's and the nation's workforce. 罗格斯大学黑尔德里希人力发展中心

11. professional degree—A professional degree is an academic degree that prepares a person to practice a profession in a field like medicine, law, engineering, psychology, science, and others. Most jobs in these fields cannot be practiced without a first professional degree. It can be awarded as undergraduate or graduate entry degrees. (Bachelors, Masters, or Doctorate). 专业学位,是相对于学术型学位而言的学位类型,培养目标侧重于适应特定行业和职业实际工作需要的人才。

12. These conditions are squeezing ... as soaring tuition fees outpace income growth. —These conditions are making young people hard to pay back the student loans that have become very common in higher education because rising tuition fees surpass income growth.

13. the College Board—a not-for-profit membership association in the US, formed in 1900 as the College Entrance Examination Board (大学入学考试委员会), composed of more than 5,900 schools, colleges, universities and other educational organizations. It sells standardized tests used by academically oriented post-secondary education institutions to measure a student's ability.

14. The public universities... their families. —Government has cut the education budget greatly so the students and their families had to pay more. This hit hard the public universities which used to be seen as a guarantee to earn more money for students from middle and low-income families 大幅削减的州预算将更多的费用负担转移到了学生和学生家庭身上,给过去被视为来自中低收入家庭的学生们获得高薪工作的保障的公立大学造成了严重冲击。这里是指中低收入的学生原来青睐于公立大学,而随着学费更多被转嫁在学生身上,他们可能转而选择私立大学或社区大学等。

15. FinAid. org—A website that was established in the fall of 1994 as a

public service, and provides a comprehensive source of student financial aid information, advice and tools on or off the web. Access to FinAid is free for all users and there is no charge to link to the site. Being comprehensive, informative and objective, it has grown to be the first stop on the web for students looking for ways to finance their education. 一个提供关于学生经济援助信息等全面信息来源的免费公共服务性网站

16. community colleges—sometimes called junior colleges, technical colleges, or city colleges. They are primarily two-year public institutions providing higher education and lower-level tertiary education, granting certificates, diplomas, and associate's degrees. Many also offer continuing and adult education. After graduating from a community college, some students transfer to a four-year liberal arts college or university for two to three years to complete a bachelor's degree. 社区学院，两年制的专科学校，技术学院

17. the Pew Research Center—an American think tank（智库）organization based in Washington, D.C. that provides information on issues, attitudes and trends shaping the United States and the world. The Center and its projects receive funding from The Pew Charitable Trusts(皮尤慈善信托基金会). 皮尤研究中心

18. US Senate—the upper house of the bicameral legislature（两院制立法机构之上院，虽不同于英国无权之贵族院，亦称之为上院）of the US, and together with the House of Representatives makes up the US Congress 美国参议院

19. Barack Obama—1961— , US President, the first African American to hold the office since 2009.

20. Mitt Romney—1947— , an American businessman, served as the 70th Governor of Massachusetts (2003—2007). the first Mormon （摩门教徒）to be a major and Republican party presidential nominee, but defeated by incumbent（在职的）Obama.

21. New York's Barnard College—a private women's liberal arts college founded in 1889 and a member of the Seven Sisters(七姐妹学院，此处省去了 colleges。美国早期的七所女子文理学院联盟). It has been affiliated with Columbia University since 1900. 巴纳德学院

22. strike a sombre note—to express and communicate a serious and

grave opinion

23. Just as you were starting out ... when we were sitting where you are now. —Just as you began your college life and started to prepare for your future, an economic crisis attacked the US, which would lead to more than 5 million jobs lost before you finished your first-year study in the college....... you may be feeling worried about your future just as my generation did as we were freshmen too when the early 1980's crisis struck. 这里的 economic crisis 就是指美国2008年爆发的金融危机而引发的经济危机。(见《导读》"经济用语")奥巴马在1981年至1983年期间就读于加利福尼亚州洛杉矶的西方学院[Occidental College],当时的美国经济也不景气。

Questions

1. Does the 2008 financial crisis influence the university graduates?
2. What can be learned from the result of Rutgers University's study?
3. Why does Chelsea Katz want to study business?
4. What conditions are squeezing American young people's ability to repay the student loans?
5. Why do American students have to borrow more money to finish their higher education?
6. Why do you think the authors cite Mr. Obama's speech in the last paragraph?

语言解说

金融危机催生新词

有人说,金融危机是 Pax Dollarium(美元主宰下的和平)闹的,要跟美元脱钩(decoupling),就像反对 Pax America(美国主宰下的和平)一样。欧洲还有人主张搞欧美元 Doro(Dollar+Euro)或 Eullar(Euro+Dollar)。我国在G20伦敦峰会(2009年4月)前夕提出了改革国际货币体系的新设想,即用超越主权、并能保持货币值长期稳定的国际储备货币取代美元,这就是"a super-sovereign currency"(超主权国际储备货币),得 BRIC(金砖四国)(由 Brazil, Russia, India 与 China 四国首字母组成,与 brick 谐音)的支持。俄也提出类似中国的货币设想,称之为"a super-national reserve currency"。经济危机后,欧盟内又出现了两个新词

PIGS 和 PIIGS。这两个字始于希腊的债务危机蔓延至西班牙、葡萄牙和爱尔兰等欧元区成员国。四国英语国名首字母缩合成 PIGS(猪)，一些媒体不客气地称为"笨猪四国"。另一种说法就是再加上意大利，成为 PIIGS，称为"欧猪五国"。为应付危机，各国都要实行"严格节约措施""siege economics"。"保守的经济政策""old time religion"又会吃香。自由派也推出"量入宽松政策""quantitative easing money policy"。

金融危机还带来"recession chic"，经济衰退时尚，这个销售用语指大堆高价品牌商品打折降价成时髦。另一个是仿 fashionista(时尚达人[粤语：时髦之人])的"recessionista"，找老牌知名公司（established company）打折的名牌货，就是经济衰退时购物迷的特点（recession ＋-ista）。经济出现萧条，那么"depressionista"就会取代"recessionista"成为时髦。还有的国家提议将 G8(西方七国加俄罗斯的八国集团)改为 G20。G2(中美两强)也随着 Chimerica 或 Chindia(由 Cina＋India)(中印大同)走俏起来。有的词语不解释不好理解。再如：China ＋ India ＋ ME (Middle East)＋Africa 等于投资市场＋石油＋非洲原料与市场。

奥巴马拨款救市（bailouts）还加进"buy American"（买国货）条款。美国各大银行及有的公司都"向政府财政求助""go to the well"，不可能"一毛不拔""zero out"，是否"愿意发放信贷""nation's credit window"或"将黄金兑换美元""nation's gold window"。美国常挥舞的贸易大棒301 (the 301st provision of the U. S. Trade Act)（301条款）或 Special/Super 301(对歧视其产品的国家采取带有破坏性的一般和特别的报复)更会频繁了。

商业和企业领域随着全球化和高新技术不断创新，人才便成了具有决定意义的时代。金融危机带来大批裁员，也引起趁机高薪征求人才。head hunters 猎头公司造出了诸如"golden handcuffs/cuffs"（金手铐，指高薪留人）、"golden hello"（高薪）、"golden parachute"（黄金降落伞，人去薪留，直到合同期满）和"golden handshake"（补偿金）等词语，随之出现了"gold collar"金领阶级和"new collar"（新领阶级，指比其父辈更富裕和受过更高深教育的白领工人），对中老年人的"ageism"（年龄歧视）。公司要"brand extension"（品牌延伸或扩展），suitor 也由"求婚者"引申为"企图收购竞争者"，feeding frenzy 由"拼命争食"引申为"疯狂的竞争"。仿 blackmail 造出了"greenmail"（以套购股票作兼并威胁）。还出现了诱人用信用卡疯狂购物的"merchants of debt"（债商）(仿 merchant of death [军火商])。

企业丑闻与政治丑闻如 Watergate 一样，引申出新义。加之媒体跟风造词能力强。例如 2002 年是美国大公司会计丑闻频发年，Enron(安然)、World Com(世通)和 Xerox(施乐)等大公司为虚报利润而做假账(cook the books),股民损失惨重,证券业和公司诚信扫地。Enron 曾在美国 500 强大企业中名列第七,"massive accounting scandal"破产后,Enron 转化成普通名词或动词,成为"cheat"的同义词,《纽约时报杂志》举例称:

a. The verb is simply the name, as in "He got **enroned** last Thursday."

b. "I don't want to **Enron** the American people," said the Democrat Tom Daschle, defining the new verb in his next sentence, "I don't want to see them holding the bag at the end of the day just like Enron employees have held the bag."

不但如此,enron 还衍生出 enronesque(做假账的)、enronish(靠不住的)、enronism(造假风)、enronista(安然式破产责任人,大骗子)、enronite(冤大头)、enronitis(造假症,指其他大公司也有此或大或小的问题)、enronlike(像安然公司那样的)等新字。这些词语,除 enron 外,只能风靡一时,但是熟悉这些字,抓住 cheat 核心义便会举一反三,见一知十,根据这些后缀,增强猜词(义)能力,加深阅读理解,就不那么困难了。

上面以 enron 为例,举出一批后缀造词,这里再举几个加前缀造词的例子。outsourcing/offshore outsoucing(外包),又类比造出 crowdsourcing(群包)和 insourcing(内包)。加拿大还提出与其 offshoring 还不如 nearshoring(让邻国如加拿大和墨西哥等国干的近包)等等不同想法的新词。

世贸组织(WTO)组织的一些缩略词和用缩略造词也大行其道,令人目眩。为"BIT"(bilateral investment treaties)(双边投资条约)、"BTA"(border tax adjustments)(边境税调整)、"NAMA"(nonagricultural market access)(非农业市场准入)、"NTB"(nontariff barriers)(非关税壁垒)、"TRAIPS"(trade related aspects of intellectual property)(有关智力产权方面的贸易)以及"Everything but arms"(允许最贫穷国家除武器外的所有产品进入欧盟市场)等等。内地与香港实现 CEPA(Closer Economic Partnership Arrangement),与台湾也达成 ECFA(Economic Cooperation Framework Agreement),同时还创造了个"Chiwan"新词。

此外,以前还发生过 dotcom crash 或 bursting of the (high) tech bubble(高科技股尤其网络经济股市泡沫的破灭)。

早有人料到这次金融危机会演变成经济危机。如英国记者 Larry Elliot 在 2007 年就以"Three bears that ate Goldilocks economy"(2007/9/24 *The Guardian*)为题发表警世文章。"Goldilocks economy"这里"金

发姑娘经济"是 20 世纪 90 年代中期新词,指美国既不冷也不过热的"称心如意的经济"。文章借用《格林童话》里 Goldilocks and the Three Bears 的故事。

Lesson Eight

课 文 导 读

美国高中毕业生因为学费而对择校问题左右为难。据报道,在获得学士学位的毕业生中,有 2/3 的学生通过贷款支付高等教育费用,许多大学生毕业时已经负债累累。能进入常春藤名校,自然有利于求职及事业发展,许多研究显示,名校毕业生确实收入较高,申请就读名牌大学研究生的机率也较高。不过,常春藤名校学费昂贵,学生在读学士学位阶段较难获得助学金。目前就业市场情况不佳,不禁令人质疑,花高额学费上常春藤名校值得吗? 本文为我们讲述了几个大学生的真实故事,他们的选择看似"明智",却充满了无奈和迷茫:虽然公立学校学费低廉,但是学生们需要面对有限的选课条件、水平参差不齐的同学、薄弱的师资力量等问题,未来还要面临不能按时毕业、就业机会减少等风险。文章视角客观,多用引语;语言洗练,使用了很多动词词组和缩略语(如 land jobs, take on debt, med);文字生动,细致描绘了几个学生的心路历程。

我国学生与美国学生不同的是,他们不愁学费和吃住,有政府为他们撑腰,而担心自己是否是北大、清华等名牌学校的那块料。

Pre-reading Questions

1. How many Ivy League Universities do you know?
2. Which do you think is more important, the best college or the best major?

Text

Is an Ivy League[1] Diploma Worth It?
Fearing Massive Debt, More Students Are Choosing
to Enroll at Public Colleges Over Elite Universities.
By Melissa Korn

1   Daniel Schwartz could have attended an Ivy League school if he wanted to. He just doesn't see the value.

2   Mr. Schwartz, 18 years old, was accepted at Cornell University[2] but enrolled instead at City University of New York's Macaulay Honors College, which is free.

3   Mr. Schwartz says his family could have afforded Cornell's tuition, with help from scholarships and loans. But he wants to be a doctor and thinks medical school, which could easily cost upward of $45,000 a year for a private institution, is a more important investment. It wasn't "worth it to spend $50,000-plus a year for a bachelor's degree," he says.

4   As student-loan default rates climb and college graduates fail to land jobs, an increasing number of students are betting they can get just as far with a degree from a less-expensive school as they can with a diploma from an elite school—without having to take on debt.

5   More students are choosing lower-cost public colleges or commuting to schools from home to save on housing expenses. Twenty-two percent of students from families with annual household incomes above $100,000 attended public, two-year schools in the 2010—2011 academic year, up from 12% the previous year, according to a report from student-loan company Sallie Mae.

6   Such choices meant families across all income brackets spent 9% less—an average of $21,889 in cash, loans, scholarships and other methods—on college in 2010—11 than in the previous year, according to the report. High-income families cut their college spending by 18%, to $25,760. The report, which is released annually, was based on a survey of about 1,600 students and parents.

7   The approach has risks. Top-tier colleges tend to attract recruiting visits from companies that have stopped visiting elsewhere. A diploma from an elite school can look better to many recruiters and graduate schools, as well. And overcrowding at state schools means students could be locked out of required courses and have difficulty completing their degrees in four years.

8   Mr. Schwartz started at the Macaulay Honors program at Queens College this fall with "nagging" disappointment but has come to terms with his decision.

9   "I have to grow up. I have to incorporate what I want and what I can have," he says. "Even though people say money shouldn't be everything, in this situation, money was the most important thing."

10   He says he had grown enamored with the "prestige" of an Ivy

League degree. His teachers cited the networking opportunities and academic rigor. It didn't help that his father attended Princeton University and his uncle, Columbia University.

11 "I thought that the Ivy League title would really, really boost my chances of getting into a good med school," Mr. Schwartz says. Now, he is aiming for top grades at Macaulay to remain competitive with Ivy League candidates.

12 There is little question that having a college degree gives candidates an edge in the job market. The unemployment rate for people with a bachelor's degree was 4.9% last month, compared with 10.5% for high-school graduates with no degree, according to the Bureau of Labor Statistics.

13 But a degree from a private college also is expensive and piles on debt. The average debt load for students who took out loans hit a record $27,200 for the class that graduated this year, says Mark Kantrowitz, publisher of student-aid websites Fastweb.com and FinAid.org. That comes as general per capita debt reached $47,260 in the second quarter, a figure that has been dropping in recent years, according to the Federal Reserve Bank of New York.

14 Jesse Yeh, a 20-year-old California resident, chose the University of California at Berkeley over Stanford University. Tuition at Berkeley, a state school, is about $14,460 for in-state students. At Stanford, it's $40,050.

15 Now he worries about graduating on time, having been locked out of some overcrowded courses, including Spanish and a public-policy elective. Berkeley says 71% of students who entered in 2006, the latest period available, graduated within four years. At Stanford, that number is closer to 80%.

16 Attending a private university still can pay off. Schools with large endowments have beefed up their aid programs in recent years, which can make them less expensive than their public, cash-strapped counterparts. Brown University, for example, offers grants instead of loans for students whose families earn less than $100,000 a year. Harvard College doesn't expect any contribution from families with annual incomes below $60,000.

17 But Carl Van Horn, director of the John J. Heldrich Center for Workforce Development at Rutgers University, says graduate outcomes often have more to do with major and how a student takes advantage of

networking and internship opportunities, than with school choice.

18   Natasha Pearson, 19, questions her decision to attend the City University of New York's Hunter College. She says she turned down an offer from Boston College after the school said her family would need to pitch in $30,000 annually.

19   She says there's a "wide variety" of academic ability among her Hunter classmates and that many of her courses are taught by graduate students, rather than by full professors.

20   "I can't help but wonder, had I gone to BC, where that could have taken me," she says.

(From *The Wall Street Journal*, November 8, 2011)

New Words

beef /biːf/ *v.* to make strong or stronger, improve

boost /buːst/ *vt.* contribute to the progress or growth of

candidate /ˈkændɪdət/ *n.* a person who is being considered for a position 候选人

cash-strapped *adj.* not having enough money to buy or pay for the things they want or need 手头紧的；资金短缺的

diploma /dɪˈpləʊmə/ *n.* a document certifying the successful completion of a course of study 毕业文凭；学位证书

endowment /ɪnˈdaʊmənt/ *n.* a gift of money that is made to an institution or community in order to provide it with an annual income 资助；捐款

enamored /ɪˈnæməd/ *adj.* marked by foolish or unreasoning fondness 倾心的，迷恋的

grant /ɡrɑːnt/ *n.* an amount of money that a government or other institution gives to an individual or to an organization for a particular purpose such as education or home improvements 助学金

nagging /ˈnæɡɪŋ/ *adj.* continually complaining or faultfinding 唠叨的，挑剔的；使人不得安宁的

networking /ˈnetwɜːkɪŋ/ *n.* social network 社会或人脉关系

pitch /pɪtʃ/ *vt.* to throw or toss something, such as a ball 投；扔

rigor /ˈrɪɡə/ *n.* excessive sternness 严格；严酷；严密

top-tier *adj.* of the highest degree, quality, or amount 顶级的；顶尖的

Notes

1. The Ivy League—a group of eight universities in the north-eastern part of the US which have high academic and social status. The Ivy League is an athletic conference (体育赛事联盟) composed of sports teams from eight private institutions of higher education in the Northeastern US. The eight institutions are Brown University, Columbia University, Cornell University, Dartmouth College, Harvard University, Princeton University, the University of Pennsylvania, and Yale University. 常春藤联盟
2. Cornell University—located in Ithaca, New York, founded in 1865
3. City University of New York's Macaulay Honors College—纽约市立大学麦考利荣誉学院

    City University of New York (*abbrev*. CUNY)—public(公立的), located in all five New York City boroughs(行政区). Its administrative offices are in Yorkville in Manhattan.
4. Sallie Mae—or SLM Corporation, a publicly traded U. S. corporation whose operations are originating, servicing, and collecting on student loans. 萨利美(学生贷款)公司
5. across all income brackets—包括所有收入阶层的家庭
6. Queens College—one of the senior colleges of the City University of New York 皇后区学院
7. It didn't help that his father attended Princeton University and his uncle, Columbia University.—His father's and his uncle's diplomas at the two famous Universities did not help him change the school-choosing decision. .

    a. Princeton University—private(私立的), located in Princeton, New Jersey, founded in 1746.

    b. Columbia University—private, located in New York City, founded in 1754.
8. med school—medical school, med = medical 报刊英语偏爱用那些短缩略的词, 也称截短词, 如: biz = business, sec = secretary, expo = exposition, vet = veteran 等。
9. the Bureau of Labor Statistics—a unit of the Department of Labor. It is the principal fact-finding agency for the U. S. government in the broad field of labor economics and statistics and serves as a principal agency of the U. S. Federal Statistical System. 美国劳工统计局

10. the Federal Reserve Bank of New York—the largest of the 12 Federal Reserve Banks of the United States. Working within the Federal Reserve System, the New York Federal Reserve Bank implements monetary policy, supervises and regulates financial institutions and helps maintain the nation's payment systems. 纽约联邦储备银行
11. the University of California at Berkeley—also referred to as UC Berkeley, public, located in Berkeley, California, established in 1868. 加州大学伯克利分校
12. Stanford University—founded in 1891. 斯坦福大学
13. beef up—to increase, strengthen, or improve 改善;提高;加强
14. Brown University—private, located in Providence, Rhode Island, founded in 1764.
15. Harvard College—one of two schools within Harvard University granting undergraduate degrees
16. Rutgers University—public, the largest institution for higher education in New Jersey. 罗格斯大学
17. the City University of New York's Hunter College—纽约市立大学亨特学院
18. Boston College—a private Jesuit(教会的) university, located in the village of Chestnut Hill, Massachusetts, founded in 1863. 波士顿学院

Questions

1. Why did not Mr. Schartz enroll at Cornel University?
2. What was the general annual cost of top-tier colleges or Ivy League such as Cornell university?
3. What is the meaning of the phrase "land jobs" in the seventh paragraph?
4. What is the reason for those students at state schools who are locked out of required courses and have difficulty completing their degrees in four years?

读报知识

Ivy League, Seven Sisters & Russel Group

The Ivy League　常春藤联合会

指美国东部八所名牌大学。原为这些大学体育联合组织的名称。它们以历史悠久、教学和研究成果卓著而享有社会声誉,因砖楼墙上有常春藤蔓延而得名。这些学校是:在罗得岛州的布朗大学(Brown University)、在纽约市的哥伦比亚大学(Columbia University)、在纽约州的康奈尔大学(Cornell University)、在新罕布什尔州的达特默思学院(Dartmouth College)、在马萨诸塞州的哈佛大学(Harvard University,创建于1636年,是美国历史最悠久的高等学府)、在宾夕法尼亚州的宾夕法尼亚大学(University of Pennsylvania)、在新泽西州的普林斯顿大学(Princeton University)和在康涅狄格州的耶鲁大学(Yale University)。这些学校大多建于18世纪,哈佛最早,始于1636年。

The Seven Sisters　七姐妹女子学院

美国七所最著名的女子学院及其组成的联合会,原名七学院联合会(the Seven Colleges Conference),1915年由马萨诸塞州的霍利奥克山(Mount Holyoke)、史密斯(Smith)、韦尔斯利(Wellesley)和纽约州的瓦萨(Vassar)等四所学院组成,后又有纽约市的巴纳德(Barnard)、宾夕法尼亚州的布林马尔(Bryn Mawr)和马萨诸塞州的拉德克利夫(Radcliffe)等三所学院加入。作为联合会成员,七所学院的校长及其他领导人经常商讨共同的教学目标与问题,制订互利的招生政策。这些学校教学标准较高,相当于常春藤联合会(the Ivy League)大学。七所学校均建于19世纪。瓦萨学院现也招收男生。

The Russel Group　罗素大学集团

1994年成立,现有24所英国最卓越的公立研究性大学,其中以金三角名校　Oxford/Cambridge/London Universnty(牛津、剑桥和伦敦大学)为代表。该联盟被誉称为英国的常春藤联合会。

Lesson Nine

> 课文导读

　　自1620年一群英国清教徒乘坐"五月花号"横穿大西洋来到马萨诸塞南部的科德角,希望建立一个自由、平等、没有宗教迫害的"天堂"起,"美国梦"已开始悄然萌芽:机会均等,自由民主,只要通过勤奋、坚忍、勇气和决心就能实现梦想,迈向繁荣。这些均在"五月花协议"中有所体现。随着时代的变化,而今的美国梦也在不断拓展,产生了新的诠释。发财致富,拥有不动产是否还是美国人一成不变的梦想?金融动荡,政治僵局是否熄灭了美国民众对美国梦的信心和热情?这个曾经自诩为自由、平等、努力奋斗就能收获幸福成功的美国梦正面临新一轮的种种困惑、误解及挑战。

Pre-reading Questions

1. What do you often associate the U. S. A. with?
2. Do you think the American dream achievable?

Text

Five Myths about the American Dream
By Michael F. Ford

1. The American dream is about getting rich.

1　　In a national survey of more than 1,300 adults that we completed in March, only 6 percent of Americans ranked "wealth" as their first or second definition of the American dream. 45 percent named "a good life for my family," while 34 percent put "financial security"—material comfort that is not necessarily synonymous with Bill Gates[1]-like riches—on top.

2　　While money may certainly be part of a good life, the American dream isn't just about dollars and cents. 32 percent of our respondents pointed to "freedom" as their dream; 29 percent to "opportunity"; and 21 percent to the "pursuit of happiness." A fat bank account can be a means to these ends, but only a small minority believe that money is a worthy end in itself.

2. Homeownership is the American dream.

3 In June, a New York Times[2]-CBS News[3] poll found that almost 90 percent of Americans think that homeownership is an important part of the American dream. But only 7 percent of Americans we surveyed ranked homeownership as their first or second definition of the American dream. Why the discrepancy? Owning real estate is important to some Americans, but not as important—or as financially rewarding—as we're led to believe.

4 Federal support of homeownership greatly overvalues its meaning in American life. Through tax breaks[4] and guarantees, the government boosted homeownership to its peak in 2004, when 69 percent of American households owned homes. Subsidies for homeownership, including the mortgage interest deduction, reached $230 billion in 2009, according to the Congressional Budget Office[5]. Meanwhile, only $60 billion in taxbreaks and spending programs aided renters.

5 The result of this real estate spending spree? According to the Federal Reserve[6], American real estate lost more than $6 trillion in value, or almost 30 percent, between 2006 and 2010. One in five American homeowners is underwater, owing more on a mortgage than what the home is worth[7].

6 Those who profit most from homeownership are far and away the largest source of political campaign contributions[8]. Insurance companies, securities and investment firms, real estate interests, and commercial banks gave more than $100 million to federal candidates and parties in 2011, according to the Center for Responsive Politics[9]. The National Association of Realtors[10] alone gave more than $950,000—more than Morgan Stanley[11], Citigroup[12] or Ernst & Young[13].

7 Homeownership is more important to special interests than it is to most Americans, who, according to our research, care more about "a good job," "the pursuit of happiness" and "freedom."

3. The American dream is American.

8   The term "American dream" was coined in 1931 by James Truslow Adams[14] in his history "The Epic of America." In the midst of the Great Depression[15], Adams discovered the same counterintuitive optimism that we observe in today's Great Recession[16], and he dubbed it "the American dream"—"that dream of a land in which life should be better and richer and fuller for every man, with opportunity for each according to his ability or achievement."

9   However, the American dream pre-dated 1931. Starting in the 16th century, Western European settlers came to this land at great risk to build a better life. Today, this dream is sustained by immigrants from different parts of the world who still come here seeking to do the same thing.

10   Perceptions of the dream today are often more positive among those who are new to America. When asked to rate the condition of the American dream on a scale of one to 10, where 10 means the best possible condition and one means the worst, 42 percent of immigrants responded between six and 10. Only 31 percent of the general population answered in that range.

4. China threatens the American dream.

11   Our surveys revealed that 57 percent of Americans believe that "the world now looks to many different countries," not just ours, to "represent the future." When we asked participants which region or country is charting that future, more than half chose China. Nearly two-thirds of those surveyed mistakenly believe that the Chinese economy is already larger than the U.S. economy—it is actually one-third the size, with a population four times larger. China does own more than $1.1 trillion of U.S. debt, however; it is our largest creditor.

12   But the problem isn't just one nation. Japan holds almost $1 trillion of U.S. debt. Britain owns more than $400 billion. In 1970, less than 5 percent of U.S. debt was held by non-citizens. Today, almost half is. Neither China nor these other countries can be blamed for U.S. choices that have placed our financial future increasingly out of our hands.

13   Still, no matter how much we owe, the United States remains the world's land of opportunity. In fact, the largest international group coming to America to study is from China—157,000 students in the 2010—2011 academic year. As recently reported in *The Washington Post*, the number of Chinese undergraduates at U.S. colleges increased 43 percent over the previous year.

5. Economic decline and political gridlock are killing the American dream.

14   Our research showed a stunning lack of confidence in U.S. institutions. 65 percent of those surveyed believe that America is in decline; 83 percent said they have less trust in "politics in general" than they did 10 or 15 years ago; 79 percent said they have less trust in big business and major corporations; 78 percent said they have less trust in government; 72 percent reported declining trust in the media. These recent figures are more startling when contrasted against Gallup[17] polling from the 1970s, when as many as 70 percent of Americans had "trust and confidence" that the government could handle domestic problems.

15   Even so, 63 percent of Americans said they are confident that they will attain their American dream, regardless of what the nation's institutions do or don't do. While they may be worried about future generations, their dream today stands defiantly against the odds.
(From *The Washington Post*, January 6, 2012)

New Words

chart /tʃɑːt/ v. to make a plan of what should be done to achieve a particular result 描绘

counterintuitive /ˌkaʊntərɪnˈtjuːɪtɪv/ adj. contrary to what intuition or common sense would indicate 违反直觉的

defiant /dɪˈfaɪənt/ adj. clearly refusing to do what someone tells you to do 挑战的 defiantly adv.

discrepancy /dɪsˈkrepənsɪ/ n. a difference between two amounts, details, reports etc. that should be the same 矛盾,差异

dub /dʌb/ v. to give sth or sb a name that describes them in some way 授予称号

gridlock /'grɪdlɒk/ *n.* a situation in which nothing can happen, usu. because people disagree strongly 僵局

mortgage /'mɔːgɪdʒ/ *n.* a legal arrangement by which you borrow money from a bank or other financial organization in order to buy a house, and pay back the money over a period of years 抵押借款,按揭

myth /mɪθ/ *n.* an idea or story that many people believe, but which is not true 传说,神话

respondent /rɪ'spɒndənt/ *n.* someone who answers questions, esp. in a survey 回应者

spree /spriː/ *n.* a short period of time when you do a lot of one activity, esp. spending money or drinking alcohol 无节制的狂热行为

stunning /'stʌnɪŋ/ *adj.* very surprising or shocking 使人震惊的

subsidy /'sʌbsədɪ/ *n.* money that is paid by a government or organization to make prices lower, reduce the cost of producing goods etc. 补贴,津贴

synonymous /sɪ'nɒnɪməs/ *adj.* a situation, quality, idea etc. that is synonymous with sth else is the same or nearly the same as another 同义的

underwater /ˌʌndə'wɔːtə(r)/ *adj.* (of a stock option or other asset) having a market value below its purchase value 价值缩水的,资不抵债的

Notes

1. Bill Gates—1955—, born in Seattle, former chief executive (CEO) and current chairman(董事长,董事会主席)of Microsoft, the world's largest personal-computer software company, which he co-founded with Paul Allen. Gates is not only one of the best-known entrepreneurs of the PC revolution, in the later stages of his career, he also has pursued a number of philanthropic(慈善的)endeavors, donating large amounts of money to various charitable organizations and scientific research programs through the Bill & Melinda Gates Foundation(比尔及梅琳达·盖茨基金会).
2. The New York Times—a serious daily newspaper which is based in New York City. It is sold elsewhere in the US and in many other countries, and people in the US often just call it "the Times"《纽约

时报》

3. CBS News——the news tycoon corporation of American television and radio network CBS(Columbia Broadcasting System). CBS News' flagship program is the *CBS Evening News*(CBS 晚间新闻). Other programs include a morning news show called, *CBS This Morning* (CBS 今晨), news magazine programs *CBS News Sunday Morning* (CBS 周日早间), *60 Minutes* (CBS 每周日晚 8 点一小时的专题报道栏目), *&48 Hours*, and Sunday morning political affairs program *Face the Nation*. 美国哥伦比亚广播公司新闻频道

4. tax breaks——a special reduction in taxes（减税优惠，税额优惠）

5. Congressional Budget Office（CBO）——a federal agency within the legislative branch of the United States government that provides economic data to Congress. The CBO was created as a nonpartisan agency by the Congressional Budget and Impoundment Control Act of 1974, which was signed into law by President Richard Nixon on July 12, 1974. Official operations began on February 24, 1975. 国会预算局

6. The Federal Reserve——(＝Federal Reserve System) the central banking system of the United States. It was created on December 23, 1913, largely in response to a series of financial panics, particularly a severe panic in 1907. 美国联邦储备系统

7. One in five American homeowners is underwater, owing more on a mortgage than what the home is worth. ——One in five American are faced with assets shrinking, the mortgage loan they have to repay exceeds the real value of their property. 每 5 名美国房主就有一人资不抵债，也就是说他们要偿还的贷款超过他们住房本身的价值。

   underwater——having a market value below its purchase value 美国房地产泡沫产生了一大批溺水房，即房屋所欠抵押贷款价值高于房屋价值，溺水房房主拥有的是负资产。这样的房子就像是沉在水底，等房价回升到贷款金额以上的价值时才算是浮出水面。于是很多房主就选择了放弃还贷，结果贷款银行收走房屋，房主失去住所。

8. Those who profit most from homeownership are far and away the largest source of political campaign contributions. ——Those organizations who have got the most interest from real estate mortgage donate the biggest part of money for political election campaign. 获利最大的抵押贷款银行为政治竞选捐款最多。

far and away—by a great deal or amount; very much
9. The Center for Responsive Politics—a non-profit, nonpartisan research group based in Washington, D. C. that tracks the effects of money and lobbying on elections and public policy. It maintains a public online database of its information. Their database OpenSecrets. org allows users to track federal campaign contributions and lobbying. 政治反应中心
10. The National Association of Realtors (NAR)—Headquartered in Chicago, whose members are known as Realtors. NAR is the largest trade association and one of the most powerful lobbying groups in North America with over 1. 2 million members including NAR's institutes, societies, and councils, involved in all aspects of the residential and commercial real estate industries. NAR also functions as a self-regulatory organization for real estate brokerage. 美国房地产经纪人协会
11. Morgan Stanley—an American multinational financial services corporation headquartered in the Morgan Stanley Building, New York City. Morgan Stanley operates in 42 countries, and has more than 1300 offices and 60,000 employees. The main areas of business for the firm today are Global Wealth Management, Institutional Securities, and Investment Management. (摩根·士丹利投资公司)
12. Citigroup (or Citi)—an American multinational financial services corporation headquartered in Manhattan, New York, United States. Citigroup was formed from one of the world's largest mergers in history by combining the banking giant Citicorp and financial conglomerate(大型联合企业) Travelers Group in October 1998. It is currently the third largest bank holding company in the United States by assets. Citigroup has the world's largest financial services network, spanning 140 countries with approximately 16,000 offices worldwide. 花旗集团
13. Ernst & Young—one of the largest professional service firms in the world and one of the "Big Four" accounting firms, along with Deloitte, KPMG and PricewaterhouseCoopers (PwC). Ernst & Young is a global organization of member firms with 167,000 employees in more than 140 countries, headquartered in London, England. It was ranked by *Forbes* magazine as the eighth-largest

private company in the United States in 2011. http://en. wikipedia. org/wiki/Ernst_%26_Young-cite_note-7♯cite_note-7 安永会计师事务所

14. James Truslow Adams—(1878－1949) an American writer and historian, also the editor of a scholarly multi-volume Dictionary of American History. http://en. wikipedia. org/wiki/James_Truslow_Adams-cite_note-4♯cite_note-4 His *Epic of America*(《美国史诗》) was an international bestseller.
15. Great Depression—It refers to the severe economic problems that followed the Wall Street Crash of 1929. In the early 1930s, many banks and businesses failed, and millions of people lost their jobs in the US and in the UK and the rest of Europe. 大萧条时期
16. Great Recession—It refers to a major global recession characterized by various systemic imbalances and was sparked by the outbreak of the U. S. subprime mortgage(次级房贷)crisis and financial crisis of 2007－2008. 经济大衰退
17. Gallup—The Gallup Organization is a firm founded by George Gallup in 1935, well known for its opinion poll by profession. 盖洛普咨询公司,最早以预测总统候选人的民调而著名。

Questions

1. What is the core of American dream?
2. Is the American dream American?
3. Do you believe that American dream reflects human nature and could be shared by other peoples?
4. Why isn't homeownership ranked first or second by most people in the American dream?
5. Do you think China is a threat to the American dream?
6. How do economic decline and political gridlock influence the American dream?

新闻写作

报刊语言主要特点

报刊语言的主要特点是简约、时尚、创新、引经据典、修辞色彩浓、

(插)图文(章)并茂和程式化。这些特点与报刊体裁有关,报道性文章语言是非正式的,与公文体不同,也与高雅的文学语言有别,介于雅俗之间。本节所谈简约、创新等例子,是从语言运用的角度而言的,不是严格的语言学分析。省略、用缩略词、短字、句法上等的"简约",突出一个"短"字,其中有的用法与汉语很相似,尤其是名词代替形容词作定语用,这早在20世纪30年代就曾有学者指出过。所谓"时尚",主要指语言时尚,时髦词大量涌现,与创新有关。"创新"指报刊语言新、奇、活的特点,体现在新言新语层出不穷,旧词不断引申出新义,推陈出新,标新立异。语句、语法也在发展创新,只要读了《导读》"跟踪语言的变化和发展"这一节,就一目了然。"修辞色彩浓",主要指报刊常运用各种修辞手段,引经据典,成语典故多,用语新颖别致,形象生动。与文学语言相比,报刊语言在这些方面紧贴现实,更突出些。"图文并茂",主要指插图等与文章配合,交相辉映。文章里所插图表、漫画等加上简练的语言,形象生动、幽默等特点得到充分体现。程式化指读者能理解和明白的常用套语及新闻报道中固定的几种形式。应该说明的是,简约、时尚、创新和修辞色彩浓这四方面相互关联,创新是动力,而这些特点则正在推动当代英语向前发展。(详见《导读》四章二节)

Unit Four
United States（Ⅱ）

Lesson Ten

课文导读

提到现代战争,大多数人脑海里浮现的是美国电影中展现的航母战斗群、核潜艇、隐形飞机、导弹等先进武器,以及美国在20世纪末、21世纪初主导的科索沃、阿富汗、伊拉克、利比亚等战争。我们不禁要问:未来的战争会是什么样的呢?它将向何方向演变?

美国成天叫嚷遭到中国网络攻击。然而,天有不测风云,它却被一无名小将打蒙了。据前CIA和NSA雇员斯诺登（Edward Snowden）披露,NSA对全球电话和网络通信实行监听和攻击,甚至连美国公民、在美外国人和机构也不放过。此事使美国颜面尽失。不断指责他国对其进行网络攻击,到头来它才是最大始作俑者,可见其多么虚伪。Edward揭密的同时生出两个新词:PRISM（personal record information system for management）scandal,（棱镜门丑闻）和surveillancegate。

随着信息技术的大量应用和普及,我们社会生活的各个方面越来越离不开网络,网络信息已成为保持社会正常运行的神经中枢。信息时代,一旦神经系统遭到破坏,社会就会陷入全面瘫痪。然而,网络信息安全面临的威胁已不是理论上的想象和推测,而是每天都在人们身边发生的事实。近年来,网络攻击和入侵事件从数量规模到危害程度不断升级,已对国家安全构成严重危害。美国不断装扮成网络领域的受害者,借此,它大力招募网络高手,建立培训学校和网战司令部,欲成为军力更加无敌的超级大国。

通过本文的学习,我们深刻体会到网络战争的时代已经来临,网络空间已成为继陆地、海洋、空中和太空之后的第五维作战空间。为我国安全计,人们必须提高警惕。

Pre-reading Questions

1. Do you know anything about cyberwar?
2. What is your view of cyberwar in the future?

Text

Pentagon Digs In on Cyberwar Front[1]
Elite School Run by Air Force Trains Officers to Hunt
Down Hackers and Launch Electronic Attacks
By Julian E. Barnes

1 The U. S. military is accelerating its cyberwarfare training programs in an aggressive expansion of its preparations for conflict on an emerging battlefield.

2 The renewed emphasis on building up cyberwarfare capabilities comes even as other defense programs have been trimmed. Along with unmanned aircraft[2] and special operations, cyberwarfare is among the newer, more high-tech and often more secretive capabilities favored by the Pentagon's current leadership.

3 In June, the U. S. Air Force's elite Weapons School[3]—the Air Force version of the Navy's famed "Top Gun" program[4]—graduated its first class of six airmen trained to fight in cyberspace. The new course, at Nellis Air Force Base in Nevada[5], trains airmen working at computer terminals how to hunt down electronic intruders, defend networks and launch cyberattacks.

4 "While cyber[6] may not look or smell exactly like a fighter aircraft or a bomber aircraft, the relevancy in any potential conflict in 2012 is the same," said Air Force Col.[7] Robert Garland, commandant of the Weapons School. "We have to be able to succeed against an enemy that wants to attack us in any way."

5 The training effort comes amid a push by the Obama administration to rapidly deploy offensive and defensive techniques across the government, including at the Central Intelligence Agency[8], other intelligence agencies and the Department of Homeland Security[9].

6 Cyberwarfare techniques have been deployed in an apparent U. S. and Israeli campaign to undermine Iran's nuclear program[10], elements of which were reported last month by the *New York Times*. The U. S.

also contemplated using cyberweapons to incapacitate Libyan air defenses in 2011, before the start of U. S. airstrikes.

7 The military's cyber buildup began in 2008, leading to creation of a formal "U. S. Cyber Command[11]." The command marshals computer-warfare capabilities from across the military and integrates them with expertise at the National Security Agency[12]. Some of the defenses could someday be extended to the private sector.

8 Overall the Air Force spends about $4 billion a year on its cyber programs, though the training initiatives are a fraction of that cost.

9 Other military services also are taking steps to strengthen cyberwarfare capabilities and training. The Navy is revamping courses for 24,000 people trained each year at the Center for Information Dominance[13] each year.

10 "It is that full span, from peace time to war and everything in between," said Capt. Susan Cerovsky, commander of the Center for Information Dominance.

11 James Cartwright, a retired Marine general and former vice chairman of the U. S. Joint Chiefs of Staff[14], argues the new emphasis on cyber training is critical. But he said the military should do a better job publicizing that it is working to hone all of its cyber capabilities—both defensive and offensive.

12 "For cyber deterrence to work, you have to believe a few things: One, that we have the intent; two, that we have the capability; and three, that we practice—and people know that we practice," Gen. Cartwright said.

13 The full range of U. S. cyberweapons is a closely guarded secret. U. S. officials have said the military is developing weapons aimed at cutting off power to precise, limited locations.

14 "Our curriculum is based on attack, exploit and defense of the cyber domain," said Lt. Col. Bob Reeves, who oversees the cyber course as commander of the 328th Weapons Squadron[15].

15 The U. S. also has acknowledged it has cyberweapons that could help suppress enemy air and sea defenses. Israel used cyber techniques to hide its aircraft in a 2007 attack on a Syrian nuclear facility, according to current and former officials.

16 Such methods are taught at Weapons School, officials acknowledge. The course focuses on combining cyber power with more traditional combat, said

Lt. Col. Reeves. That includes "affecting an adversary's computer system in a way that allows us to fly in an airstrike more effectively, with less resistance," he said.

17   Lt. Col. Steven Lindquist, one of the inaugural students, said the course asks officers to study how an attacker could launch a cyberattack against an Air Force command center or an individual airplane, and to construct defenses. An Air Force "aggressor" team at Nellis then tests the defenses.

18   "The Air Force aggressor acts as a hacker coming against us and we see how our defensive plan measured up," said Lt. Col. Lindquist.

19   The Air Force Weapons School provides advanced training for a handful of elite officers each year in traditional skills, like teaching aerial combat, reconnaissance and bombing, and also for the growing ranks of drone pilots. Adding the cyberwarfare course to the most elite school, officials say, is important to changing the mindset of the military, where many still regard radios, telephones and computers as communications tools—not targets and weapons.

20   "We know this is a contested domain," said Lt. Col. Timothy Franz, staff director for the Air Force Office of Cyberspace Operations[16]. "There are people out there trying to get into your telephones and networks for military purposes[17], and we recognize that having similar capabilities is imperative for the future fight." (From *The Wall Street Journal*, July 9, 2012)

New Words

adversary /ˈædvəsəri/ *n.* a country or person you are fighting or competing against 敌手;对手

aerial /ˈeəriəl/ *n.* (of an attack, etc.) from an aeroplane

aggressor /əˈgresə(r)/ *n.* a person or country that starts a fight or war with another person or country

buildup /ˈbɪldˌʌp/ *n.* a building up, as of military forces; increase in amount or number; a process of growth; strengthening; development 集结;累积;形成

commandant /ˈkɒməndænt/ *n.* the army officer in charge of a place or group of people 司令官;〈美〉(陆军军官学校的)校长

contemplate /ˈkɒntəmpleɪt/ *v.* to think about sth. that you might do in the future 企图,打算

cyber- *prefix* relating to computers, esp. to messages and information on the Internet 计算机(网络)的，信息技术的

cyberwarfare /ˈsaɪbəwɔːfɛə/ *n.* politically motivated hacking to conduct sabotage and espionage 网络战

cyberspace /ˈsaɪbəspeɪs/ *n.* all of the data stored in a large computer or network represented as a three-dimensional model through which a virtual-reality user can move 网络空间

deploy /dɪˈplɔɪ/ *v.* *fml* to use sth. for a particular purpose, esp. ideas, arguments etc. 采用；部署

deterrence /dɪˈterəns/ *n.* the prevention of sth, esp. war or crime, by having sth. such as weapons or punishment to use as a threat 威慑，阻吓

domain /dəʊˈmeɪn/ *n.* an area of activity, interest, or knowledge; realm 领域，……界

drone /drəʊn/ *n.* an aircraft that does not have a pilot, but is operated by radio 无人机

fraction /ˈfrækʃn/ *n.* a very small amount of sth

hacker /ˈhækə(r)/ *n.* sb who secretly uses or changes the information in other people's computer systems

hone /həʊn/ *v.* to improve your skill at doing sth, esp. when you are already very good at it 磨炼(技能)

imperative /ɪmˈperətɪv/ *adj.* extremely important and needing to be done or dealt with immediately

inaugural /ɪˈnɔːgjərəl/ *adj.* marking the beginning of a new venture, series, etc. 开始的，揭幕的

incapacitate /ˌɪnkəˈpæsɪteɪt/ *v.* to stop a system, piece of equipment etc. from working properly

intruder /ɪnˈtruːdə(r)/ *n.* sb. who illegally enters a building or area, usu. in order to steal sth 入侵者

Iran /ɪˈrɑːn/ *n.* a country in southwest Asia, between Iraq and Afghanistan 伊朗

Israeli /ɪzˈreɪli/ *adj.* relating to Israel or its people

Libyan /ˈlɪbɪən/ *adj.* relating to Libya or its people

marshal /ˈmɑːʃl/ *v.* to organize all the people or things that you need in order to be ready for a battle, election etc. 整理，排列，集结

mindset /ˈmaɪndset/ *n.* one's general attitude, and the way in which they think about things and make decisions 思维模式

Nevada /neˈvɑːdə/ *n.* a state in the western U.S, between California and Utah. Nevada is mostly desert, and it is the driest part of the U.S. 内华达州

oversee /ˌəʊvəˈsiː/ *v.* to be in charge of a group of workers and check that a piece of work is done satisfactorily 监督；监管

reconnaissance /rɪˈkɒnɪsns/ *n.* the military activity of sending soldiers and aircraft to find out about the enemy's forces

relevancy /ˈreləvənsiː/ *n.* the condition of being connected with the matter at hand; the state of having practical value or importance

revamp /ˌriːˈvæmp/ *v. infml* to change sth. in order to improve it and make it seem more modern 改进，更新

secretive /ˈsiːkrətɪv/ *adj.* Liking to keep one's thoughts, intentions, or actions hidden from other people

squadron /ˈskwɒdrən/ *n.* a military force consisting of a group of aircraft or ships 中队

trim /trɪm/ *v.* to reduce a number, amount, or the size of sth.

Notes

1. Pentagon Digs In on Cyberwar Front——五角大楼决心在网络战领域发力

  a. the Pentagon——the headquarters of the U.S. Department of Defense. The Pentagon is often used metonymically to refer to the U.S. Department of Defense rather than the building itself. 五角大楼借指美国国防部

  b. dig in——to go resolutely to work

2. unmanned aircraft——commonly known as a drone, is an aircraft without a human pilot on board. Its flight is controlled either autonomously by computers in the vehicle, or under the remote control of a pilot on the ground or in another vehicle.

3. the U.S. Air Force's elite Weapons School——a unit of the U.S. Air Force, assigned to the 57th Wing (第 57 联队). It is stationed at Nellis Air Force Base, Nevada. Its mission is to teach graduate-level instructor courses, which provide advanced training in weapons and tactics employment to officers of the combat air forces. 美国空军军械学院

4. "Top Gun" program——The U.S. Navy Strike Fighter Tactics Instructor program, more popularly known as TOPGUN. 美国海军

战斗机武器学校培训课程。TOPGUN 其实是一个空战训练课程的代号，它开创了假想敌训练模式的先河，目的是为了训练"海军飞行员毕业后的空中格斗技能"。好莱坞曾以此为背景，拍摄《壮志凌云》，其英文原名就是 TOPGUN。

5. Nellis Air Force Base in Nevada—a U. S. Air Force Base, located NE of Las Vegas, Nevada. 内利斯空军基地

6. cyber—Here it is short for "cyberwar."("cyber"并不是一个独立的单词，常用以构成复合词成分。本课中除"cyberwar"以外，还出现了"cyberspace"、"cyberattack"、"cyberweapon"，另外还有"cyber capabilities"、"cyber domain"、"cyber power"、"cyber program"等。在后面四例中，都以独立的单词形式出现，这反映了它正在从构词成分演化成词的过程。)

7. Col.—*abbrev.* Colonel（上校）。本课还出现了"Capt.（Captain 上尉）"，"Gen.（General 上将）"，"Lt. Col.（Lieutenant Colonel 中校）"等军衔的缩写形式。

8. the Central Intelligence Agency—CIA, the department of the US government that collects information about other countries, esp. secretly. 中央情报局

9. the Department of Homeland Security—a cabinet department of the U. S. federal government, created in response to the September 11 attacks, and with the primary responsibilities of protecting the U. S. and U. S. territories from and responding to terrorist attacks, man-made accidents, and natural disasters. 国土安全部

10. Iran's nuclear program—launched in the 1950s with the help of the U. S. as part of the Atoms for Peace program. The participation of the U. S. and Western European governments in Iran's nuclear program continued until the 1979 Iranian Revolution that toppled the Shah of Iran（伊朗国王）。Later, the West has to destroy the program. The US and Israil used stuxnet（震网病毒）to undermine it in 2011.

11. U. S. Cyber Command—an armed forces sub-unified command subordinate to U. S. Strategic Command. It centralizes command of cyberspace operations, organizes existing cyber resources and synchronizes（使同步）defense of U. S. military networks. 美国网战司令部

12. the National Security Agency—NSA, an intelligence agency of the

U. S. Department of Defense responsible for the collection and analysis of foreign communications and foreign signals intelligence, as well as protecting U. S. government communications and information systems, which involves information security and cryptanalysis（密码分析）. Former CIA website blower（揭密者）Edward Snowden, the former NSA contract employee provided the Guardian in July 2013 with top-secret NSA documents leading to revelations about US global surveillance on phone and internet communications. 国家安全局

13. the Center for Information Dominance—a branch of the U. S. Navy. Whose mission is to deliver full spectrum Cyber Information Warfare, and Intelligence Training to achieve decision superiority. 信息控制中心

14. the U. S. Joint Chiefs of Staff—a body of senior uniformed leaders in the U. S. Department of Defense who advise the Secretary of Defense, the Homeland Security Council, the National Security Council and the President on military matters. 美国参谋长联席会议，其主席为军中最高首长。

15. the 328th Weapons Squadron—a USAF Weapons School training unit located at Nellis Air Force Base, Nevada. 美国空军第328武器中队

16. Cyberspace Operations—The term has been proposed to mean the employment of cyber capabilities where the primary purpose is to achieve military objectives or effects in or through cyberspace. Such operations include computer network operations and activities to operate and defend the Global Information Grid. 网络空间战，即通过网络或在网络内部，以达成军事目的或影响为主要目标而对网络功能的运用。这样的作战是指为了操控和防护全球信息网格，所进行的计算机网络作战和行动。

17. There are people... for military purposes. —这是美国最典型的贼喊捉贼伎俩。

Questions

1. Why does the Pentagon show much interest in cyberwarfare?
2. What is the Air Force version of the Navy's "Top Gun" program mainly about?

3. How does the U. S. Cyber Command deal with the cyber world?
4. Why does the Air Force set up the "aggressor" team?
5. Why is it important to add the cyberwarfare course to the most elite school?

读报知识

美英等国情治机构简介

国家安全为头等大事,称为 high foreign policy,经济援助政策则为 low foreign policy。美英等国情报和治安机构常见诸报端,有的一般词典中查不到,行话更费解。为此,特在此先将机构简介如下:

1. 美国

到 2008 年为止,美国共有 16 个情治机构,下面将常见诸报端的几个简介如下:

FBI(Federal Bureau of Investigation) 联邦调查局成立于 1908 年,负责国内治安和反间反颠覆活动的政府机构,属司法部管辖。

CIA(Central Intelligence Agency) 中央情报局是 1947 年建立的独立机构,从事国外的情报与反情报活动,搜集有关国家安全情报。总部设在弗吉尼亚州兰利(Langley,Langley 可指代 CIA)。

中情局控制的情报机构,据称由于在"9·11"事件和伊拉克战争中情报工作失误,地位已大大削弱。原来控制的其他机构有向总统汇报工作,此任务已划归国家情报总监(DNI, Director of National Intelligence)。

Defense Intelligence Agency (DIA) 国防情报局是总局,听取国防部所属情报机构汇报。

National Security Agency/No such Agency(NSA) 国家安全局是国防部情报机构,保护本国通信安全和通过截收、破译、监听来搜集国内外国通信情报的密码机构,成立于 1952 年。又名 Central Security Service,属绝密单位,已有 50 多年历史,美国政府一直讳莫如深,总说"No Such Agency"(没有这个部门),缩写与国家安全局一样。媒体讽刺说,美国国家安全局的英文名字不是"National Security Agency",而是"No Such Agency"。直到 20 世纪 70 年代初,美国政府才肯认账。

National Counterterrorism Center (NCC) 国家反恐中心,是为防止"9·11"事件重演于 2005 年成立。

Terrorist Threat Integration Center(TTIC) 防止恐怖威胁综合中心,由国土安全部、国家反恐中心、国防部和其他有关机构的成员组成,旨在防止恐怖分子袭击美国机构。

United States Secret Service 特工处,常简称 Secret Service,原隶属美国财政部,2002年国土安全部(Department of Homeland Security)成立后,划归新部管辖。原从事查抄伪币等经济事务,现专司保卫总统和其他高官、来访领导人的人身安全。

2. 英国

英国主要有三大情报机构,因为 GCHQ 太机密,常见报的是 MI5 和 MI6。

MI5 (Military Intelligence, Section Five) 军(事)情(报)五处是沿用战时旧称,并非军方情报部门,事实上是英国两个情报局之一,正式名称为 the Intelligence Service(安全局),相当于美国 FBI,负责国内安全及国内反间活动。

MI6 (Military Intelligence, Section 6) 军(事)情(报)六处也是沿用战时旧称,正式名称为 the Secret Intelligence Service(SIS)(情报局),职能相当于美国 CIA。

GCHQ (Government Communications Headquarters) 政府电信总局是英国从事保障电信安全、搜集外国通讯情报、破译密码等任务的政府机构,职能相当于美国的 NSA。据揭露,美英对伊战前夕,曾窃听联合国秘书长科菲·安南(Kofi Annan)的谈话。

3. 苏联

提到情报机构或斗争,至今这两个机构常映入读者的眼帘:**KGB** (Komitet Gosudarstvennoi Bezopastnosti) 克格勃(1954—1991)起美国 CIA 负责对外情报活动及 FBI 负责对内的反间和维持治安的双重作用的苏联政府机构(英译 Committee/Commission for/of State Security[国家安全委员会]);**GRU** 格鲁乌即苏联军队总参谋部情报总局(英译 Chief Directorate of Intelligence of the General Staff)

4. 俄罗斯

Federal Security Service/Federal Service of Security(FSS) 联邦安全局系由联邦反间谍局改组而成,前身是 KGB。1995年,叶利钦总统将原联邦反间局改组为联邦安全局,强化其内外职能,不仅反间,还刑侦,恢复了因改组剥夺掉的一系列特权,拥有预审权、侦讯室及特种部队。

5. 法国

DGSE(Direction Generale de la Securite Exterieure) 对外安全总局

6. 以色列

Mossad 莫萨德,以色列情报和特务局(英译 the Institution for Intelligence and Special Duties),负责对外的情报机构,创建于1951年。

Al 意为至高无上,是 Mossad 的化名(Al 为希伯来文,等于英文 above)。

Shin Bet/Beth 辛贝特:以色列"国家安全总局",负责对内的安全机构。(详见《导读》五章四节)

Lesson Eleven

课文导读

2010年6月28日,美国情报部门和司法部门逮捕了10名在美国为俄罗斯搜集情报的秘密特工。这些"俄罗斯对外情报局秘密特工"被指在美国多年"深度潜伏",借助高技术暗中联络,采取多种手段向美国政府决策层渗透,搜集核武器、美国对俄政策等情报。该消息一传出立刻引发世界各大媒体的广泛关注,7月8日,这10名被告在纽约一家法庭认罪,被判驱逐出境。作为交换条件,俄罗斯同意释放4名被控与西方情报机构有接触的在押人员。7月10日,美俄在维也纳机场交换间谍。至此,这起美俄落网特工交换事件尘埃落定。这起引人注目的间谍案处理得如此默契,说明双方政府对情报工作都心照不宣。冷战时代,美国和苏联曾在柏林多次进行过 spy swap,故这并非鲜为人知。

通过此课,我们可以了解不同层面和地域当代情报活动的特点,熟悉英美情报机构,并学习到和情报工作相关的词汇和行话。

Pre-reading Questions

1. What do you know about CIA?
2. Do you think James Bond and Jason Bourne typical spies in modern espionage? Why?

Text

Spies Among Us: Modern-Day Espionage

Long after the Cold War's[1] end, nations still send secret agents[2] across borders. But corporations, terrorists, and private investigators are also part of the sleuthing underground.

By Mckay Coppins

1   The startling discovery of an undercover Russian spy ring last month no doubt shocked many Americans who assumed that

international espionage was mostly a product of the Cold War and, these days, Hollywood[3].

2 But intelligence experts weren't the least surprised. "We forget that states like Russia have been conducting espionage for centuries," says Peter Earnest, a former member of the CIA[4] who is now director of the Spy Museum[5] in Washington, D. C. "It didn't stop with the Cold War and start again recently. It simply continued." Of course, diplomatic relations between the U. S. and Russia have improved in recent years, and Earnest says the two governments work together with an unspoken understanding that they are still spying on each other. "It's just the cost of doing business," he says.

3 While professional spying was once about nation-states looking over other governments' shoulders, today it's largely about tracking terrorists' activities and monitoring public communications for suspicious chatter[6]. In fact, intelligence experts say espionage of all shades has actually increased since the Cold War, amplified by new technology and soaring demand for information in the public and private sectors. Just this week, The Washington Post reported that "some 1,271 government organizations and 1,931 private companies work on programs related to counterterrorism, homeland security, and intelligence in about 10,000 locations across the United States" as part of the paper's report on the top-secret world created by Washington after 9/11[7].

4 Here's a look at who's spying on whom, circa 2010:

OTHER NATIONS

5 When it comes to state-backed espionage, experts say the U. S. has focused much of its recent spying on Iran, North Korea, and China. And these countries, it appears, are returning the favor.

6 Earnest says the U. S. is the recipient of "hundreds of thousands" of cyberattacks every day, many of which emanate from Beijing. "They want to find out if they can penetrate our firewalls and actually learn

intelligence. We believe a good deal has been learned."

7   But, of course, computers and satellites can do only so much. Secret agents, like the ones recently deported to Russia, still play a significant role in international spy games, though Earnest says the number of "illegals" currently undercover in the U. S. is unknowable. "The problem with counting spies is that their nature is not to be counted," he says.

8   Even longtime strong allies may spy on each other. An Israeli report in 2008 documented a long history of American spying on Israel, particularly in regard to Israel's secret nuclear program. And there have been several known instances of Israel spying on America, including the famous case of Jonathan Pollard[8], a U. S. intelligence analyst sentenced to life in prison after an espionage conviction.

TERRORISTS

9   Many Americans are under the false impression that "cave-dwelling terrorists" are too primitive to support effective intelligence operations, Earnest says. The most dangerous spies, however, are often the ones not working for recognized governments (which are bound, at least theoretically, by diplomacy and international law).

10   Independent terror networks have proved adept at the art of deception and intelligence gathering. The 2008 attack on Mumbai[9], says Earnest, "required a tremendous amount of planning as well as some relatively low-tech, but well-used, technology." And this January, a double agent[10] of Al Qaeda[11] successfully infiltrated a CIA base in Afghanistan and killed seven agents in a suicide bombing, temporarily crippling America's intelligence operations in the country.

MAJOR CORPORATIONS

11   Spying isn't just the stuff of war and international politics. While researching his 2010 book *Broker, Trader, Lawyer, Spy: The Secret World of Corporate Espionage*[12], journalist Eamon Javers uncovered the dealings of private-sector spy firms employed by companies to detect deception in negotiators, surveil competing investors, and glean intelligence that could give them an edge in their dealmaking. Espionage has become so ubiquitous in the corporate world, Javers says, that

billion-dollar merger-and-acquisition deals are almost never made these days without highly skilled spies getting involved.

12   Using some of the most sophisticated technology in the world (like a laser that can record conversations from a kilometer away by picking up the slightest vibrations on an office window), these firms are staffed almost entirely by former military and intelligence officials, from the U. K. 's MI5[13] to Russia's KGB[14]. The CIA even has a policy that allows its analysts to "moonlight" for major corporations. And there's no shortage of demand. One hedge-fund executive told Javers he used corporate spies to keep tabs on the entire board of directors for every company he invested in[15]. "There is even a whole network of people who do nothing but track corporate jets," Javers says.

13   It's not only competitors snooping around these major corporations. Both Earnest and Javers say foreign governments regularly spy on U. S. companies. "The Chinese have an extremely elaborate intelligence network aimed at penetrating defense and technology firms," Javers says. "Every piece of technology they steal is a piece they don't have to invent for themselves."

PRIVATE INVESTIGATORS

14   The advent of the Internet transformed the private-eye industry, shifting its focus from background checks (which can now be completed for a small price on myriad Web sites) to surveillance[16].

15   Skipp Porteous, president of New York-based Sherlock Investigations, says much of his business is derived from spouses who suspect infidelity. "A lot of times we get calls from a wife whose husband is coming to New York, usually on business, and she's afraid he's going to fool around," Porteous says. "So she hires us and we get the goods." (Incidentally, Porteous says women are right in their suspicions about 90 percent of the time; when men think their wives are cheating, they're usually wrong.)

16   Sherlock dispatches teams of two licensed private investigators, experts at blending into crowds and going unnoticed, to follow the suspected cheater and snap photos. In one case, a woman from Bermuda hired Sherlock to follow her husband while he was in New York. Investigators took pictures of him with six prostitutes (at once) and e-

mailed them to their client before her spouse returned home.

17   Additionally, since the Internet has enabled people to easily purchase illegal audio and video transmitters, Sherlock has seen a boom in "bug sweep" business[17], especially among celebrities who believe the paparazzi have infiltrated their homes or cars. As new technologies emerge, experts expect intelligence and counterintelligence methods to grow in sophistication, and generate even more job opportunities for a new generation of supersleuths. (From *The Daily Beast*[18], July 21, 2010)

New Words

adept /əˈdept/ *adj.* good at sth. that needs care and skill 熟练的,擅长的,内行的

advent /ˈædvent/ *n.* the time when sth. first begins to be widely used (重要事件、人物、发明等的)到来

Afghanistan /æfˈgænɪstæn/ *n.* a country in Asia that is west of Pakistan and east of Iran 阿富汗

amplify /ˈæmplɪfaɪ/ *v. fml.* to increase the effects or strength of sth. 增强

Bermuda /bə(ː)ˈmjuːdə/ *n.* a group of islands in the West Atlantic Ocean which is a popular place for tourists. Bermuda is a British colony, but has its own local government. 百慕大群岛(英国)

circa /ˈsɜːkə/ *prep.* used before a date to show that sth. happened close to but not exactly on that date(用在日期、数字等前面)大约在,接近于

counterterrorism /ˈkaʊntəˌterərɪzəm/ *n.* a strategy intended to prevent terrorist acts or to get rid of terrorist groups 反恐怖主义

cripple /ˈkrɪpl/ *v.* to damage sth. badly so that it no longer works or is no longer effective 削弱,使……瘫痪

cyberattack /ˌsaɪbəəˈtæk/ *n.* illegally getting access to others' computer system in order to obtain secret information or cause damage by means of email and other tools of the Internet 网络攻击

deception /dɪˈsepʃn/ *n.* the act of deliberately making someone believe sth. that is not true 欺骗

deport /dɪˈpɔːt/ *v.* to force someone to leave a country and return to the country they originally came from, esp. because they do not have a legal right to stay or have committed crimes 驱逐出境

elaborate /ɪˈlæbəreɪt/ *adj.* carefully planned and organized in great detail 精心制作的

emanate /ˈeməneɪt/ *v.* to produce a smell, light etc., or to show a particular quality 散发，发出

espionage /ˈespɪənɑːʒ/ *n.* the activity of secretly finding out secret information and giving it to a country's enemies or a company's competitors 间谍行为，谍报活动

firewall /ˈfaəwɔːl/ *n.* (computing) a security system consisting of a combination of hardware and software that limits the exposure of a computer or computer network to attack from crackers; commonly used on local area networks that are connected to the internet 防火墙

glean /gliːn/ *v.* to find out information slowly and with difficulty 费力地收集，四处收集（信息、知识）

hedge-fund /ˈhedʒ fʌnd/ *n.* a flexible investment company for a small number of large investors (usu. the minimum investment is $1 million) 对冲基金

infidelity /ɪnfɪˈdelətɪ/ *n.* an act of sex with someone other than one's marriage partner（夫妇间的）不忠实，不贞行为

infiltrate /ˈɪnfɪltreɪt/ *v.* to secretly join an organization or enter a place in order to find out information about it or harm it 使悄悄进入，潜入

intelligence /ɪnˈtelɪdʒəns/ *n.* information about the secret activities of foreign governments, the military plans of an enemy 情报，情报工作，情报机关

Iran /ɪˈrɑːn/ *n.* a country in southwest Asia, between Iraq and Afghanistan. 伊朗

Israel /ˈɪzreɪl/ *n.* a country on the eastern side of the Mediterranean Sea, surrounded by Egypt, Jordan, and Lebanon 以色列

Israeli /ɪzˈreɪlɪ/ *adj.* relating to Israel or its people 以色列的

moonlight /ˈmuːnlaɪt/ *v.* to have a second job in addition to your main job, esp. without the knowledge of the government tax department（暗中）兼职，从事第二职业

Mumbai /mʌmˈbaɪ/ *n.* a city in western India and India's 2nd largest city（印度城市）孟买

myriad /ˈmɪrɪəd/ *adj.* very many 无数的

North Korea a country in East Asia, west of Japan and east of China, which is officially called the Democratic People's Republic of Korea 朝鲜

paparazzi /ˌpæpəˈrætsɪ/ n. pl. photographers who follow famous people in order to take photographs they can sell to newspapers 狗仔队

penetrate /ˈpenətreɪt/ v. to enter sth and pass or spread through it, esp. when this is difficult 穿透,渗透

primitive /ˈprɪmətɪv/ adj. belonging to a simple way of life that existed in the past and does not have modern industries and machines 原始的

prostitute /ˈprɒstɪtjuːt/ n. someone, esp. a woman, who earns money by having sex with men 卖淫者,娼妓

ring /rɪŋ/ n. a group of people who illegally control a business or criminal activity 团伙,帮派,集团

sleuth /sluːθ/ v. to track or follow; to act as a detective 跟踪,侦查

snap /snæp/ v. to take a photograph

snoop /snuːp/ v. to try to find out about someone's private affairs by secretly looking in their house, examining their possessions etc 窥探,打探

sophistication /səˌfɪstɪˈkeɪʃn/ n. the state of being developed or produced with a high level of skill and knowledge 复杂,尖端

staff /stɑːf/ v. to provide the workers for 为……配备职员

supersleuth /ˈsjuːpəsluːθ/ n. a special law-enforcement agent of the Federal Bureau of Investigation(美国联邦调查局)高级特工

surveil /sɜːˈveɪl/ v. to keep under surveillance 使受监视(或监督)

surveillance /sɜːˈveɪləns/ n. a close watch kept on someone, esp. someone who is believed to have criminal intentions(对有犯罪意图者的)监视

ubiquitous /juːˈbɪkwɪtəs/ adj. seeming to be everywhere, sometimes used humorously 普遍存在的,无所不在的

undercover /ˌʌndəˈkʌvə(r)/ adj. working secretly using a false appearance in order to get information for the police or government 秘密从事的,从事间谍活动的

Notes

1. Cold War—unfriendly and hostile relationship between the US and the Soviet Union after the Second World War(1947—1991)冷战
2. secret agents—someone whose job is to find out and report on the military and political secrets of other countries 特工人员,间谍

3. Hollywood—movie studios in Los Angeles, California where films are made, often used to refer to the U.S film industry in general 好莱坞
4. CIA—Central Intelligence Agency is a federal US bureau created in 1947 to conduct espionage and intelligence activities.
5. Spy Museum—a privately owned museum dedicated to the field of espionage located in Washington, D.C. 间谍博物馆
6. While professional spying... for suspicious chatter. —Although in the past, the focus of professional spying had been investigating other governments' intelligence in all aspects for the sake of their sovereign nation, today, tracking terrorists' activities and monitoring public communications for anti-governments or suspicious comments had been a very important part of their undercover investigation. 虽然职业间谍的工作重点曾是为主权国家监视他国,但现在追踪恐怖分子的活动和监控公众通信中的可疑言论则成了他们隐秘调查的重头戏。

　　look over one's shoulder—keep close watch over 严密监视
7. 9/11—Also the September 11 attacks/September 11. It refers to a series of four coordinated terrorist attacks launched by the Islamic terrorist group al-Qaeda(伊斯兰恐怖主义基地组织) upon the United States in New York City and the Washington, D.C. area on September 11, 2001. 9·11事件
8. Jonathan Jay Pollard—1954— , is an American who passed classified information to Israel while working as an American civilian intelligence analyst. He pleaded guilty and received a life sentence in 1987. Because his crime occurred prior to November 1, 1987, he is eligible for parole(假释), and may be released on November 21, 2015.
9. The 2008 attack on Mumbai—The twelve coordinated shooting and bombing attacks across Mumbai by members of Lashkar-e-Taiba(虔诚军). The attacks, which drew widespread global condemnation, began on 26 November and lasted until 29 November 2008, killing 164 people and wounding at least 308. 孟买恐怖袭击(2008)
10. double agent—someone who finds out an enemy country's secrets for their own country but who also gives secrets to the enemy 双重间谍

11. Al Qaeda—also the Base, is a global militant terrorist organization founded by Osama bin Laden at some point between August 1988 and late 1989, with its origins being traceable to the Soviet War in Afghanistan. It operates as a network comprising both a multinational, stateless army and a radical Sunni Muslim(逊尼派穆斯林) movement calling for global Jihad(全球圣战) and a strict interpretation of sharia law(伊斯兰教教法). It has attacked civilian and military targets in various countries, including the September 11 attacks, 1998 U. S. embassy bombings and the 2002 Bali bombings(巴厘岛爆炸案).
12. *Broker, Trader, Lawyer, Spy: The Secret World of Corporate Espionage*—a book written by Award-winning reporter Eamon Javers. It is a penetrating work of investigative and historical journalism about the evolution of corporate espionage, exploring the dangerous and combustible power spies hold over international business.
13. MI5—The Security Service, commonly known as Military Intelligence, Section 5, is the UK's internal counter-intelligence and security agency.
14. KGB—the Committee for State Security, more commonly known by its transliteration "KGB," was the main security agency for the former Soviet Union from 1954 until its collapse in 1991.
15. he used corporate spies to keep tabs on the entire board of directors for every company he invested in—For the company he invested in, the hedge-fundexecutive employed corporate spies to keep all the board members of these companies under his surveillance. 他利用公司探子监视他所投资公司的董事会。

    keep tabs on—to keep an eye on, watch attentively 监视
16. The advent of the Internet... to surveillance. —As the Internet becoming widely used, the private detective industry had changed markedly. The focus of private detective agency had been investigating individuals' identity for security purposes before, such as membership in groups or organizations, criminal convictions, work experience, education, etc. , which can be done now on numerous websites for a small price. But nowadays its focus has been oriented on attentively observing a person or group, especially one under suspicion. 因特网的出现改变了私家侦探行业。他们的工

作重点从背景调查(现在,背景调查只要付一点费用就可以在海量的网站上完成)变为监视。

17. "bug sweep" business——the business of detecting and sweeping away any concealed electronic listening devices equipped in a room or telephone circuit, etc. "清除窃听器"业务

18. *The Daily Beast*——"每日野兽"(thedailybeast.com)是美国曼哈顿的互联网公司 IAC/ InterActiveCorp 公司拥有的一家新闻报道和评论网站,成立于 2008 年 10 月 6 日,由《纽约客》和《名利场》前总编蒂娜·布朗(Tina Brown)创办,被称为"野兽"级《新闻周刊》。每日野兽的名字来自于伊夫林·沃(Evelyn Waugh's)的小说《独家新闻》(*Scoop*)中的一份虚构报纸。据美国《纽约时报》报道称,每日野兽拥有自己独特的客户群,每月大约有 300 万访问量,2010 年 11 月 12 日,每日野兽与美国新闻周刊合并,成立新闻周刊与每日野兽公司(The Newsweek Daily Beast Company)。该网站的新闻涉及政治、经济、娱乐、时尚、女性和艺术等领域,同时刊登《新闻周刊》电子版。以突发新闻和尖锐的时评著称。后来有变(见 *Newsweek* 介绍)。

Questions

1. Is espionage mostly a product of the Cold War? Why or why not?
2. What is the focus of modern professional spying?
3. How many "secret agents" are there currently undercover in the U.S.?
4. According to experts, who are the most dangerous spies?
5. What is the focus of modern corporation espionage?
6. According to the passage, what contributes most to modern espionage?

语言解说

间谍行话

间谍用语大多是从泛指到特指而词同义异的一些俚语行话,其中有不少是 CIAese, KGBese 等(见二课)spookspeak(间谍行话),一般词典大多语焉不详。例如本课第 10 段就有一字把编委将住了:

... the number of "illegals" currently undercover in the U. S. is unknowable.

此处的"illegals"是何意?虽经编委劳顿也未能阐释其意,直至看了

《导读》"间谍行话"和"报刊词典"才知非"非法移民"等意思。下面从《导读》附录"间谍行话"选若干对读者看间谍书刊或许有参考价值的行话：

agent of influence 旨在影响舆论（而不是从事破坏、暗杀等间谍活动）的特工：散布假情报、反宣传等活动的人员；在美收买权势人物的特工

agent provocateur（鼓励涉嫌者从事非法活动而加以逮捕的）坐探，密探

asset（尤指美国中央情报局在搜集情报的国家所建立的）关系，眼线

bagman 从事收买拉拢的特工

black bag (job) 黑袋（活计）：指警察或特工人员为获取证据而"非法入室秘密搜查"。黑袋子是从事非法秘密搜查的象征，里面装着搜查用具。

blown（间谍）被发现的

boxed 被测谎过的

brainwashed（谍报人员的）心理经过调试的：如用测谎器就不一定能测准

burnt 身份暴露的，活动曝光的

compromised＝burnt 可能死了

country team 见 U.S. country team

cut-off man（地方情报站的）联络员，交通

cut-out（情报联络或交易的）中间人

desk man（情报总局负责间谍活动部门的）总管，主管

destabilize 颠覆

drop（间谍用于传递情报、转交赏金等的）"信箱"：如树根、古庙等均可用作这样的地点；如"无人情报交接处"则为 **dead (letter) drop**（见 dubok）；（为获取情报而进行的）成功讹诈

dubok（俄语）无人情报交接处，无人材料、信息交换处：一方将"信"放在隐蔽之处，另一方然后再去取，两方不见面。

Farm（中央情报局设在弗吉尼亚的）培训学校

field agent/man 外调特工，派遣特工

flaps and seals（美国中央情报局给学员开设的邮检）启封课：a ～ man 邮检专家

front（为非法活动、间谍活动而装的）门面，（作）掩护者

G-men 联邦调查局特工；美国特工处：源于一同名电影和美国特工处设在华盛顿G Street之故。

illegals（无外交身份和豁免权的）间谍（网），情报站

legals（具有外交官身份的）间谍（网）

legend 间谍的化名和伪造的履历

mole 鼹鼠，（打入敌对情报机关而）长期潜伏的间谍（见 sleeper）

naked 无掩护和支援的

nash 我们的一个人，我方的一员

onetime pad 简单的、只能用一次的编码法

paroles（未见过面的间谍接头时确认双方身份的）主要暗号

playback（被捕间谍）被迫继续向

己方发送(情报)
plumbing(为进行颠覆等重大活动前而设的)秘密机构
resident director(驻在某国的)情报站站长,间谍网头头
safe house(接待或安排特情或投靠者用的)密点,秘密招待所,秘密旅馆,(旅馆的)秘密套间
secret secret service officer 秘密机关从事秘密工作的官员或人员,情报机关的情报人员或特工,保卫机关的安全人员。

... and it is likely that the former **secret secret service officer**[Peter Wright] with a Government pension of £2,000 a year (or 3,200) is already a millionaire. (The *Guardian*)

sleeper(随时待机活动的)潜伏间谍(见 **mole**)

stringer(非情报机关的)兼职间谍
swim(间谍的)外出活动,旅行
take(因间谍活动而取得的)情报成果
terminate with extreme prejudice(婉)暗杀,干掉:指美国中央情报局常选择"暗杀"政界要人甚至国家元首,原指其在越南战争期间"暗杀"北越村长
turned 被说服(而倒向另一方)或被收买的
U.S. country team 由驻某国大使和情报站长组成的美在驻在国的情报班子
walk-in 主动提供情报或支持的志愿人员
watcher 主管监视怀疑对象的情报人员
wet job(间谍进行的)流血行动,暗杀行动

Lesson Twelve

课文导读

　　反恐战已在美国形成了一种恐惧氛围,"反恐反恐,越反越恐"一文就是其生动写照。2001年"9·11"事件发生后,小布什政府认为美国在阿富汗和第二次伊拉克战争取得了军事上胜利,却遭到不断的反抗和恐怖袭击,于是又进行反恐战,并将此作为美国长期的首要任务,其经费支出总额到2008年9月竟高达8,580亿美元。

　　本文作者认为,小布什政府不断为反恐战辩解和为发动伊拉克战争开脱,并在2006年国会中期选举和2004年大选中利用"9·11"事件和反恐战不断恐吓选民,使共和党人和他自己在竞选连任中取胜。难怪 Newsweek 在总结其竞选策略时仿 F. 罗斯福说的名言"The only thing we have to fear is fear itself",而写道:"The only thing we have to use is fear itself."[我们什么竞选策略都不用,就用(袭击)恐惧这一招。]另一方面,因惧怕恐怖袭击而使人产生了一种被围困的心态(siege mentality),弄得草木皆兵,杯弓蛇影,机场、公路、办公楼都得安检,给美国人民的工作和生活带来诸多不便,使他们产生了"terror fatigue"。尤为重要的是,美国各民族之间产生了不应有的裂痕,阿拉伯人成了受歧视和怀疑的对象,迫使其对美国政府不满。美国政府的这种做法最终严重地削弱了它在全世界的地位和声誉。

Pre-reading Questions

1. What do you know about terrorism and terrorist attacks?
2. What do you think are the causes of terrorism?

Text

Terrorized by "War on Terror"
How a Three-Word Mantra[1] Has Undermined America
By Zbigniew Brzezinski[2]

　　The "war on terror" has created a culture of fear in America. The

Bush administration's elevation of these three words into a national mantra since the horrific events of 9/11[3] has had a pernicious impact on American democracy, on America's psyche and on U.S. standing in the world. Using this phrase has actually undermined our ability to effectively confront the real challenges we face from fanatics who may use terrorism against us.

2 The damage these three words have done—a classic self-inflicted wound—is infinitely greater than any wild dreams entertained by the fanatical perpetrators of the 9/11 attacks when they were plotting against us in distant Afghan caves. The phrase itself is meaningless. It defines neither a geographic context nor our presumed enemies.[4] Terrorism is not an enemy but a technique of warfare-political intimidation through the killing of unarmed non-combatants.

3 But the little secret here may be that the vagueness of the phrase was deliberately (or instinctively) calculated by its sponsors. Constant reference to a "war on terror" did accomplish one major objective: It stimulated the emergence of a culture of fear. Fear obscures reason, intensifies emotions and makes it easier for demagogic politicians to mobilize the public on behalf of the policies they want to pursue.[5] The war of choice in Iraq could never have gained the congressional support it got without the psychological linkage between the shock of 9/11 and the postulated existence of Iraqi weapons of mass destruction[6]. Support for President Bush in the 2004 elections was also mobilized in part by the notion that "a nation at war" does not change its commander in chief in midstream.[7] The sense of a pervasive but otherwise imprecise danger was thus channeled in a politically expedient direction by the mobilizing appeal of being "at war."[8]

4 To justify the "war on terror," the administration[9] has lately crafted a false historical narrative that could even become a self-fulfilling prophecy. By claiming that its war is similar to earlier U.S. struggles against Nazism (while ignoring the fact that Nazi Germany was first-rate military power, a status al-Qaeda[10] neither has nor can achieve), the administration could be preparing the case for war with Iran. Such war would then plunge America into a protracted conflict spanning Iraq, Iran, Afghanistan and perhaps also Pakistan.

5 The culture of fear is like a genie that has been let out of its

bottle[11]. It acquires a life of its own and can become demoralizing. America today is not the self-confident and determined nation that responded to Pearl Harbor[12]; nor is it the America that heard from its leader, at another moment of crisis, the powerful words "the only thing we have to fear is fear itself"[13]; nor is it the calm America that waged the Cold War with quiet persistence despite the knowledge that a real war could be initiated abruptly within minutes and prompt the death of 100 million Americans within just a few hours[14]. We are now divided, uncertain and potentially very susceptible to panic in the event of another terrorist act in the United States itself.

6   That is the result of five years of almost continuous national brainwashing on the subject of terror, quite unlike the more muted reactions of several other nations (Britain, Spain, Italy, Germany, Japan, to mention just a few) that also have suffered painful terrorist acts. In his latest justification for his war in Iraq, President Bush even claims absurdly that he has to continue waging it lest al-Qaeda cross the Atlantic to launch a war of terror here in the United States.

7   Such fear-mongering, reinforced by security entrepreneurs, the mass media and the entertainment industry, generates its own momentum. The terror entrepreneurs, usually described as experts on terrorism, are necessarily engaged in competition to justify their existence. Hence their task is to convince the public that it faces new threats. That puts a premium on the presentation of credible scenarios of ever-more-horrifying acts of violence, sometimes even with blueprints for their implementation. [15]

8   That America has become insecure and more paranoid is hardly debatable. A recent study reported that in 2003 Congress identified 160 sites as potentially important national targets for would-be terrorists. With lobbyists weighing in[16], by the end of that year the list had grown to 1,849; by the end of 2004, to 28,360; by 2005, to 77,769. The national database of possible targets now has some 300,000 items in it, including the Sears Tower[17] in Chicago and an Illinois Apple and Pork Festival[18].

9   Just last week, here in Washington, on my way to visit a journalistic office, I had to pass through one of the absurd "security checks" that have proliferated in almost all the privately owned office

buildings in this capital and in New York City. A uniformed guard required me to fill out a form, show an I. D. and in this case explain in writing the purpose of my visit. Would a visiting terrorist indicate in writing that the purpose is "to blow up the building"? Would the guard be able to arrest such a self-confessing, would-be suicide bomber? To make matters more absurd, large department stores, with their crowds of shoppers, do not have any comparable procedures. Nor do concert halls or movie theaters. Yet such "security" procedures have become routine, wasting hundreds of millions of dollars and further contributing to a siege mentality.

10   Government at every level has stimulated the paranoia. Consider, for example, the electronic billboards over interstate highways urging motorists to "Report Suspicious Activity" (drivers in turbans)[19]. Some mass media have made their own contribution. The cable channels and some print media have found that horror scenarios attract audiences, while terror "experts" as "consultants" provide authenticity for the apocalyptic visions fed to the American public.[20] Hence the proliferation of programs with bearded "terrorists" as the central villains. Their general effect is to reinforce the sense of the unknown but lurking danger that is said to increasingly threaten the lives of all Americans.

11   The entertainment industry has also jumped into the act. Hence the TV serials and films in which the evil characters have recognizable Arab features, sometimes highlighted by religious gestures, exploit public anxiety and stimulate Islamophobia[21]. Arab facial stereotypes, particularly in newspaper cartoons, have at times been rendered in a manner sadly reminiscent of the Nazi anti-Semitic campaigns[22]. Lately, even some college student organizations have become involved in such propagation, apparently oblivious to the menacing connection between the stimulation of racial and religious hatreds and the unleashing of the unprecedented crimes of the Holocaust[23].

12   The atmosphere generated by the "war on terror" has encouraged legal and political harassment of Arab Americans (generally loyal Americans) for conduct that has not been unique to them. A case in point is the reported harassment of the Council on American-Islamic Relations (CAIR)[24] for its attempts to emulate, not very successfully, the American Israel Public Affairs Committee (AIPAC)[25]. Some House Republicans recently described CAIR

members as "terrorist apologists" who should not be allowed to use a Capitol[26] meeting room for a panel discussion.

13   Social discrimination, for example toward Muslim air travelers, has also been its unintended byproduct. Not surprisingly, animus toward the United States even among Muslims otherwise not particularly concerned with the Middle East has intensified, while America's reputation as a leader in fostering constructive interracial and interreligious relations has suffered egregiously.

14   The record is even more troubling in the general area of civil rights. The culture of fear has bred intolerance, suspicion of foreigners and the adoption of legal procedures that undermine fundamental notions of justice. Innocent until proven guilty has been diluted if not undone, with some—even U.S. citizens—incarcerated for lengthy periods of time without effective and prompt access to due process.[27] There is no known, hard evidence that such excess has prevented significant acts of terrorism, and convictions for would-be terrorists of any kind have been few and far between.[28] Someday Americans will be as ashamed of this record as they now have become of the earlier instances in U.S. history of panic by the many prompting intolerance against the few.

15   In the meantime, the "war on terror" has gravely damaged the United States internationally. For Muslims, the similarity between the rough treatment of Iraqi civilians by the U.S. military and of the Palestinians by the Israelis[29] has prompted a widespread sense of hostility toward the United States in general. It's not the "war on terror" that angers Muslims watching the news on television, it's the victimization of Arab civilians. And the resentment is not limited to Muslims. A recent BBC poll of 28,000 people in 27 countries that sought respondents' assessments of the role of states in international affairs resulted in Israel, Iran and the United States being rated (in that order) as the states with "the most negative influence on the world." Alas, for some that is the new axis of evil[30]!

16   The events of 9/11 could have resulted in a truly global solidarity against extremism and terrorism. A global alliance of moderates, including Muslim ones, engaged in a deliberate campaign both to extirpate the specific terrorist networks and to terminate the political conflicts that spawn terrorism would have been more productive than a demagogically proclaimed and largely

solitary U. S. "war on terror" against "Islamo-fascism[31]." Only a confidently determined and reasonable America can promote genuine international security which then leaves no political space for terrorism.

17　　Where is the U. S. leader ready to say, "Enough of this hysteria, stop this paranoia"? Even in the face of future terrorist attacks, the likelihood of which cannot be denied, let us show some sense. Let us be true to our traditions. (From *The Washington Post*, March 25, 2007)

New Words

animus /ˈænɪməs/ *n.* a feeling of hatred or ill will; hostility 仇视；敌意

apocalyptic /əˌpɒkəˈlɪptɪk/ *adj.* foreboding imminent disaster; terrible 预示大动乱或大灾变的；预示世界末日恐怖景象的

authentic /ɔːˈθentɪk/ *adj.* representing facts accurately or reliably; trustworthy

blueprint /ˈbluːprɪnt/ *n.* a detailed programme of action

brainwashing /ˈbreɪnˌwɒʃɪŋ/ *n.* a systematic attempt to instill a particular set of beliefs into sb 洗脑

calculate /ˈkælkjʊˌleɪt/ *v.* to figure out in one's head; intend or arrange for a particular purpose

channel /ˈtʃænl/ *v.* to direct

comparable /ˈkɒmpərəbl/ *adj.* approximately equivalent; similar

craft /krɑːft/ *v.* to make as if by using skill and dexterity 精心制作

demagogic /ˌdeməˈɡɒdʒɪk/ *adj.* of or like a political speaker or leader who plays upon the passions of the people to win their support for himself or his party 蛊惑人心的

demoralize /dɪˈmɒrəlaɪz/ *v.* to weaken the morale of; discourage

dilute /daɪˈljuːt/ *v.* to weaken

egregious /ɪˈɡriːdʒəs/ *adj.* conspicuously or shockingly bad; flagrant 惊人的，利害的　egregiously *adv.*

elevate /ˈelɪveɪt/ *v.* to raise gradually

emulate /ˈemjʊleɪt/ *v.* to rival; strive to do as well as or better than; imitate closely 努力赶上或超过；仿效，模仿

engage /ɪnˈɡeɪdʒ/ *v.* to participate

expedient /ɪksˈpiːdɪənt/ *adj.* characterized by concern with what is opportune rather than what is right or just; specifically governed by self-interest, rather than by concern with what is moral 谋取本身利益的；出于私利考虑的；权宜之计的

exploit /ˈeksplɔɪt/ v. to take unfair advantage of for financial or other gain
extirpate /ˈekstɜːpeɪt/ v. to destroy completely 灭绝；根除
fanatic /fəˈnætɪk/ n. sb who is excessively and often uncritically enthusiastic 狂热者
harass /ˈhærəs/ v. to annoy or worry persistently 骚扰，扰乱；烦扰 harassment n.
hysteria /hɪsˈtɪərɪə/ n. unmanageable emotional excess, esp. fits of laughing or weeping
implement /ˈɪmplɪmənt/ v. to carry out; accomplish, esp. to give practical effect to
imprecise /ˌɪmprɪˈsaɪs/ adj. not precise, inexact, vague
incarcerate /ɪnˈkɑːsəreɪt/ v. to confine (as if) in a prison 监禁；囚于
instinctive /ɪnˈstɪŋktɪv/ adj. of, being, or prompted by instinct; arising spontaneously and being independent of judgment 本能的；天性的；直觉的
intimidate /ɪnˈtɪmɪdeɪt/ v. to frighten, esp. to compel or deter (as if) by threats 恫吓；威胁
lurking /lɜːk/ adj. latent; lying hidden waiting for attack 潜在的，隐藏的
mantra /ˈmʌntrə/ n. a sacred word or sound used as an invocation or incantation (e.g. in Hinduism or Buddhism)（印度教和大乘佛教中的）祷文；咒符
menace /ˈmenɪs/ v. to threaten or show intent to harm
mentality /menˈtælɪtɪ/ n. mental power or capacity; a person's habitual way of thinking; character 智能；心态
mobilize /ˈməʊbɪlaɪz/ v. to put into movement or circulatoin
moderate /ˈmɒdərɪt/ n. one who holds moderate views or who belongs to a group favouring a moderate course or programme (e.g. in politics or religion) 持温和观点者；（政党中的）稳定派；温和派
momentum /məʊˈmentəm/ n. force or speed of movement; impetus, as of a physical object or course of events 动力，势头
monger /ˈmʌŋɡər/ v. to sell; hawk 贩卖；兜售
muted /ˈmjuːtɪd/ adj. being mute; subdued（批评等）温和的；（争吵等）已趋缓和的
non-combatant /ˌnɒnˈkɒmbətənt/ n. a civilian in wartime（战争时期的）平民
obscure /əbˈskjʊə/ v. to conceal (as if) by covering

paranoia /ˌpærəˈnɔɪə/ *n*. a tendency towards excessive or irrational suspiciousness and distrustfulness of others 妄想狂倾向；偏执
paranoid /ˈpærənɔɪd/ *adj*. 有妄想狂倾向的；偏执狂的；多疑的
pernicious /pɜːˈnɪʃəs/ *adj*. highly injurious or destructive; deadly 有害的，恶劣的；恶性的，致命的
perpetrate /ˈpɜːpɪtreɪt/ *v*. to commit, perform (sth bad) 作恶；行凶
pervasive /pɜːˈveɪsɪv/ *adj*. spreading throughout and into every part
plunge /plʌndʒ/ *v*. to force (sth or sb) into a new set of circumstance 使突然陷入或遭受
postulate /ˈpɒstjʊleɪt/ *v*. to assume or claim to be existent or true 假定或认定……存在
proliferate /prəˈlɪfəreɪt/ *v*. to increase in number or quantity suddenly and quickly; multiply
protract /prəˈtrækt/ *v*. to prolong in time or space protracted *adj*.
psyche /ˈsaɪki/ *n*. the mind or soul; that which makes up the self 心灵，精神，自我
reminiscent /ˌremɪˈnɪsnt/ *adj*. recalling particulars and ideas believed to have been known in a previous existence; thinking about past experiences 令人联想的；起提醒作用的
render /ˈrendə/ *v*. to reproduce or represent by artistic or verbal means; depict 表现，描绘
resentment /rɪˈzentmənt/ *n*. a feeling of bitterness or persistent hurt and indignation at sth regarded as an insult, injury, or injustice (愤恨；怨恨)
respondent /rɪˈspɒndənt/ *n*. a person who replies to a poll (民意测验等的)调查对象；(调查表、问题表的)答卷人
scenario /sɪˈnɑːriəʊ/ *n*. a possible event or situation 可能发生的事；可能出现的局面
self-fulfilling *adj*. happening as a result of having been asserted or assumed beforehand (预言等)本身会实现的
self-inflicted *adj*. imposed by oneself 加于自身的
siege /siːdʒ/ *n*. a military blockade of a city or fortified place to compel it to surrender
solitary /ˈsɒlɪtəri/ *adj*. being, living, or gong alone or without companions
solidarity /ˌsɒlɪˈdærəti/ *n*. unity (e.g. of a group or class) that produces or is based on community of interests, objectives, and standards
spawn /spɔːn/ *v*. to bring into existence, esp. in large numbers; generate (引起, 酿成，使大量产生)

standing /'stændɪŋ/ *n.* position, status, or condition in relation to a society, group, or profession, esp. good reputation 地位；级别；名声

status /'steɪtəs/ *n.* a position

stereotype /'steriətaɪp/ *n.* sb or sth that conforms to a fixed or general pattern; esp. a standardized, usu. oversimplified, mental picture or attitude that is held in common by members of a group 陈规；老套；刻板模式

stimulate /'stɪmjʊleɪt/ *v.* to excite to growth or to (greater) activity; animate

susceptible /sə'septəbl/ *adj.* easily moved or emotionally affected; impressionable, responsive

terminate /'tɜːmɪneɪt/ *v.* to bring to an end; close

turban /'tɜːbən/ *n.* a headdress worn esp. by Muslims and Sikhs and made of a long cloth wound either round a cap or directly round the head（穆斯林和锡克教徒用的）包头巾

unleash /'ʌn'liːʃ/ *v.* to free (as if) from a leash; loose from restraint or control 发泄；发动；发出

victimize /'vɪktɪmaɪz/ *v.* to cause to be a person made to suffer 使牺牲；使受害；使受骗

villain /'vɪlən/ *n.* a scoundrel, rascal

Notes

1. Three-Word Mantra——三字经，此处指"war on terror"
2. Zbigniew Kazimierz Brzezinski——1928— , a Polish-American political scientist, geostrategist（地缘政治战略家）, and statesman who served as United States National Security Advisor to President Jimmy Carter (1977—1981). Currently professor of American foreign policy at Johns Hopkins University's School of Advanced International Studies and Barack Obama's guru（顾问）during the 2008 presidential election, and known for his hawkish（鹰派的）foreign policy at a time when the Democratic Party was increasingly dovish（鸽派的）, he is a foreign policy realist and considered by some to be the Democrats' response to Republican realist Henry Kissinger.
3. the horrific events of 9/11——the attacks on the World Trade Center in New York City and on the Pentagon on September 11, 2001, often referred to simply as "9/11"

4. It defines neither a geographic context nor our presumed enemies. ——它既没有能界定出地域范围(即究竟在何国何地),也没有能确定出我们的假想敌。

5. Fear obscures reason... to pursue. ——恐惧使人们失去理性、情绪激动,使蛊惑人心的政客们更容易鼓动民众,推行有利于他们的政策。

　　on behalf of——for the benefit of; for the interest of

6. the postulated existence of Iraqi weapons of mass destruction——认定伊拉克存有大规模杀伤性武器。为消除后患就只有"先发制人",以"大规模杀伤性武器"打击并毁灭"大规模杀伤性武器"。这就是小布什政府(the Bush Administration)发动伊拉克战争的借口或理由。

7. Support for President Bush... in midstream——布什总统在 2004 年大选的竞选连任中能调动民意获得支持,在一定程度上是因为"处于战争中的国家"不应中途更换统帅。美国的古话说:"Don't swap horses in the middle of the stream."

　　that "a nation at war"... in midstream——The clause is in apposition(同位语) to "the notion".

8. The sense of... being "at war."——通过"处于战争状态"这种蛊惑做法,民众普遍存在但又不能确定的恐惧危险感又被小布什政府为了达到其政治目的所利用(其竞选连任成功就是例证)。

9. the administration——referring to the Bush Administration 小布什政府

10. al-Qaeda——alternatively spelled al-Qaida, al-Qa'ida or al-Qa'idah,(translation: The Base), an international terrorist movement founded in 1988. It has attacked civilian and military targets in various countries, the most notable being the September 11 attacks in 2001. These actions were followed by the US government launching a military and intelligence campaign called the War on Terror. al-qaeda 源于阿拉伯语 qaf-ayn-dal,是"基地"、"营地"、"家"、"根本"、"组织"、"原则"、"方式"、"方法"和"普遍真理"等意思。1988年,本·拉登(Osama bin Ladan)在阿富汗建立了"基地"组织(又译"卡达"或"凯达")。成立之初,其目的是为了训练和指挥与入侵阿富汗的苏联军队战斗的阿富汗义勇军,但是从苏军撤退后的 1991 年前后开始,该组织将目标转为打倒美国和所谓伊斯兰世界的"腐败政权"。

11. The culture of fear... its bottle. ——恐惧气氛就像一个被从瓶子里释放出的妖怪。妖怪一旦从囚禁它的瓶子里放了出来,就会到处肆虐,造成难以收拾的后果。(语出阿拉伯故事)

genie—a spirit or jinnee (in Arabian stories), esp. one trapped in a bottle, lamp, etc. and capable of granting wishes

12. Pearl Harbor—referring to the attack on Pearl Harbor, or the Hawaii Operation, as it was called by the Imperial General Headquarters (日本帝国大本营). It was a surprise attack against the United States' naval base at Pearl Harbor, Hawaii, by the Japanese navy, on the morning of Sunday, December 7, 1941, resulting in the United States becoming involved in World War II. It was intended as a preventive action to remove the U.S. Pacific Fleet as a factor in the war Japan was about to wage against Britain, the Netherlands, and the United States.

13. "the only thing we have to fear is fear itself"—A statement from the first inaugural address of President Franklin D. Roosevelt in 1933. Roosevelt was speaking at one of the worst points of the Great Depression (大萧条). 我们什么都不怕,怕就怕自己害怕。

14. nor is it the calm America...a few hours—更不是不动声色地坚持推行冷战的那个冷静的美国了,尽管它知道,几分钟之内就能突然触发一场真正的战争,短短几个小时内就能导致1亿美国人丧生。

    Cold War—the state of conflict, tension and hostility that existed between the US and the Soviet Union and their respective allies (mid-1940s—1991) (cf. cool/hot/shooting war)

15. That puts a premium on the presentation...for their implementation. —这就使人们相信他们所展示的种种更加可怕的暴力行动场景是可信的,有时甚至还展示其执行计划。

    put/place a (high) premium on—cause (a quality or action) to be advantageous 鼓励,重视;使……有利

16. With lobbyists weighing in—due to the influence of lobbyists

    a. lobbyist—a person who tries to influence (legislation) in favor of a certain policy by constantly seeking interviews, writing letters, bringing external pressures to bear ect. 院外游说集团人员,游说政府者,政治说客。

    b. weigh in—play an important role; take strong action in order to deal with a situation etc.

17. the Sears Tower—a skyscraper in Chicago, Illinois, the tallest building in North America since 1973. The tower is named after its commissioner, Sears, Roebuck and Company. 西尔斯大厦

18. Apple and Pork Festival—Since 1968, the Apple N' Pork Festival with its delightful aroma (氛围) of smoked ham and spicy apple butter, has ushered in autumn for Dewitt County. From its beginning as a modest event, centered around a kettle of soup and stack of sandwiches, the festival has grown to one of the state's favorite fall festivals.
19. "Report Suspicious Activity" (drivers in turbans) —"报告可疑行为"(包着穆斯林头巾的驾驶员)。此例说明反恐已搞得草木皆兵。
20. The cable channels...the American public. —有线电视频道及一些印刷媒体发现恐怖情景能吸引受众，用反恐"专家"作"顾问"能使美国公众被灌输的大灾难情景真实可信。
21. Islamophobia—a neologism (新词) that refers to prejudice or discrimination against Islam or Muslims. 对伊斯兰教或穆斯林的非理性的恐惧和憎恶。此词由 Islamo-和 phobia 两部分拼缀而成，Islamo-指伊斯兰教或穆斯林，phobia 意为"fear"。
22. Nazi anti-Semitic campaigns—In the Nazis' paranoid conspiracy theory, "Jewry" comprised powers behind the scenes in London, Moscow, and Washington. In response to the "war of extermination (消灭，灭绝)" that Jewry had supposedly launched against Germany, the Nazi leadership publicly threatened to "exterminate" and "annihilate" the Jews as an act of justified retaliation. The phrase is generally used to refer to such a social ideology and act prevailing here and there in the world in modern times. 纳粹反犹太主义运动。反犹太主义主要指近现代仇视、排斥、压迫和残害流落于世界各地的犹太人的社会思潮与行为。亦称排犹主义。
23. the Holocaust—the genocide (种族灭绝) of approximately six million European Jews during World War II, as part of a program of deliberate extermination planned and executed by the National Socialist German Workers' Party (Nazi) regime in Germany led by Adolf Hitler. 纳粹对犹太人的大屠杀
24. the Council on American-Islamic Relations (CAIR)—a civil liberty and advocacy group for Muslims in North America, created in 1994. Its professed goals are to enhance understanding of Islam, promote justice and empower American Muslims. "In its work, the group has been a party to lawsuits," testified before the United States

Congress, and met with President George W. Bush.
25. the American Israel Public Affairs Committee (AIPAC)—an American lobbying（游说）group that advocates what it believes are pro-Israel policies to the Congress and Executive Branch of the United States. It has been consistently ranked among the most powerful and most influential lobbies in Washington. Describing itself as "America's Pro-Israel Lobby," AIPAC is a mass-membership organization whose members include Democrats, Republicans, and independents. AIPAC is funded through contributions from its members. 美以公共事务委员会
26. Capitol—referring to the building where the US Congress is housed; (metonymically) the US Congress. Don't get it confused with capitol or capital.
27. Innocent until proven guilty... to due process. —无罪推定原则就算没有被废除，也遭到了削弱，因为有些人（甚至是美国公民）被长时间监禁而无法有效迅速地进入法定诉讼程序。

  innocent until proven guilty—The presumption of innocence being innocent until proven guilty is a legal right that the accused in criminal trials has in many modern nations.
28. There is no... such excess... have been few and far between. —This is a coordinate sentence connected by the conjunction "and." So far there has not been any very strong evidence that we know to prove that the actions taken to a greater extent than necessary have prevented severe acts of terrorism, and firm evidences for any kind of terrorists that are supposed to be in the future have been scarce in number.

  a. excess—the amount by which sth is greater than what is usual, necessary, or permitted

  b. few and far between—scarce in number 稀少
29. rough treatment of Iraqi civilians... by the Israelis—指美军虐待伊拉克战俘事件及在巴以为期14个月的冲突中，以色列执法人员曾严刑拷打和虐待逮捕的巴勒斯坦人事件。
30. the new axis of evil—referring to Iran, Syria and North Korea by the Bush Administration 邪恶轴心
31. Islamo-fascism—a controversial neologism suggesting an association of the ideological or operational characteristics of certain Islamist

movements from the late 20th century on, with European fascist movements of the early 20th century, neofascist movements, or totalitarianism 极权主义

Questions

1. What is the "three-word mantra" in the author's opinion? What is his attitude to this mantra? Can you explain it in your own words?
2. What's the Bush Administration's main objective to refer to "war on terror" constantly?
3. What phenomena can show that "America has become insecure and more paranoid"?
4. Why does the author say that "the 'war on terror' has encouraged legal and political harassment of Arab Americans"?
5. What is the reason for the author's view that "the 'war on terror' has gravely damaged the United States internationally"?

语言解说

Culture/Cultural

现在不少人见到"culture"或"cultural"就不加思考地译为"文化(的)",什么企业文化、汽车文化、西瓜文化、土鳖文化等等,不一而足。本课的"culture of fear",是否也是"恐惧文化"? 这样的理解和翻译犹如一个小孩戴了一顶大人的帽子——不合适。"文化"涵盖的范围广,世界各国对其定义各异。所以此处只从具体例句的上下文加以商榷。

1. Air Force whistle-blower Ompal Chauhan warned against "a type of cultural conditioning" in which a typical Pentagon manager "thinks more about his future employer than his current one. Loyalties become confused." (*U. S. News & World Report*)

2. If the government sets the right climate, Thatcher believes, new business will flourish. But is modern-day Britain capable of creating the kind of enterprise culture Thatcher envisions? The plain truth is that Britain companies do not, for the most part, work as efficiently as their competitors. "Yes, we're creating new companies," says Stuart Slatter, director of the Institute of Small Business Management of the London Business School, "but there is very little evidence that they will

be a major source of new jobs." Slatter cites what amounts to a cultural handicap: "People lack the get-up-and-go to go out and succeed." (*Newsweek*)

例1中 a type of cultural conditioning 指五角大楼出现的"一股习以为常的损人利己的歪风",因为其管理军工企业的官员假公济私,满脑子想的是离任后到他所监管的企业谋个肥缺。

例2中 enterprise culture 在第一句已指明是"right climate",根据语境,意为"良好的企业环境"或"企业发展的良好氛围"。a cultural handicap 也在后面做了解释,即缺乏企业家那种奋斗创新的进取精神。

可见,以上两句中"cultural"和"culture"分别意味着"风气"、"环境"或"氛围"、"进取精神"。在本课出现的"The 'war on terror' has created a culture of fear in America",亦作"氛围"讲为宜。(详见《导读》六章二节)

Unit Five
United States (Ⅲ)

Lesson Thirteen

课文导读

2008年美国大选期间,奥巴马喊着"变革"(change)的口号,先后击败党内竞争对手前第一夫人希拉里和共和党总统候选人资深参议员麦凯恩,成为美国历史上第一位非洲裔总统。四年后的奥巴马打着"前进"(forward)旗号与共和党候选人展开角逐,他是否光环依旧?四年间他的好多竞选承诺都没有兑现,美国依然经济疲软,失业率高。共和党候选人罗姆尼打的是经济牌,他抓住奥氏执政四年依然经济没有起色的弱点加以抨击,说他能把美国经济整好(fix the economy)。但美国人最终还是选择了奥巴马。原因何在?是由于对手太弱,抑或奥巴马做出的决定正确和应对大事的能力强?本文自有分析。通过学习本课,可以了解一些关于美国选举方面的知识。

美国高官和富翁都想过总统瘾,接二连三的竞选,大有不达目的不罢休的气势,读了《导读》美国"总统"和"总统选举"就明白了,并能对本文理解得更深刻。

Pre-reading Questions

1. Did Mr. Obama win a landslide victory in the election?
2. How much do you know about President Obama?

Text

Obama Wins a Second Term as U. S. President

By David A. Fahrenthold

1   Barack Obama was elected to a second presidential term Tuesday, defeating Republican Mitt Romney[1] by reassembling the political coalition that boosted him to victory four years ago, and by remaking himself from a hopeful uniter into a determined fighter for middle-class

interests.

2 Obama, the nation's first African American president, scored a decisive victory by stringing together a series of narrow ones. Of the election's seven major battlegrounds[2], he won at least six.

3 "While our journey has been long, we have picked ourselves up," Obama told a cheering crowd of supporters in his home town of Chicago early Wednesday morning. "We have fought our way back. And we know in our hearts that, for the United States of America, the best is yet to come."

4 Obama also made an oblique reference to the hard, negative edge of his campaign, saying that even this bitter election was something to be envied in nations around the world that enjoy fewer freedoms: "These arguments we have are a mark of our liberty."

5 Romney, a former Massachusetts governor, had built his campaign around the single contention that the U.S. economy is battered and adrift because of Obama's failures, and that his business experience uniquely qualified him to fix it.

6 "This is a time of great challenges for America, and I pray that the president will be successful in guiding our nation," a slightly hoarse Romney told his supporters in Boston early Wednesday morning. He said he and his running mate, Rep. Paul Ryan[3] (Wis.), had left "everything on the field,"[4] adding: "I so wish that I had been able to fulfill your hopes."

7 As of early Wednesday, Florida was too close to call—but also irrelevant, as Obama had passed the threshold of 270 electoral votes.

8 Romney was beaten by a different Obama than the one who defeated Republican Sen. John McCain (Ariz.)[5] four years ago. Back then, Obama had run as a symbol of limitless hope.

9 The president no longer pledged to sweep away Washington's old partisan politics[6]. He had tried that and was unable to do so. Now, he was pledging to plunge into those old politics and fight—battling Republicans whom Obama said favored the rich and waged a "war on women."

10 As the election results came in, they showed that Obama's promises had won over the groups for which he had promised to fight the hardest. He lost among white men by a large margin, as expected.

But he performed strongly among African Americans, won by double digits among women, and routed Romney among a key and expanding demographic, taking 69 percent of the Latino vote in early exit polls[7].

11　　Early returns also indicated that Capitol Hill's[8] balance of power would not change. Democrats would keep control of the Senate, after winning key races in Indiana, Massachusetts, Missouri and Virginia. Republicans were expected to keep the House, with virtually the same number of seats.

12　　So now, ironically, the bruised Obama of 2012 has the job that the hopeful Obama of 2008 said he wanted: to conjure "change" out of a capital that is split and paralyzed by partisan battling.

13　　For Romney, 65, Tuesday's loss ends a personal marathon that began in June. But, in a broader sense, it started with his first presidential run, nearly six years ago. A longtime executive and investor, Romney ran a campaign that promised to bring a businessman's clear-eyed conservatism to the problems of the U.S. economy.

14　　He was helped immensely by a new breed of political action group, the free-spending super PACs that the Supreme Court legalized in 2010[9]. Outside groups, including super PACs, poured an estimated $350 million into the race on his behalf, with pro-Obama groups spending an estimated $100 million.

15　　For Romney's family, it was the third unsuccessful attempt to capture the White House: Romney's father, George, a Republican governor of Michigan, ran in 1968.

16　　He had spent years fighting a perception that he was too moderate, too malleable, for the swashbuckling, tea-partying modern GOP[10]. But in this campaign's final days, he became a bona-fide Republican hero.

17　　Romney's close loss was also a milestone for his religion, the Church of Jesus Christ of Latter-day Saints[11]. Mormons had once been persecuted to the desert edge of American civilization. Now, with 15 of the church's members in Congress, a devout Mormon had fallen just short of the White House.

18　　In the immediate aftermath of the election, it seemed that three of Obama's actions as commander in chief had played significant roles in his reelection.

19　　One was his decision to bail out the U. S. auto industry[12]. In Ohio, a battleground where that industry is a major presence[13], 59 percent of voters in early exit polls favored the bailout. Obama did better than usual there among a group he usually loses by a lot: white men without a college education.

20　　Another key decision was Obama's choice to offer some young illegal immigrants who were brought to the United States as children the temporary right to live and work in this country legally without the fear of being deported. In Florida, Obama won 60 percent of Latino voters, up three percentage points from four years ago, exit polls showed.

21　　A third was Obama's handling of Hurricane Sandy[14], which earned him plaudits from New Jersey Gov. Chris Christie (R), a major Romney backer. In early exit polls, percent of voters said the hurricane was an important factor in their vote: More than 60 percent of them voted for the president.

22　　Now, Tuesday's victory illuminates the next arc of Obama's career[15]. In the past decade, he was transformed from an unknown Illinois state senator, to a U. S. senator, to a political cause, and then into a president who struggled to deliver on his promises of far-reaching hopes and changes.

23　　Obama's victory seems to guarantee that the landmarks of his first term—the Dodd-Frank financial reforms[16] and the health-care law—will remain in effect. Romney said he wanted to repeal both.

24 It was difficult, even after months of campaigning, to say what Obama's next big idea would be. He did not lay out a broad new agenda in the campaign. Instead, his vague slogan, "Forward," was a sign that the election was about voters trusting him, rather than a set of specific ideas.

25 Already, Obama's chief antagonists—the House's leaders[17]—have signaled that they do not intend to change. Whatever mandate Obama gained Tuesday, Speaker John A. Boehner (R-Ohio)[18] said, the GOP got an equal mandate to oppose him.

26 "For two years, our majority in the House has been the primary line of defense for the American people against a government that spends too much, taxes too much and borrows too much[19] when left unchecked," Boehner said at a Republican event Tuesday night.

27 On Election Day, Boehner said, "they've responded by renewing our majority."

28 At the end of the campaign trail, Romney voted Tuesday morning in his home town of Belmont, Mass. Then, with swing-state polls leaning against him, he headed back out. Romney made a stop in Cleveland. Then he went to Pittsburgh, as part of a last-minute push for Pennsylvania.

29 Ryan made eleventh-hour stops in Cleveland and Richmond.

30 On Tuesday, Obama played his traditional Election Day game of basketball in Chicago. Other players included campaign staff members, friends, and NBA Hall of Famer Scottie Pippen. Obama's team won by about 20 points, one participant told reporters.

31 He also visited a Chicago field office. There, Obama made three calls to the most harassed constituency in the nation this year: swing-state voters.

32 When one Wisconsin woman picked up, however, he had a moment that might have put his win—and this long campaign—in perspective[20].

33 "This is Barack Obama," he said.

34 But the woman at the other end of the phone didn't recognize the name.

35 "You know, the president?" (From *The Washington Post*,

November 7, 2012）

New Words

antagonist /æn'tægənɪst/ *n.* your opponent in a competition, battle, quarrel etc.
batter /'bætə(r)/ *v.* to hit sb or sth again and again, in a way that hurts sb or causes damage
bona-fide /'bɒnəˈfaɪd/ *adj.* real, true, and not intended to deceive anyone
conjure /'kʌndʒə/ *v.* to effect, produce, or bring, etc. by or as by magic(如用魔力般)使……产生
constituency /kən'stɪtjʊənsɪ/ *n.* an area of a country that elects a representative to a parliament or the people who live and vote in a particular area
demographic /ˌdeməˈɡræfɪk/ *adj.* a section of the population sharing the same characteristics, such as age, sex, class, etc.
contention /kənˈtenʃn/ *n.* a strong opinion that sb expresses 论点
deport /dɪˈpɔːt/ *v.* to make sb leave a country and return to the country they came from, esp. because they do not have a legal right to stay 驱逐出境
Gov. = governor
harassed /ˈhærəst/ *adj.* anxious and tired because you have too many problems or things to do
illuminate /ɪˈluːmɪneɪt/ *v.* to make sth much clearer and easier to understand
marijuana /ˌmærəˈwɑːnə/ *n.* an illegal drug smoked like a cigarette, made from the dried leaves of a type of plant that is used to make rope and sometimes to produce the drug 大麻
malleable /ˈmælɪəbl/ *adj.* (of a person, his ideas, etc.) easily influenced or changed 可塑的；易适应的
mandate /ˈmændeɪt/ *n.* an authorization to act given to a representative (给政府或机构的代表的)授权
Mormon /ˈmɔːmən/ *n.* a member of a religious organization formed in 1830 in the U.S., officially called the Church of Jesus Christ of Latterday Saints 摩门教徒
oblique /əˈbliːk/ *adj.* not expressed in a direct way 拐弯抹角,不直截了当的,间接的
plaudit /ˈplɔːdɪt/ *n.* praise and admiration 喝彩；赞扬
plunge /plʌndʒ/ *v.* to throw oneself impetuously or abruptly into some

condition, situation, matter, etc. 投入
R = Republican 共和党人
repeal /rɪˈpiːl/ v. to withdraw a law etc. officially; revoke 废止
Rep = Representative（众议员）
rerun /ˈriːrʌn/ n. sth that happens in the same way as sth that happened before
returns /rɪˈtɜːnz/ n. here election returns 选举结果统计或报表
rout /raʊt/ v. to defeat sb completely in a battle, competition, or election
score /skɔː(r)/ v. to be very successful in sth you do
swashbuckling /ˈswɒʃbʌklɪŋ/ adj. relating to adventures in which people do brave, exciting things and fight against their enemies with swords 虚张声势的；恃强凌弱的 Read what others are sayingAbout Badges
trail /treɪl/ n. a course followed or to be followed: hit the campaign trail（开始竞选游说的行程）
Wis. = Wisconsin

Notes

1. Republican Mitt Romney—Willard Mitt Romney(威拉德·米特·罗姆尼，1947—), an American businessman who served as the 70th Governor of Massachusetts from 2003 to 2007 and President and CEO of the Salt Lake Organizing Committee for the 2002 Winter Olympics. He campaigned for the Republican nomination（共和党提名）in the presidential election, but was defeated by John McCain. He was the Republican Party's nominee for President of the United States in the 2012 election. Active in the Church of Jesus Christ of Latter-day Saints, Romney was the first Mormon to be a major party presidential nominee. He was defeated by incumbent President(在位总统) Barack Obama in the November 2012 general election at last.（米特·罗姆尼竞选过两次总统。第一次在初选就败下阵来,第二次又落选。）

2. The election's seven major battlegrounds—the seven swing states(摇摆州) in the 2012 presidential election, that is, Colorado, Florida, Iowa, Nevada, New Hampshire, Ohio, and Virginia.

　　battlegrounds—here referring to battleground states, 指两党势均力敌选情不明的州, 即两党要争夺选票的战场州。它与 toss-up/

swing states 互用，但现在由于有了 red 和 blue（分别指共和党和民主党占优势的州），两色相混便出现"purple states"，这是最时髦的说法，指举足轻重的州。

3. Rep. Paul Ryan（Wis.）—1970—，a Republican from Wisconsin, was Mitt Romney's vice-presidential running mate（竞选伙伴，如获胜即成为副总统）in the 2012 presidential election. He was the U. S. Representative for Wisconsin's 1st congressional district and chairman of the House Budget Committee. On November 6, 2012, Romney and Ryan were defeated in the general election by the incumbent Barack Obama and Joe Biden, although Ryan won reelection to his congressional seat.（保罗·瑞恩）

4. He said...on the field—They had spared no effort to campaign against Obama for the presidency.

5. Republican Sen. John McCain（Ariz.）—1936—，the senior U. S. Senator from Arizona. He was the Republican presidential nominee in the 2008 election, but lost to Democratic candidate Barack Obama in the general election.

6. partisan politics—In politics, a partisan is a committed member of a political party. In multi-party systems, the term often carries a negative connotation, referring to those who wholly support their party's policies and are perhaps even reluctant to acknowledge correctness on the part of their political opponents in almost any situation. In the U. S., it has come to refer to an individual with a psychological identification with one or the other of the major parties.（党派政治）

7. exit poll—a poll of voters taken immediately after they have exited the polling stations. Unlike an opinion poll, which asks whom the voter plans to vote for, an exit poll asks whom the voter actually voted for. Pollsters（民意调查员）conduct exit polls to gain an early indication as to how an election has turned out, as in many elections the actual result may take hours or even days to count.（投票站出口民调）

8. Capitol Hill—（喻）the U. S. Congress

9. the free-spend super PACs...in 2010—超级竞选活动委员会花钱不受限制，实际上捐款无限额限制，是由最高法院2010年宣布为合法化的。原来国会通过法律给竞选捐款数设限，后来被高法宣布非法。这充分说明美国竞选是金钱政治,富人游戏。(见《导读》"总统选举")

    a. PAC—*abbrev.* political action committee(政治行动委员会). In the U.S., it is a type of organization that campaigns for or against candidates, ballot initiatives or legislation.

    b. the Supreme Court—The highest court in the U.S. It has ultimate (and largely discretionary) appellate jurisdiction(上诉管辖权)over all federal courts and over state court cases involving issues of federal law, and original jurisdiction(初审管辖权)over a small range of cases.

10. GOP— *abbrev.* Grand Old Party:the Republican Party 老大党即共和党

11. the Church of Jesus Christ of Latter-day Saints—Informally called the LDS Church or the Mormon Church.(耶稣基督后期圣徒教会即摩门教。)

12. his decision to bail out the U.S. auto industry—The automotive industry crisis of 2008－2010 was a part of a global financial downturn. In December 2008, the three major U.S. auto industry companies—GM, Chrysler and Ford—asked the government for a $34 billion bailout(注资救助)to avoid bankruptcy. The Big 3 stated that their demise(倒闭) would trigger 3 million layoffs(临时解雇) within a year, plunging the economy further into recession. In January 2009, the Federal government used $24.9 billion of the $700 billion bank bailout fund to rescue GM and Chrysler.

13. In Ohio, a battleground where that industry is a major presence...—Ohio is a battleground state where the auto industry has a strong influence or power.

    presence—influence or power(见第 2 课"语言解说")

14. Hurricane Sandy—It devastated portions of the Caribbean and the Mid-Atlantic and Northeastern US during late October 2012. Some people believe that Obama'a reelection was helped, in part, by the hurricane because Obama reacted quickly and got good Sandy press (获得新闻界对他应对 Sandy 之好评). Polls indicated that Americans approved of Obama's Sandy response.(飓风桑迪)

15. Now, Tuesday's victory... Obama's career.—奥巴马在选举日再次当选的胜利照亮了他个人政治生涯下一阶段继续前进的历程,即再干一届。

    arc—part of a curved line or circle(弧线);here means a continuous

progression or line
16. Dodd-Frank financial reform—It is a financial reform introduced by U.S. senators Chris Dodd, and Barney Frank. On July 21, 2010, the Dodd-Frank Wall Street Reform and Consumer Protection Act was signed into a federal law by President Obama. It is an act to promote the financial stability by improving accountability and transparency in the financial system, to end "too big to fail", to protect the American taxpayer by ending bailouts, to protect consumers from abusive financial services practices, and so on. (多德—弗兰克金融改革)
17. the House's leaders—refer to "the majority leader and whip of the House of Representatives"(国会众议院领袖。因为在众议院中共和党议员占多数,所以是众院多数党领袖和督导,他们会给奥巴马推行的计划制造一些麻烦。见《导读》美国"国会"之讲解)
18. Speaker John A. Boehner (R-Ohio)—John Andrew Boehner, 1949—, served as House majority leader (2006 — 2007), and as House minority leader (2007 — 2011). After the Republicans won control of the House in the 2010 elections, he became House speaker(议长). As Speaker of the House, Boehner is second in line to the presidency. following the Vice President in accordance with the Presidential Succession Act. (众议院议长约翰·伯纳权力很大,操控着国会的钱袋。根据总统继任法,如在职总统因故死亡,他/她是仅次于副总统的继任人) Don't get Speaker confused with speaker, and spokesman(发言人).
19. spend too much... borrow too much—这是共和党人指责民主党人搞"大政府"惯用的语言,更多的用"spend and spend, tax and tax, elect and elect"(花钱多,征税多,选票多多多)。
20. When one Wisconsin woman picked up... in perspective. —When one Wisconsin woman picked up the phone to listen to Obama, he had got the chance to make a correct judgment about his running for the second term as the president.
    put sth in perspective—to judge the importance of sth correctly

Questions

1. What are the main differences between the present Obama and the one four years ago in accordance with the text?

2. In which groups of people did Obama get the most and least supports?
3. What is Obama's campaign slogan for this campaign? And what does it mean?
4. What were the three actions helping Obama win the reelection?
5. Make a comment on Mitt Romney's policy in this election.

读报知识

美国总统选举

总统选举(presidential election)也称大选(general elections)。美国宪法规定,参选总统必须是年满35岁、在美国出生的公民。选举在每隔四年的11月的第一个星期一后的星期二举行。候选人获胜后称为当选总统(President-elect),在上届总统届满之年的1月20日午时宣誓就职。一届任期四年,因任期限制(term limits),一任不得超过两届。

在大选的日子,愿意投票的合格选民把选票投给自己中意的总统候选人,这一选举方式被称为普选(popular election),他们所投的票称为普选票或民选票(popular vote)。众所周知,美国大选是全民投票进行普选,但宪法规定,总统必须经各州选出的总统选举人(presidential electors)选举产生。这就是说,总统选举实际上实行间接选举,即所谓的"选举团"(Electoral College)制度。因为选举团成员是选民选出的,所以也具有直选的内涵。

选举团诞生于1787年美国宪法会议期间。宪法制定者们原本打算挑选出一群具有远见卓识的人组成选举团,聚到一起代表全体公民来选总统。但实际上,由于全国性的党派很快就控制了选举,选举团的代表只不过是名义上的,实际上代表的是选举他们当代表的那个党在该州的势力,他们投谁的票,是事先就定下来的。尽管与别国相比有些怪,美国还是保留了选举团制度。

选民在大选日投票中选出的是"选举人"[(presidential)electors],而不是总统和副总统。选举结束后,哪个总统候选人在某一州得到的普选票最多,他就会得到该州的全部选举人票(electoral vote),即这位总统候选人有权指定选举人代表该州参加选举总统的投票。这种"胜者全得"或"赢者通吃"(winner-take-all)的制度只有缅因州和内布拉斯加州例外。在这两个州,只有两张选举人票是通过全州普选产生,而其余(九分之五)的选举人票则是看州内各国会议员选区的选民投票结果分配的,哪个候选人在某区的选举获胜，他就将获得该选区的选举人票，而不是将全州的选票投给一个党的候选人。各州在国会里有多少国会议员，就有几个选举人。尽管每个州的国会参议员的数量是相同的，都是两个，但众议员的数量则取决于各州在10年一度的人口普查中的人口数量，人口多的州在选举团中就有较多的代表。例如在2000年的大选时，加州有54个选举人，纽约州和得克萨斯州分别有33个和32个。在50个州中，阿拉斯加和特拉华等8个州，每州只有3个。因此，加州、纽约州和得州是总统候选人称为"必须取胜的州"(must-win states)。但2000年大选例外，尽管戈尔在两个大州都赢了小布什，但还是落选。

各州的选举人于12月中旬在各州首府进行选举总统和副总统的投票，但最后的选举结果要到第二年1月初由国会正式公布。全美50个州加上哥伦比亚特区共有538张选举人票，当选总统者必须赢得半数以上即至少270张以上的选举人票。在12月选举人投票时，如果所有的总统候选人都未能获得过半数的选举人票，总统将由国会众议院选出。

正是由于选举团的存在，就可能导致某位候选人在普选中获胜，却把即将得到的总统宝座拱手让给对手的咄咄怪事。2000年小布什最终赢得了佛罗里达州的25张选举人票，上面的悲剧就应验在民主党总统候选人Al Gore的身上。这种情况在美国早先已经发生过两次，分别是1876年与1888年。

General Election的单复数视情况而定，如只指总统选举，单数即可。如包括国会和地方政府和议会等选举在内就用复数。所以报刊上有时用单数有时用复数就是这个道理。英国大选只指国会选举，所以只能用单数。

Lesson Fourteen

> 课文导读

  2006年年底的华尔街,成了欢乐的海洋,并购和交易等业务快速增长,满地皆黄金。时隔一年,繁华不再,经营惨淡。投资银行的高官们纷纷离职,普通百姓的日子更糟。2008年4月,美国联邦储备委员会主席伯南克(Ben S. Bernanke)终于承认:"总体而言,短期经济前景已经减弱,2008年真正的 GDP 不会增长很多,甚至有可能收缩。"就业数字显示,2008年的美国经济衰退了,爆发了甚为严重的次贷危机。

  危机以来,美国经济持续低迷,股市大跌,楼市不振,油价大涨。这些都导致美国人的消费信心受挫,尽管美国政府为救市而将两家最大的住房抵押贷款机构房利美(Fannie Mae)和房地美(Freddie Mac)收为国有,出台了多达几千亿美元刺激消费和救市计划,但经济衰退却在加剧,导致全球金融和经济危机。

  美国经济衰退诱因有国内外因素:其一,由于大量投机活动,国际油价2007年上升58%,2008年初突破每桶100美元大关。为保存资源,美国不在本土开发,又要大量存储战略石油,成为世界最大油价干扰国。其二,长期贸易逆差和财政赤字,对美国及全球经济都是不利因素。其三,阿富汗和伊拉克战争使美军泥足深陷,至今消耗高达8,000亿美元。加之多年楼市天价,一下跌入低谷后便爆发了金融危机。

  经济形势越来越不容乐观,小布什政府终于在2008年初宣布了金额达1,450亿美元的减税计划。以前的政府也曾用过这一招,领到支票者,大多用来购物,确实刺激了经济。但这一次却不同,很多人却用来还债。对大多数美国人来说,2008年就是一个由奢入俭之年,苦日子开始之年。"经济不振,难道2008年美国大选是1992年的翻版?"老布什在1992年恰逢经济衰退,在竞选连任中败给了克林顿。选民是讲实际的,口袋里有没有钱攸关生存。所以经济常是竞选的主题(campaign message/theme)。2008年大选应验了作者的预测。此处,作者用"'92"来指代1992年的经济和大选形势,这种借喻法(metonymy)值得我们注意。

  通过此课,我们可以了解从2008年底开始的金融危机和经济危机的缘由；同时可以学到一些重要的经济词语和一些词扩展引申出的新义，如 stupid 就是一例，这对读报是非常有益的。

Pre-reading Questions

1. Do you know something about economy?
2. What policies do you know have affected economy?

Text

The Economy Sucks. But Is It '92 Redux?[1]

For the first time since Bill Clinton took the White House,
the economy could be the deciding factor.

By Daniel Gross

1   Clinton makes a gritty, unexpected comeback in New Hampshire. The contentious primaries pivot from a war in Iraq to economics.[2] Business people fret about recession. What is this, 1992?

2   Not since James Carville helped Bill Clinton take the White House 16 years ago by reminding him "it's the economy, stupid," has the nation's economic state played such a key role in a presidential campaign.[3] CNN's New Hampshire exit poll[4] found that 97 percent of Democrats and 80 percent of Republicans expressed anxiety about the economy. Of course, the economy is in a worse place than it was when Hillary Clinton's husband was on the campaign trail. Today, the nation is perilously close to sliding into a recession; in '92, the economy had already started growing, though a jobless recovery doomed George H. W. Bush's[5] re-election bid anyway. The lesson? Voters' perceptions matter more than whether the economy is technically expanding or contracting.[6]

3   The news since the ball dropped this year in Times Square[7] has been unrelentingly dour. We've learned that in December, the unemployment rate shot up from 4.7 percent to 5 percent, and the manufacturing sector unexpectedly shrank. Santa Claus left retailers lumps of coal for Christmas.[8] Macy's[9], the 850-store chain that is an excellent proxy for middle-class spending, reported that same-store sales[10] slumped 7.9 percent in December.

4   Just two years ago, Wall Street economists spoke of a Goldilocks

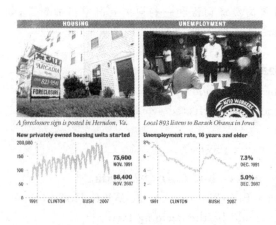

A foreclosure sign is posted in Herndon, Va.
Local 893 listens to Barack Obama in Iowa

economy[11], in which everything was just right. These days, it's the three bears.[12] As of this week, the economists at Merrill Lynch, Morgan Stanley and Goldman Sachs[13] are all predicting a recession for 2008. "I think it's already started," says David Rosenberg, chief economist at Merrill Lynch. "The real tipping point was the employment report."

5   But policymakers aren't ready to give up on the business cycle[14]. In a recent interview with NEWSWEEK, Treasury Secretary Henry Paulson, the former Goldman Sachs chief executive officer who is the administration's designated market whisperer, stayed upbeat and on message[15]. "Our economy, like any other, has its ups and downs," he says. "But you know, I believe our economy is going to continue to grow." What gives Paulson his optimism? "The president's pro growth policies, the fact that government revenues are coming in ahead of forecasts and that our deficit is now down to 1.2 percent of GDP."

6   There are bright spots, to be sure. Exports rose 13 percent in November from 2006. The farm belt[16] is thriving, thanks to record prices for grains. Regions that produce coal, gas, oil or minerals are riding the global energy boom.

7   Recessions—defined as a contraction in economic activity—are notoriously hard to predict, especially since they occur so infrequently. Since 1992 the economy has contracted for just eight months, according to the National Bureau of Economic Research, the Cambridge, Mass.-based arbiter of business cycles. Recessions usually occur after the economy hits a huge speed bump[17]. The commercial real-estate/savings-and-loan implosion precipitated the 1990 recession. In 2001 the bursting tech bubble[18] caused a sharp pullback in business investment.

8   If the economy teeters into recession this year, it will be because the hardy American consumer—who accounts for 70 percent of economic

activity—has finally hit the wall[19]. And when consumers stop spending, the companies that cater to them idle and lay off[20], which, in turn, leads to more reduced spending.

9 "Consumers were cautious in their spending at Christmas, and they're going to be cautious going forward[21]," said Rosalind Wells, chief economist at the National Retail Federation. As a result, retailers are acting swiftly to reduce costs and cut their losses. In recent weeks, Talbots[22] announced it would shutter all its Talbots Mens and Talbots Kids clothing stores.

10 At the dank CompUSA[23] store on Eighth Avenue and 57th Street in Manhattan, a lone security guard checks the bags of the handful of shoppers buying memory cards, cell phones and televisions for 15 to 30 percent off at the store's going-out-of-business sale. "As the days go by it's slowing down a bit," says assistant manager Steve Laureano, who plans to go back to school and seek work elsewhere. The outlet is one of 103 that the chain is closing.[24]

11 As you've no doubt heard, the trouble started with housing. Defaults on subprime mortgage led to a credit squeeze.[25] After enjoying several years of growth, home prices fell an unprecedented 6.1 percent in the past year. "There's never been a time where you had a real-estate deflation as deep and prolonged as this," says David Rosenberg of Merrill Lynch.

12 In the most recent recession, 2001, the areas hardest hit were those that had benefited most from the technology boom—San Francisco, Boston and Austin, Texas. Today, former housing hot spots like California are functioning as cement shoes for the national economy.[26] John Harmer, co-owner of Southland Lumber & Supply of Inglewood, Calif., says his business is off 50 percent this year. After being hit by a slowdown in sales to home-remodeling contractors, his 18-employee firm, which also supplies materials to the sets of television shows like "Boston Legal" and "Nip/Tuck," was nailed by the entertainment writers' strike[27]. "TV is out completely," Harmer says. So far, 10,500 Hollywood workers have been laid off since the strike began, says Jack Kyser, chief economist of the Los Angeles County Economic Development Corporation.

13 In California, slowing economic activity is already producing one of

the most unwelcome byproducts of an economic slump: declining government receipts. California Gov. Arnold Schwarzenegger[28] last week called for steep budget cuts to close a gaping $14 billion deficit.

14   When the economy slows, debt of all kinds begin to go bad. Subprime loans are yesterday's news. Today's news? The souring credit of middle-class consumers. Credit-card giant Capital One Financial had to set aside $1.9 billion for bad loans in the fourth quarter, thanks to higher write-offs of auto and credit-card loans.[29]

15   From Wall Street to California, eyes are turning to Washington for help. Government responses to recessions come in two forms: fiscal policy (stimulus packages[30]) and monetary policy (lowering interest rates). As the primaries roll into economically depressed Michigan, the need for the government to stimulate the economy—through tax breaks[31] or increased spending—has become a hot political issue. On Friday Hillary Clinton unveiled a $70 billion stimulus package, including aid for struggling homeowners and extended unemployment benefits. President George W. Bush, speaking in Chicago before he departed for the Middle East, shifted subtly from his position that the fundamentals are sound.[32] "Recent economic indicators[33] have become increasingly mixed," he said. Bush's upcoming State of the Union address[34] will likely include a grab bag[35] of tax proposals intended to jolt the economy back to life.

16   The Federal Reserve[36] has already taken action by slashing rates three times since September. Chairman Ben Bernanke last Thursday said the central bank is prepared to take more dramatic actions (read: more cuts) given that "the baseline outlook for real activity in 2008 has worsened.[37]" But the assumptions that a proactive Federal Reserve can bail out[38] the economy may not pan out[39] this time. Banks recovering from poor lending decisions are less willing to make mortgage loans today, regardless of the Fed's[40] interest rates.

17   Another assumption that underlay sunny economic forecasts in the past may be crumbling, as well. Economists argued that as long as the rich are getting richer, and spending—they account for a disproportionate share of consumer purchases, after all—the economy could skate by a recession[41]. But signs are mounting that even the holders of the American Express Gold Card[42] are struggling. American Express last week took a $440 million

charge for bad debt, reporting that more of its well-off customers were behind in card payments.⁴³ Cadwalader, Wickersham & Taft, the white-shoe law firm where associate pay starts at $160,000⁴⁴, just laid off 35 attorneys. And big layoffs are coming at Citigroup⁴⁵ and Merrill Lynch, two of Wall Street's biggest—and most generous—employers.

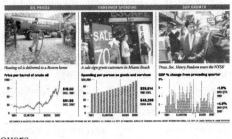

18　　Tiffany, which notched huge sales gains throughout 2007, even as many retailers suffered, on Friday reported that same-store sales during the Christmas season unexpectedly fell 2 percent. The reason: lower sales on products that cost more than $50,000. Even for the rich, breakfast at Tiffany's⁴⁶ these days is limited to the $1.99 special.

　　With Ashley Harris in New York and Andrew Murr in Los Angeles (From *Newsweek*, January 21, 2008)

New Words

arbiter /'ɑːbɪtə/ *n.* one chosen or appointed to judge or decide a disputed issue 仲裁人，公断人

attorney /ə'tɜːnɪ/ *n.* a lawyer

Austin /'ɔːstɪn/ *n.* the capital city of the State of Texas in USA 奥斯丁（美国得克萨斯州首府）

byproduct /'baɪˌprɒdʌkt/ *n.* a secondary or incidental product; the result of another action, often unforeseen or unintended

CNN *abbrev.* Cable News Network（美国）有线新闻电视网

contentious /kən'tenʃəs/ *adj.* causing, involving, or characterized by argument or controversy; quarrelsome 引起争论的；爱争论的

contraction /kən'trækʃən/ *n.* a decrease in economic and industrial activity (opposed to "expansion")收缩；紧缩

contractor /kən'træktə/ *n.* a person, business, or firm that agrees to furnish materials or perform services at a specified price, esp. for construction work 合同承保人，承包商

crumble /'krʌmbl/ *v.* to give way; collapse 失败；崩溃

dank /dæŋk/ *adj.* disagreeably damp or humid 潮湿的，阴湿寒冷的

default /dɪ'fɔːlt/ *n.* failure to perform a task or fulfill an obligation, esp. failure to meet a financial obligation 拖欠；违约

deflation /dɪˈfleɪʃən/ n. a persistent decrease in the level of consumer prices or a persistent increase in the purchasing power of money because of a reduction in available currency and credit 通货紧缩

doom /duːm/ v. to cause to suffer sth unavoidable and terrible, such as death or destruction

dour /dʊə/ adj. severe; stern; forbidding 严厉的,冷酷的

fret /fret/ v. to feel or express worry, annoyance, discontent, or the like; vex 焦虑;烦恼

gaping /ˈgeɪpɪŋ/ adj. showing a huge gap; deep and wide open

GDP abbrev. gross domestic product 国内生产总值

gritty /ˈgrɪtɪ/ adj. showing resolution and fortitude 坚定的,坚毅的

hardy /ˈhɑːdɪ/ adj. capable of enduring fatigue, hardship, exposure, etc.; strong 能吃苦耐劳的;强壮的

home-remodeling n. giving new shape or form to a home 房屋装修

implosion /ɪmˈpləʊʒən/ n. violent compression; a bursting inward (opposed to "explosion") 猛烈压缩;向心压挤

jolt /dʒəʊlt/ v. to make suddenly active or effective; to disturb 激起,唤起;震惊

nail /neɪl/ v. to hit

New Hampshire /njuː ˈhæmpʃə/ n. a state in the NE US, known for its beautiful lakes and mountains and for its many old buildings(美国)新罕布什尔州

notch /nɒtʃ/ v. to achieve; score 得到,得分

pivot /ˈpɪvət/ v. to turn on or as if on a pivot(在枢轴上)转动

precipitate /prɪˈsɪpɪteɪt/ v. to hasten 使……加速

primary /ˈpraɪmərɪ/ n. a preliminary election in which the registered voters of a political party nominate candidates for office 初选,预选

proactive /prəʊˈæktɪv/ adj. acting in advance to deal with an expected difficulty 主动的,抢先的,先发制人的

progrowth /prəʊˈgrəʊθ/ adj. supporting growth, or encouraging growth 支持增长的,鼓励增长的

proxy /ˈprɒksɪ/ n. an agent or a substitute 代理人,替代者

pullback /ˈpʊlbæk/ n. the act or process of pulling back 撤退,拉回

real estate /ˈriːəl ɪsˈteɪt/ n. property consisting of houses and land

receipt /rɪˈsiːt/ n. (pl. ~s) income

redux /riːˈdʌks/ adj. brought back; returned; resurgent 返回的;复兴的

remodel /riːˈmɒdl/ v. to reconstruct; to make over

retailer /ˈriːteɪlə/ *n.* someone who sells things in small quantities directly to consumers
revenue /ˈrevɪnjuː/ *n.* the annual income; return from investments, property, etc. 总收入；收益
shutter /ˈʃʌtə/ *v.* to close (a store or business operations) for the day or permanently
slash /slæʃ/ *v.* to reduce greatly
slump /slʌmp/ *v.* to fall or decline suddenly, as in activity, prices, or business 暴跌，跌落 *n.* a decrease, decline, or deterioration
sour /ˈsaʊə/ *v.* to become unpleasant or strained; worsen; deteriorate
special /ˈspeʃəl/ *n.* an advertised reduced price in a shop, restaurant etc
suck /sʌk/ *v.* to be very bad, disagreeable, or disgusting
teeter /ˈtiːtə/ *v.* to walk or move unsteadily or unsurely; totter 摇摆地或不稳定地行走或移动；蹒跚
tipping /ˈtɪpɪŋ/ *adj.* inclining; overturned 倾斜的；倾翻的
underlay /ˈʌndəleɪ/ *v.* to provide with a base or support 垫起；提供基础或支持
unrelenting /ˌʌnrɪˈlentɪŋ/ *adj.* merciless 严峻的；无情的 unrelentingly *adv.*
upbeat /ˈʌpˌbiːt/ *adj.* optimistic
whisperer /ˈwɪspərə/ *n.* a person who often lets out secret news
write-off /raɪt-ɔːf/ *n.* (the act of) cancelling from accounts as a loss 注销；作为亏损从账目上勾销

Notes

1. The Economy Sucks. But Is It '92 Redux? —The United States presidential elections of 1992 featured a battle between incumbent President(在位总统), George Bush(老布什), Bill Clinton, the governor of Arkansas, and independent candidate Ross Perot, a Texas businessman. Mr. Bush had alienated much of his conservative voters by breaking his 1988 campaign pledge against raising taxes, and the economy had sunk into recession. Though his foreign policy was a great success, it was regarded as much less important following the collapse of the Soviet Union and the relatively peaceful climate in the Middle East following the defeat of Iraq. The campaign came on the heels of the recession of 1990—91. During the run-up(酝酿期间) to the 1992 presidential election,

economic anxiety was fueled by stagnant(停滞的) wages and declining employment. While the recession was mild and actually ended before the election, it fueled strong discontent with him. On November 3, Bill Clinton won the general election by a wide margin. Analysts thought that the presidential election of 2008 resembled that of 1992, especially in economic terms. Both took place when the country's economy was in recession. 2008 年美国总统选举是 1992 年的翻版。经济不景气，且发生在老布什和小布什执政时，这就使反对党抓住了其对手的要害，因为选民最关心的是口袋里是否有钱。尽管老布什在任时外交上取得了成绩，但选民不买账而使他落选。'92 指1992 年的经济和大选(形势)，是借喻法。

2. Clinton makes a gritty ... to economics. —意为：希拉里·克林顿在新罕布什尔州的总统初选艰难而意外地获胜(在 Iowa 的首场初选中，她败给了奥巴马)。初选会上针锋相对的竞选演讲的话题，从伊拉克战争转向了经济问题。(Clinton here refers to Hillary Clinton, currently Secretary of State of the United States. She was the former first lady from 1993 to 2001 while her husband Bill Clinton served as president.)

　　make a comeback—achieve a success after retirement or failure

3. Not since James Carville ... in a presidential campaign. —16 年前当克林顿入主白宫前竞选时，竞选顾问詹姆斯·卡维尔提醒他，"这次竞选的要害是经济问题。"自那以后，这个国家的经济状况的好坏还从来没有像现在这样在总统竞选中起着如此关键的作用。

　　a. "stupid" 在此处并无贬义，只作"提醒"之用，即让某人集中精力于主要目标或问题。(见"语言解说")

　　b. Here in the sentence, inversion is used. The normal order should be "The nation's economic state has not played ... since James Carville helped Bill Clinton ... "

4. exit poll—a poll of voters taken immediately after they have exited the polling stations, asking them how they have voted, in order to discover the likely result of the election 选举投票后随即进行的民意调查

5. George H. W. Bush—(1924 —), U. S. President (1989 — 1993). Before his presidency, Bush held a multitude of political positions, including Vice President of the United States in the administration of Ronald Reagan (1981 — 1989) and director of the CIA. Before his

election, he promised that he would not increase taxes, using the phrase "Read my Lips—no new taxes". But after he became president, he did in fact increase some taxes.

6. Voters' perceptions ... or contracting. —不管经济事实上是发展还是萧条衰退，选民的亲身感受最重要。

   technically—actually（见"语言解说"）

7. the ball dropped this year in Times Square—Each year on New Year's Eve celebration in Times Square in Manhattan, New York City, a time ball made of crystal and electric lights is raised to the top of a pole on the One Times Square building and then lowered to mark the coming of the New Year. （纽约）时报广场水晶球降落仪式

8. Santa Claus left retailers lumps of coal for Christmas. —It is believed that Santa Claus would bring gifts to good children but coal to bad children. So lumps of coal are a kind of punishment to retailers. Business was rather low for Christmas. 此句比喻由于经济衰退和人们对未来经济的不乐观，2007年圣诞期间销售相当不景气。

   lump—a piece or mass of solid matter without regular shape or of no particular shape（形状不规则的）块

9. Macy's—Macy's, Inc., one of the leading department retail stores in the US 梅西百货公司是美国一家知名的老牌中高档百货公司。

10. same-store sales—同店销售（SSS），指同一家零售店在同期的销售额，通常以月份或季度为时间段比较每年的销售额。SSS可以衡量一家零售店在相对固定的运营成本下的盈利或亏损。这是一项衡量零售商投资回报的重要指标，反过来也将反映零售商的整体盈利能力。

11. a Goldilocks economy—a not too hot or cold economy, sustaining moderate economic growth and a low inflation allowing for a market friendly monetary policy. The name comes from the children's story *The Three Bears*. The first use of this phrase is credited to David Shulman of Salomon Brothers who wrote "The Goldilocks Economy: Keeping the Bears at Bay"（要扼制住熊而不让其近身，实际上是说要警惕经济衰退。）in March 1992. 金发女孩经济，是在20世纪90年代所创造出的名词，借用《格林童话》金发女孩和三只熊（Goldilocks and the Three Bears）中小女孩在三只熊的家里吃东西的故事，来说明华尔街对美国经济的描述：既不太冷，又不过热，是称心如意的经济。（见《导读》二版"经济用语"一节里介绍"Three

bears that ate Goldilocks economy"的文章)

12. These days, it's the three bears.—时下三只熊将 Goldilocks economy 弄糟了。这三只熊指油价和原料价格飞涨、美英的过度消费和房价泡沫破灭而引起的次贷危机。

13. Merrill Lynch, Morgan Stanley, and Goldman Sachs—美林、摩根士丹利和高盛集团

    a. Merrill Lynch—Through its subsidiaries and affiliates, Merrill Lynch & Co., Inc. provides capital markets services, investment banking and advisory services, wealth management, asset management, insurance, banking and related products and services worldwide. The firm's world headquarters is located in New York City. 美林公司，世界最著名的证券零售商和投资银行之一，总部位于美国纽约。作为世界上最大的金融管理咨询公司之一，它在金融领域占有一席之地。

    b. Morgan Stanley—a global financial services firm that, through its subsidiaries and affiliates, provides its products and services to customers, including corporations, governments, financial institutions and individuals. The Company operates in three business segments: Institutional Securities, Global Wealth Management Group, and Investment Management. 摩根士丹利，是一家全球领先的国际性金融服务公司，业务范围涵盖投资银行、证券、投资管理以及财富管理，目前在全球27个国家的600多个城市设有代表处。

    c. Goldman Sachs—a leading global investment banking, securities and investment management firm, founded in 1869, and is headquartered in the Lower Manhattan area of New York City. Goldman Sachs has offices in many financial centers in the world. The firm acts as a financial advisor and money manager for corporations, governments, and wealthy families around the world. 高盛集团，是集投资银行、证券交易和投资管理等业务为一体的国际著名的投资银行。高盛公司总部设在纽约，在全球二十多个国家设有分部，并以香港、伦敦、法兰克福及东京等地作为地区总部。高盛1869年创立于纽约，是全球历史最悠久、经验最丰富、实力最雄厚的投资银行之一。

14. business cycle—also called economic cycle or economic fluctuation. It refers to the periodic fluctuation in the rate of economic activity, as measured by levels of employment, prices, and production.

Economists have long debated why periods of prosperity are eventually followed by economic crises (stock-market crashes, bankruptcies, unemployment, etc.). Some have identified recurring 8-to-10-year cycles in market economies. 经济周期；经济波动

15. on message—offering the planned message; keeping to the authorized, prescribed policies and practices of a group 与政党或政府既定方针路线一致的；按政党或政府路线行事的(*cf.* off message)

16. farm belt—the central states of the midwestern U.S., in which agriculture is significant

17. speed bump—sleeping policeman (*BrE*); a rounded ridge built crosswise into the surface of a street, parking lot, or driveway to force vehicles to slow down 横在道路中间的驼峰式交通减速埂，此处喻指使经济发展速度放缓的问题或障碍。

18. tech bubble—here it refers to the "dot-com bubble", a speculative bubble covering roughly 1995—2001 (with a climax on March 10, 2000 with the NASDAQ peaking at 5132.52) during which stock markets in Western nations saw their value increase rapidly in the new Internet sector and related fields. The period was marked by the founding (and, in many cases, spectacular failure) of a group of new Internet-based companies commonly referred to as *dot-coms*. A combination of rapidly increasing stock prices, individual speculation in stocks, and widely available venture capital created an exuberant environment in which many of these businesses dismissed standard business models, focusing on increasing market share at the expense of the bottom line. The bursting of the dot-com bubble marked the beginning of a relatively mild yet rather lengthy early 2000s recession in the developed world. 高科技或网络泡沫，指1995—2001年期间互联网业和相关行业的迅速发展阶段，尤其是它们的股票价飞升，在2000年3月10到达顶峰，纳斯达克指数飙升到5132.52点。这期间，诞生了一批新的以互联网为基础的网络公司，这些公司通常被称为dot-coms。股票价格的上涨，尤其是股票投机以及大量的风险投资使得这一行业表面上得到飞速发展，但违背了商业的基本模式，只强调市场份额而背离了基本底线。2000年网络经济泡沫的破灭标志着在发达国家开始了一段较长的但相对温和的经济衰退时期。

19. hit the wall—(of long-distance runners) to reach a point in a race, usually after 20 miles, when the body's fuels are virtually exhausted and willpower becomes crucial to be able to finish
20. the companies that cater to them idle and lay off—the companies that provide consumers with what they need now have nothing to do and have to stop their business and dismiss their employees

　　　　a. cater to—provide or supply what amuses, is desired, or gives pleasure, comfort, etc.

　　　　b. lay off—stop work or operation; dismiss (an employee), esp. temporarily because of slack business
21. they're going to be cautious going forward—they're going to be cautious as they go forward; they're going to be very careful in spending in the future

　　　　go forward—move ahead; travel onward in time or space
22. Talbots—Operating under the brands Talbots and J. Jill, the Talbots, Inc. is a leading international specialty(精制品) retailer, cataloger(邮购商) and e-tailer of women's classic apparel, shoes, and accessories.
23. CompUSA—a retailer and reseller of consumer electronics, technology products and computer services
24. The outlet is one of 103 that the chain is closing.—The company is closing 103 of its stores and this is one of them.

　　　　outlet—store
25. Defaults on subprime mortgage led to a credit squeeze.—次级抵押贷款违约(即贷款不能按时偿还)导致信贷紧缩(即不能放贷)。

　　　　subprime mortgage—次级抵押贷款。在美国，大多数购房者需要贷款，这类贷款主要由两种金融机构运作。对于信用记录好、还贷能力健全的贷款者，他们的贷款通常由银行来运作，他们可以享受优惠利率(prime rate)，因此这类抵押贷款被称为 prime mortgage。美国银行大多不发行次级房贷，因此，对于信用不佳或者背负债务包袱的购房者(实际上是穷人)，他们的贷款通常由专门的房贷公司运作，这种贷款就叫做"次级抵押贷款"。也就是说，次级抵押贷款是指一些贷款机构向信用程度较差和收入不高的借款人提供的贷款，即银行或贷款机构提供给那些不具备资格享受优惠利率贷款的客户的一种贷款。这种贷款的利率通常比一般抵押贷款高出两个到三个百分点。美国的次级抵押贷款大多是前几年住房市场高度繁荣时贷出的。房价在1996年至2006年飞涨了80%,此后房价开始下跌,同时受美联储持续加息等种种因素的影响,贷款人拖欠应付的贷款,只能选择将房子交给银行,而银行得到的只是一批不断贬值的房产。因此,众多银行破产,尤其是业务以次级贷款为主的银行都受到了拖累,这就是"次级抵押贷款危机"(subprime mortgage crisis)。从2008年3月至10月,美国接连数十家贷款银行破产,同时引起了欧洲、亚洲市场的急剧下跌造成金融危机,对亚太国家和地区包括中国大陆的经济产生了诸多不利的影响。

26. Today, former housing hot spots ... national economy.——昔日房产业很热的地方如加利福尼亚今日已经成为全国经济的累赘。

    cement shoes—a slang term adopted by the American Mafia(黑手党)crime world for a method of execution that involves weighting down(加重物于) a victim and throwing him or her into the water to drown

27. the entertainment writers' strike—The Writers Guild of America (WGA)(美国编剧协会) launched the strike in December 2007, demanding for writers' share in the entertainment industry's online revenues. The 65th Annual Golden Globe Awards Ceremony was canceled and the Academy Awards was also affected. (美国编剧罢工)

28. Arnold Schwarzenegger—1947— , an Austrian-American bodybuilder, actor, businessman and politician, serving as the 38th Governor of the state of California 阿诺德·施瓦辛格出生于奥地利,曾任加州州长,好莱坞著名动作影星,所主演的影片均获得巨大的成功和票房收入。2004年和2007年两度获得《时代周刊》100名影响世界的人物称号。

29. Credit-card giant ... credit-card loans.——信用卡巨商Capital One Financial由于汽车和信用卡贷款的大量注销,不得不取消19亿美元的不良贷款。

    a. set aside—store up; save for a special purpose
    b. write-offs—cancellations from the accounts as a loss

30. stimulus packages—plans and actions taken to stir economy to life (刺激经济一揽子方案)

31. tax breaks—tax savings, which includes tax exemption, tax deduction and tax credit 赋税减免(包括免税、减税和税收抵免)

32. President George W. Bush ... fundamentals are sound.——布什总统原本认为经济基础是健康的,可是在他出发去中东访问前,巧妙地改变了这一说法。

33. economic indicators—statistics about the economy, which allow analysis of economic performance and predictions of future performance. Economic indicators include various indices(指数), earnings reports, and economic summaries, such as unemployment, housing starts, Consumer Price Index (a measure for inflation), industrial production, bankruptcies, Gross Domestic Product, broadband internet penetration, retail sales, stock market prices, and money supply changes. (经济指标)

34. State of the Union address—an annual message which the President of the United States gives to Congress, usually an address to a joint session of Congress (the House of Representatives and the Senate). It has occurred in January (except for six occasions in February) since 1934. The address is most frequently used to outline the President's legislative proposals for the upcoming year. So a State of the Union address is generally not given in years in which a new president is inaugurated. In his speech, Bush assured American people that "In the long run, Americans can be confident about our economic growth. But in the short run, we can all see that growth is slowing." Bush said, "The economy is still basically strong but going through a rough time right now." 国情咨文,是美国总统每年向国会两院联席会议发表的演讲,相当于我国总理在人大作的政府工作报告。自1934年以来,国情咨文一般发表于1月,一般被认为是在新的一年中总统对于国家的建议。因此在新总统就任当年没有国情咨文。

35. grab bag—(Am. E) a container with articles, from which a person at a party or the like draws a gift without knowing what it is; any miscellaneous collection 运气袋,摸彩袋;百宝囊

36. the Federal Reserve—the Federal Reserve Board(美国联邦储备委员会)

37. Chairman Ben Bernanke ... has worsened.—美国联邦储备委员会主席伯南克上周四说,考虑到对2008年经济活动的预期底线降低,中央银行准备采取更强烈的行动(意思是:继续减税)。

   a. Ben Bernanke—1953— ,Chairman and a member of the Board of Governors of the Federal Reserve System since 2006. Dr. Bernanke also serves as Chairman of the Federal Open Market

Committee, the System's principal monetary policymaking body. 伯南克，第14任美联储主席。伯南克曾就读于哈佛大学，在麻省理工学院获得博士学位。2002年伯南克成为美联储理事会成员。2005年6月宣誓就职总统经济顾问委员会主席，此前一直任普林斯顿大学经济系主任。

  b. read—*fml* understand (the stated printed or written words) to be a mistake for or to have the meaning of

  c. baseline—a basic standard or level; guideline

38. bail out—relieve or assist (a person, company, etc.) in an emergency situation, esp. a financial crisis
39. pan out—turn out well; be successful
40. the Fed—Here it refers to the Federal Reserve Board.
41. the economy could skate by a recession—经济可以与衰退擦肩而过

  skate by—(*Am. E*) avoid narrowly

42. American Express Gold Card—美国运通金卡

  American Express—founded in 1850 and sometimes known as "AmEx" or "Amex", is a diversified global financial services company, headquartered in New York City. The company is best known for its credit card, charge card and traveler's cheque businesses. It is the largest company providing independent credit card. Among the varieties of financial and travel products and services, American Express Card enjoys the highest popularity. American Express Gold Card is a credit card providing favorable terms to customers. American Express is one of the 30 stocks that comprise the Dow Jones Industrial Average and is ranked as the 74th largest company by *Fortune*. 美国运通公司创立于1850年，总部设在美国纽约，是国际上最大的旅游服务及综合性财务、金融投资及信息处理的环球公司，在信用卡、旅行支票、旅游、财务计划及国际银行业占领先地位，美国运通公司是全球最大的独立信用卡公司，是在反映美国经济的道琼斯工业指数30家公司中唯一的服务性公司，《财富》杂志将其列为全球第74大公司。在美国运通公司提供的众多金融及旅游产品及服务中，美国运通卡为知名度最高的产品。运通金卡为信用卡客户提供优惠的条件。

43. American Express ... card payments.—美国运通上周由于不良贷款损失了4.4亿美元，报告称越来越多的有钱顾客在信用卡还款方面滞后。

take charge for—take the responsibility for
44. white-shoe law firm where associate pay starts at ＄160,000—律师最低薪金为16万美元的一流法律事务所

  a. white-shoe firm—a phrase used to describe the leading professional services firms in America, particularly firms that have been in existence for more than a century and represent Fortune 500 companies. The term is derived from the white shoes favored by the upper class. It frequently—but not always—refers to securities, law and management consulting firms, and frequently (but not always) refers to firms in New York City. A similar phrase, Magic Circle, refers to law firms in the UK, while the Big Six refers to leading Australian law firms and Seven Sisters to similar Canadian firms.

  b. associate—the lowest level of attorney in a United States law firm（法律事务所的）初级律师

45. Citigroup—Citigroup Inc. is a major American financial services company based in New York City. The company employs approximately 358,000 staff around the world, and holds over 200 million customer accounts in more than 100 countries. It is the world's largest bank by revenues as of 2008. It is a primary dealer in US Treasury securities(美国财政部证券)and its stock has been a component of the Dow Jones Industrial Average since March 17, 1997. 花旗(银行)集团

46. Tiffany—1837年Charles Tiffany在美国纽约第五大道与57街交叉口创办了蒂芙尼公司(TIFFANY & CO.)，主要经营珠宝、银器、文具和餐具等产品。

Questions

1. In what ways are the 2008 and 1992 presidential elections similar?
2. What is the position of policymakers towards the slowdown of economy?
3. What is the root of the financial crisis in the Unites States?
4. How did the U.S. government respond to recessions? Why did it become a hot political issue?
5. Why did economists think that the economy could skate by a recession as long as the rich are getting richer and spending?
6. Along with the subprime loan problem, what are the other financial

problems that banks are faced with?
7. According to this article, can the government bail out the economy? Why or why not?

语言解说

Stupid 和 Technical(ly)

本课中引用的"It's the economy, Stupid!"是1992年克林顿竞选美国总统期间,谋士 James Carville 在克竞选总部办公桌上放的一块牌子上写的字,提醒克林顿要抓住竞选对手老布什在经济上乏善可陈的弱点不放。现在这个竞选口号已成为报刊标题的模仿句型,如"It's the Deficit, Stupid!"及"The Foreword Was the Mideast, Stupid!"等。在这个句型中,Stupid 并无贬义,只作提醒之用。

另外,我们还应该注意本课中的一个副词"technically"及其形容词"technical"的意思,要视上下文,不能简单地一律理解为"技术的(地)",新闻词语常扩展引申。见下列例句:

1. Technical

(1) 规则的,规章的,章程的:

The university admits its Asian-American acceptance rate dipped three years ago, after some **technical** changes in admission procedures, but denies discrimination and says the rate is going back up. (*Time*)

(2) 细节的,法规详细条文的:

technical talks

(3) 机械的:

a **technical** fault

(4) 专门技术的,专长的:

When Kissinger enrolled at Harvard, Elliott, then about fifty, was already a legend, an irascible Professor of Government, who in Kissinger's words, "lived as a grand seigneur in a world where eminence has become **a technical** achievement."

2. Technically

(1) 以下两例的 technically 的词义是"确切地说";"严格地讲"。这是从"技术"这个本义引申而来,因技术要求一丝不苟。

a. The method of electing the President is peculiar to the American system. Although the names of the candidates appear on the ballot,

technically the people of each state do not actually vote directly for the President (and Vice President). (*An Outline of American Government*)

b. In the U. S. , the words college and university are often used interchangeably. **Technically**, there is a difference.

(2) 事实上：

More substantively, Aldrich claims to have been told directly by former White House Associate Counsel William Kennedy that it was Mrs. Clinton who got Livingstone his White House job. Kennedy last week denied that. After some backing and filling, Livingstone said that while Kennedy **technically** hired him, the person he consulted about a White House job was Christine Varney, a former senior White House aide and currently a Federal Trade Commissioner. (*Time*)(详见《导读》二章一节)

Lesson Fifteen

课文导读

美国会衰落吗？这是个让美国人忧虑且具有周期性特点的问题。冷战时期，苏联抢先发射了第一颗人造卫星，此后，这种忧虑就萦绕在美国人心头。20世纪80年代，当苏联已经不是威胁的时候，美国却又遭遇到经济强劲发展的日本在经济上的挑战，于是另一个忧虑的时代开始了。今天，中国、印度等新兴国家（emerging powers）经济快速发展，似乎又成了美国新一轮忧虑的理由。

此论不但引起美国的热议，还使全球关注。本文介绍了美国专家、学者和政府研究机构负责人的观点，具有权威性。他们都认为美国独霸世界和单极时代的日子已经结束，美国已进入相对衰落时期，从这篇文章里的插图也可以看出，美国（头带花旗帽的 bald eagle 秃鹰指代美国）已垂垂老矣！不然怎么会拄着拐杖，步履蹒跚呢？但是，也有人对新衰落论不以为然。那么，美国的新衰落论是真有其事，还是像以往的重复论或杞人忧天？看来只有等待时间去检验。伊阿战争是美衰落的一个标志。与翱翔的中国相比，衰老的美国鹰在世界上的相对实力显得比以前弱小了，现在已是多极世界。任何国家达到鼎盛时，如不与时俱进，定会一步步走下坡路，这是历史发展不可抗拒的规律，美国也不能例外。

Pre-reading Questions

1. Do you think the US is the most powerful country in the world? In what respects is it powerful?
2. Can you give some examples to illustrate its power?

Text

Is America's New Declinism for Real?
By Gideon Rachman

1   Texas A&M[1] is not the obvious place to pick if you want to discuss American decline. The university sends more of its graduates straight

into the military than any other civilian college in the US. Its officer training corps prowl the campus in crisply pressed uniforms and knee-high leather boots, greeting each other with brisk "howdys". Agonised introspection and crises of confidence are not Texan traits.[2]

2　　But last week the Scowcroft Institute of International Affairs at Texas A&M hosted a conference designed to discuss the latest, markedly gloomy world view issued by America's intelligence establishment[3]. Every four years the National Intelligence Council[4]— which oversees America's baroque collection of intelligence agencies— releases a global trends report, which is given to the new president.

3　　The latest report, published on November 20, has made headlines around the world. The front page of Britain's *Guardian* newspaper[5] shouted "2025: the end of US dominance". For once, the headline is broadly accurate. As the NIC frankly notes, "the most dramatic difference" between the new report and the one issued four years ago is that it now foresees "a world in which the US plays a prominent role in global events, but the US is seen as one among many global actors". The report issued four years ago had projected "continuing US dominance".

4　　The NIC report has made people sit up because it comes from the heart of the US security establishment. But it is part of a broader intellectual trend in America: a "new declinism". This mood marks a complete break with the aggressive confidence of the Bush years[6] and the "unipolar moment"[7]. Its starting assumption is that America, while still the most powerful country in the world, is in relative decline.

5　　Three developments have fed the new declinism.[8] First, the wars in Iraq and Afghanistan have underlined that US military supremacy does not automatically translate into political victory. Second, the rise of China and India suggest that America's days as the world's largest economy are numbered. Third, the financial crisis has fed the notion that the US is living beyond its means and that something is badly wrong with the American model.

6   This gloomy mood was captured by the opening address to the NIC's conference, given by none other than General Brent Scowcroft[9] himself, returning to the institute named after him. The general noted that the US had found itself in a position of huge global power after the end of the cold war, which was "heady stuff". But "we exercised that power for a while only to realise that it was ephemeral".

7   This new awareness of the constraints on American power is reflected in a number of new books and articles. The most influential is probably Fareed Zakaria's *The Post-American World*[10], which is said to be the only book on foreign affairs read by Barack Obama this year. Although Mr Zakaria strives to present the rise of China, India and "the rest" as unthreatening to the US, the inescapable conclusion is that the Bush years marked the apogee of American power.

8   Another influential book to capture this new mood is Andrew Bacevich[11]'s *The Limits of Power*. Professor Bacevich, a conservative historian and military veteran whose son was killed in the Iraq war, argues: "American power ... is inadequate to the ambitions to which hubris and sanctimony have given rise.[12]" Richard Haass[13], who as head of the Council of Foreign Relations[14] is arguably the doyen of the foreign policy establishment, is another important voice arguing: "The United States' unipolar moment is over."

9   But as William Wohlforth of Dartmouth College[15] reminded the NIC conference in Texas last week, America has been through phases of declinism before. The current debate is reminiscent of the arguments unleashed by the publication in 1988 of Paul Kennedy[16]'s *The Rise and Fall of the Great Powers*. Professor Kennedy's argument that previous great powers had succumbed to "imperial over-stretch" resonated in the US at a time when many were worried by Reagan-era[17] budget deficits and Japan's growing economic power.

10   But the "declinism" represented by Prof Kennedy was quickly dissipated by victory in the cold war, Japan's lost decade of economic growth and the high-tech boom of the Clinton years[18]. All this set the stage for a resurgence of American confidence and the swagger of the Bush presidency.

11 Odd as it is to recall now, there were people during the early phases of the cold war who were also genuinely worried that the USSR[19] might outperform the US. There was also a national crisis of confidence caused by the Vietnam war[20], when Richard Nixon[21] warned his fellow countrymen they risked looking like a "pitiful, helpless giant". In the 1980s, Japan became the new challenger to American supremacy. Now it is China.

12 Professor Wohlforth argues that the NIC report reflects "a mood change, not a change in the underlying assessment of power". As he says, rising powers do not always complete their climb and economic strength does not always translate into political power.

13 This is all true. But there are still reasons for thinking that the new declinism may be more soundly based than its predecessors. China has a record of sustained and dynamic economic growth that the Soviet Union was never capable of. And China's sheer size makes it a more plausible challenger than a relatively small nation, such as Japan.

14 This time it really does feel different. But then it always does, does it not? (From *Financial Times*, November 24, 2008)

New Words

apogee /ˈæpədʒiː/ *n.* the highest or most distant point; climax

assessment /əˈsesmənt/ *n.* the act of assessing; appraisal; evaluation

baroque /bəˈrəʊk/ *adj.* extravagant, complex, or bizarre; verging on excessive 巴洛克风格的；奇异的；过分雕琢和怪诞的

crisp /krɪsp/ *adj.* clean-cut, neat, and well-pressed; well-groomed 整洁的；干净利落的 crisply *adv.*

dissipate /ˈdɪsɪpeɪt/ *v.* to scatter in various directions; disperse; dispel 驱散；使消失

doyen /ˈdɔɪən/ *n.* the senior member, as in age, rank, or experience, of a group, class, profession, etc. 老资格，老前辈；首席

dynamic /daɪˈnæmɪk/ *adj.* characterized by continuous change, activity, or progress; vigorously active or forceful; energetic 有活力的

ephemeral /ɪˈfemərəl/ *adj.* lasting a very short time; short-lived; transitory 短暂的，瞬息的

heady /ˈhedɪ/ *adj.* intoxicating; affecting the mind or senses greatly; exciting; exhilarating 令人陶醉的；使人发晕的

howdy /'haʊdɪ/ n. (pl. howdys or howdies) hello; how do you do (used as an expression of greeting)

hubris /'hjuːbrɪs/ n. excessive pride or self-confidence; arrogance 骄傲自大

introspection /ˌɪntrəʊ'spekʃən/ n. observation or examination of one's own mental and emotional state, mental processes, etc.; the act of looking within oneself 反省,自省

outperform /ˌaʊtpə'fɔːm/ v. to surpass in excellence of performance; do better than

plausible /'plɔːzəbl/ adj. seemingly or apparently valid, likely, or acceptable; credible; believable

predecessor /'priːdɪsesə/ n. a person who precedes another in an office, position, etc.; sth succeeded or replaced by something else

project /prə'dʒekt/ v. to present (an idea, program, etc.) for consideration or action 表达

prowl /praʊl/ v. to rove over or through in search of what may be found 徘徊

reminiscent /ˌremɪ'nɪsnt/ adj. tending to recall or suggest sth in the past 使人想起……的;暗示的

resonate /'rezəˌneɪt/ v. to resound; to evoke a feeling of shared emotion or belief 产生回声或共鸣

resurgence /rɪ'sɜːdʒəns/ n. a renewal or revival 复苏

sanctimony /'sæŋktɪmənɪ/ n. pretended, affected, or hypocritical religious devotion, righteousness, etc.; sanctity; sacredness (假装的)神圣;正义

sheer /ʃɪə/ adj. unmixed with anything else 完全的,十足的

succumb /sə'kʌm/ v. to give way to superior force; yield 屈从

supremacy /sjuː'preməsɪ/ n. the state of being supreme; supreme authority or power 霸权

sustained /səs'teɪnd/ adj. maintained; continued 持续不变的

swagger /'swægə/ n. ostentatious display of arrogance and conceit; boastful or conceited expression 自鸣得意

unipolar /'juːnɪ'pəʊlə/ adj. having, acting by means of, or produced by a single magnetic or electric pole 单极的

unleash /ʌn'liːʃ/ v. to release from or as if from a leash; to abandon control of 把(感情、力量等)释放出来;发泄

Notes

1. Texas A&M—Texas Agricultural &Machinary University. It is a state supported university. Its main campus is located at College Station, Texas. 得克萨斯农业机械大学。美国各州几乎都有农机大学。
2. Agonised introspection and crises of confidence are not Texan traits.—Texan people (here students of Texas A&M University) are not inclined to lose confidence and indulge in painful thinking and examination of themselves.
3. America's intelligence establishment—美国的情报界。本课中还出现了"US security establishment(美国安全部门)"和"the foreign policy establishment(对外政策部门)"。(见"语言解说")
4. National Intelligence Council—the center for midterm and long-term strategic thinking within the United States Intelligence Community (IC,美国情报部门). It was formed in 1979. The NIC's goal is to provide policymakers with the best information: unvarnished(不加修饰的), unbiased and without regard to whether the analytic judgments conform to current US policy. 国家情报委员会
5. Britain's *Guardian* newspaper—It refers to *The Guardian*, a British newspaper owned by the Guardian Media Group. 英国的《卫报》
6. the Bush years—the years when George W. Bush was US President (2001—2009)
7. unipolar moment—the period of time after the end of the cold war, when the United States is the single dominant super power in the world 单极时期
8. Three developments have fed the new declinism.—Three significant events or states of affairs have contributed to the new declinism.
9. General Brent Scowcroft—(1925—) Chairman of the President's Foreign Intelligence Advisory Board under President George W. Bush (2001—2005). He was the National Security Advisor under Presidents Gerald Ford and George H. W. Bush. He also served as Military Assistant to President Nixon and as Deputy Assistant to the President for National Security Affairs in the Nixon and Ford administrations. 布伦特·斯考克罗夫特将军
10. Fareed Zakaria's *The Post-American World*—Fareed Zakaria (1964—), is an India-born American journalist, author, and

television host specializing in international relations. *The Post-American World* was published in 2008.

11. Andrew Bacevich—(1947—) a professor of international relations at Boston University, former director of its Center for International Relations, and author of several books, including *American Empire: The Realities and Consequences of US Diplomacy* (2002), *The New American Militarism: How Americans are Seduced by War* (2005) and *The Limits of Power: The End of American Exceptionalism* (2008). He has been "a persistent, vocal critic of the US occupation of Iraq, calling the conflict a catastrophic failure." In March 2007, he described Bush's endorsement(赞同)of such "preventive wars" as "immoral, illicit, and imprudent." His son died fighting in the Iraq war in May of 2007.

12. American power ... is inadequate to the ambitions to which hubris and sanctimony have given rise. —America is not powerful enough to accomplish the ambitions that have been conceived as a result of their arrogance and pretended righteousness.

13. Richard·Haass—1951— , president of the Council on Foreign Relations (2003—). Before this, he was Director of Policy Planning for the United States Department of State and a close advisor to Secretary of State Colin Powell. He has been US Coordinator for the Future of Afghanistan. He succeeded George J. Mitchell as the United States Special Envoy for Northern Ireland to help the peace process in Northern Ireland, for which he received the State Department's Distinguished Service Award.

14. Council of Foreign Relations—an American bipartisan foreign policy organization founded in 1921. Located at 58 East 68th Street (Park Avenue) in New York City, with an office in Washington, D. C. Some international journalists believe it to be "the most influential foreign-policy think tank." It publishes a bi-monthly journal *Foreign Affairs*. 美国对外关系委员会,成立于1918年,是美国最知名的领袖智囊团之一,其宗旨是通过"了解国际形势"对"美国的政治、经济和财政问题的国际方面"进行持续不断的研究,帮助政府制定"明智的美国对外政策"。它在外交方面的影响力无与伦比,曾经为美国制定了许多对外政策方针,是这方面的权威。成员有政府、工商界、教育界和新闻界中一批最有影响的人物。

15. Dartmouth College—见第 4 课读报知识 "Ivy League & Seven Sisters Colleges"
16. Paul Kennedy—1945 — , a British historian specializing in international relations and grand strategy. He has published books on the history of the Royal Navy, Great Power struggles, the Pacific War and many others.
17. Reagan-era—The period of time when Reagan was President (1981 — 1989), who influenced American culture, esp. American politics.
18. the high-tech boom of the Clinton years—the rapid development of the computer science and the Internet in the 1990s when Bill Clinton was President (1993—2001).
19. USSR—The Union of Soviet Socialist Republics (usu. the Soviet Union) was a socialist state that existed from 1922 to 1991.
20. the Vietnam war—conflict in Southeast Asia, primarily fought in South Vietnam between government forces aided by the US and guerrilla forces aided by North Vietnam. The war began in 1957 after the Geneva Conference divided (1954) Vietnam into the North Vietnam and South Vietnam. It escalated from a Vietnamese civil war into a limited international conflict in which the US was deeply involved, until North Vietnam's successful offensive(进攻)in 1975 resulted in South Vietnam's collapse and the unification of Vietnam by the North.
21. Richard Nixon—1913—1994, US President (1969—1974). Because of the Watergate affair, he was the only person to resign from that office.

Questions

1. What is the difference between the latest global trends report and the one issued four years ago?
2. What does "new declinism" mean?
3. What are the reasons of the new declinism?
4. What does William Wohlforth of Dartmouth College think of the new declinism?
5. Why does the writer think that the new declinism may be more soundly based than the previous ones?
6. What do you think of America's decline and China's rise?

:::语言解说:::

Establishment

　　establishment 是报刊中常见的多义词，读者切忌见之就理解为"建立"。《泰晤士报》曾载文称，在现代报纸上，一个词有五六个意思是很平常的。见以下解说：

　　1. 界。作"界"讲，在美语里已成了贬义词，在英国却不然。本课第 2 段便是例证。

　　Intelligence **establishment** became intelligence community because establishment became pejorative. (*The New York Times Magazine*)

　　2. 建立起来的机构，单位

　　a. The hotel is a well-run **establishment**. (*Los Angles Times*)

　　b. "It is truly regrettable. It is deplorable that a diplomatic **establishment** has been mistakenly hit," Keizo Obuchi was quoted as saying by Kyodo News Agency. (*AP*)

　　3. 编制，建制

　　The Pentagon argues for a leaner military **establishment**... (*Time*)

　　4. 当局，当权派，官方，统治集团

　　a. Indeed the West German **establishment**, like the Polish and East German governments, seems to be cordially displeased with Judge Stern's judgment. (*Newsweek*)

　　b. Khomeini's curious blend of mysticism and activism still made him slightly suspect in the eyes of the Islamic **Establishment**—as a holy man who tried to run around with the Mob, one might say—but his following was growing steadily. (*Time*)

　　c. Some **establishment** figures remain wary of Byrne because she defeated their candidate, but the new mayor has moved to patch up differences. (*Time*)

　　5. 权势集团，社会既成权力机构；门阀，财阀

　　a. Despite his contribution in the field of social progress President Johnson "was never accepted by the liberal Eastern **Establishment**," Carter said. "I don't know why."(*Washington Star News*)

　　b. The Church of England is the official (established) church of the United Kingdom, created in the 16th century as a protestant church by the Act of Supremacy. Its secular head is the sovereign, and its religious head, the Archbishop of Canterbury. Its senior clergy—archbishops, bishops and deans—are appointed by the Prime Minister. It is one of the main forces of the **Establishment** in Britain. (*Adrian Room*)

6. 当权派；实力集团

a. But Dole had the near-unanimous support of the GOP **establishment** and wrapped up the nomination after a shaky start. (*The World Almanac*)

b. Several senior strategists recommended that the White House adopt an **anti-Establishment** strategy, taking on organized labor, civil-rights groups, feminists and other GOP foils. (*U.S. News & World Report*) （详见《导读》二章一节）

Lesson Sixteen

课文导读

2003年3月20日,美国和英国未经联合国授权,以所谓的伊拉克拥有大规模杀伤性武器为借口而一意孤行地发动了第二次伊拉克战争。这是因为当时小布什政府里的新保守派(neocon)试图将伊建成以美国价值观为准则的"民主国家的榜样",以它来推动其他中东国家的改革,使之最后都成为美式国家。这就是"改造中东"说;另一说是"独霸伊拉克的石油"。本文写于战争爆发5周年纪念日来临之际,此时诸多无可辩驳的事实业已表明,这场战争使伊拉克生灵涂炭、文明遭殃、基础设施损毁,至今恐怖袭击事件不断,人们成天生活在恐惧气氛中;而美英等发动战争的国家在人员、经济、政治等诸多方面也付出了惨痛代价。单就金钱而言,美国政府自2001年"9·11"事件后发动阿富汗和伊拉克战争至2008年9月,已经花掉了纳税人几千亿美元。

虽说战争总是在制造失败者,但事实上有输家就有赢家。那么这场伊战的赢家是谁呢?他们既非美国和英国,更非美国所谓的被从专制统治下解放出来的伊拉克平民,西方认为政治上的赢家是伊朗和"基地"组织。伊朗是穆斯林什叶派占绝对多数的国家,而伊拉克战争将掌权的逊尼派打垮后,什叶派掌握了大权,所以与伊朗关系密切。基地组织一直与美作对,至今未被打垮,力量反而增强了。在经济上获利的是私营承包商、美英与官方有瓜葛的石油公司(如Halliburton等,他们可未经竞标就赢得合同),以及与这场战争有关的商人,他们从中发了横财。

通过此课我们不但了解了伊战的真相、官商勾结的内幕,还可学到一些在一二年级课本上学不到的对读报非常有用的 new words,因而值得好好学习。

Pre-reading Questions

1. Why have the US and the UK built so many military bases abroad?
2. What are the principles of our foreign policy?

Text

Iraq: Who Won the War?

Not the 90,000 Iraqi civilians or the 4,200 US and UK troops killed since 2003. The big winners are the money men who have made billions.

By Raymond Whitaker and Stephen Foley

1 Five years ago today, Britain stood on the brink of war. On 16 March 2003, United Nations weapons inspectors were advised to leave Iraq within 48 hours, and the "shock and awe" bombing campaign[1] began less than 100 hours later, on 20 March. The moment the neocons[2] around President George Bush[3] had worked so long for, aided by the moral fervour of Tony Blair[4], was about to arrive.

2 "I believe demolishing Hussein's[5] military power and liberating Iraq would be a cakewalk," Kenneth Adelman[6], a leading neocon, had said a few weeks before, and so it proved. Within barely a month, Saddam's bronze statue in Baghdad's Firdaus Square was scrap metal. But every other prediction by the Bush administration's hawks[7] proved wrong.

3 No weapons of mass destruction[8] — Britain's key justification for war — have been found. The Pentagon[9] acknowledged last week that a review of more than 600,000 captured Iraqi documents showed "no evidence that Saddam Hussein's regime had any operational links with Osama bin Laden's al-Qa'ida[10] terrorist network".

4 In 2008, there are still more American troops in Iraq than during the invasion, with no exit yet in sight[11]. Britain's Ministry of Defence has just admitted that it has been unable to withdraw as many British troops as it planned — there are 4,000 still based just outside Basra, instead of the projected 2,500. So far 3,987 American soldiers and 197 British troops have died in Iraq.

5 So, five years on, who can be said to have won the war? Certainly not Iraqi civilians, at least 90,000 of whom have died violently since 2003, at the most conservative estimate. Other studies have multiplied that figure by five or six.[12] Two million Iraqis have fled the country, and at least as many again are internally displaced. Baghdad households suffered power cuts of up to eight hours a day in Saddam's time; now

they can expect less than eight hours of electricity a day on average. The US troop "surge"[13] has cut the number of murders, but there are still 26 a day in the capital. The list goes on.

6   Nor have the eager promotors of the war, such as Mr Adelman, fared well. (By October 2006 he was admitting: "We're losing in Iraq.") The most arrogant of them all, Donald Rumsfeld[14], the ex-secretary of defence, was reluctantly dropped by Mr Bush in his second term. His former deputy, Paul Wolfowitz[15], who famously said that WMD had been used as the excuse for war because it was the only topic Washington's bureaucracy could agree on, was forced to resign as president of the World Bank[16] after arranging a pay rise for his girlfriend. The Senate refused to confirm John Bolton[17] as US ambassador to the UN.

7   George Bush is the most unpopular President since opinion polls[18] began, mainly because of Iraq. Tony Blair, his partner in the reckless venture, has already gone[19]; those in a position to know[20] believe he would still be Prime Minister had it not been for the war. The standing of both Britain and the US has suffered immeasurably, and the international scepticism engendered by manipulation of the evidence on WMD has hampered efforts to deal with nuclear threats from the likes of North Korea[21].

8   The main winners of the war are not the ones its instigators planned: Iran and al-Qa'ida. No one in Washington appeared to have calculated that to unseat Saddam, whom the US once supported as a bulwark against the Iranians, would empower the majority community in Iraq, the Shias[22], or that many of them would look to the world's only Shia nation, Iran. The US insists that Tehran retains nuclear ambitions, despite its own intelligence estimate that work on a weapon has stopped, but its occupation of Iraq has given Iran a hostage it could never have imagined having.[23]

9   As for al-Qa'ida, it never had a foothold in Iraq until the chaos created by the invasion gave it the opportunity to establish one. And while the US is preoccupied in Iraq, the conflict it neglected, in Afghanistan, is getting worse. Al-Qa'ida has re-established itself in the lawless tribal areas of Pakistan, while its old host, the Taliban[24], regains ground on the other side of the Afghan border.

10 In early 2003, Mr Rumsfeld mused on what might be the cost of the war to come: $50bn (£25bn) or $60bn, he and White House planners thought. Five years on, the bill is already 10 times that, while here the Commons Defence Committee[25] has just warned of a "surprising" 52 per cent increase in the cost of operations in Iraq to nearly 1.45bn in the current financial year, despite the reductions in troop levels. An unprecedented amount has been funnelled to the private sector[26]. The big winners have been the money men[27].

11 Another army of private security guards escorts, convoys, protects infrastructure projects and ferries military equipment around Iraq. These have been followed by business consultants, building project planners and government advisers, many of whom have put their lives at risk in the pursuit of a reconstructed Iraq while their companies earn billions.

12 An estimate last October put the number of private contractors working in Iraq at 160,000 from up to 300 separate companies. About 50,000 were private security guards from companies such as Blackwater[28]—whose killing of 17 Iraqi civilians last September in a gun battle shone a spotlight on[29] the US military's reliance on poorly controlled private armies. Each Blackwater guard in Iraq, of whom there have been up to 900, costs the US government $445,000 per year.

13 British firms have also been operating in Iraq. After courting controversy in the Nineties, Tim Spicer—whose previous company, Sandline International, was accused of breaking a United Nations embargo by selling arms to Sierra Leone[30]—has re-emerged as a powerful player with his latest venture, Aegis Defence Services. Aegis won a $293m Pentagon contract in 2004, which has since been extended, and employs more than 1,000 contractors in the country. Another British company, Global Strategies, which calls itself a

A security guard from Blackwater in Iraq

"political and security risk-management company", employs cheaper Fijian contractors for its Iraq operations.

14   At one point, ArmorGroup[31], chaired by the former foreign secretary Sir Malcolm Rifkind, was getting half its revenues from Iraq. It carried out convoy protection at rates estimated at between $8,000 and $12,000 a day, and helped to guard polling stations during the country's elections. By far the biggest winner of contracts in Iraq, though, is Halliburton, the oil and related services company run by Dick Cheney[32] before he became US vice-president and a key architect of the war. The connections between the company and the Bush administration helped to generate $16bn in contracts in Iraq and Afghanistan in the three years from the start of 2004—nine times as much as any other company. Halliburton decided last year to spin off the division[33] operating in Iraq. That business, KBR[34], has generated half its revenues there each year since the invasion, providing private security to the military and infrastructure projects and advising on the rebuilding of the country's oil industry.

The Relationship between Cheney and Halliburton[35]

15   The Washington-based Center for Public Integrity, which tracks Iraqi contracts in its investigation "Windfalls of War"[36], says the total value of contracts tendered by the US government in Iraq rose 50 per cent each year from 2004 to 2006. That had been planned to slow in 2007, but KBR said recently that the US military "surge" meant more business than previously expected. After KBR, the US security contractor DynCorp[37] secured the most work, worth $1.8bn over the three years to the end of 2006.

16   Many of the biggest contract winners have extensive lobbying budgets and funds for targeting political donations[38]. Public records

show that BearingPoint[39], the consulting firm appointed to advise on the economic reconstruction of Iraq, has paid hundreds of thousands of dollars into Republican Party coffers, including $117,000 to the two Bush presidential campaigns. The company is being paid $240m for its work in Iraq, winning an initial contract from the US Agency for International Development (USAID)[40] within weeks of the fall of Saddam. It was charged with supporting the then Coalition Provisional Authority[41] to introduce policies "which are designed to create a competitive private sector".

17   Last year, The IoS[42] revealed that a BearingPoint employee based at the US embassy in Baghdad was involved in drafting the controversial hydrocarbon law[43] that was approved by Iraq's cabinet last March. The legislation opens up the country's oil reserves to foreign corporations for the first time since 1972.

18   Western companies will be able to pocket up to three-quarters of profits from new drilling projects in their early years. Supporters say it is the only way to get Iraq's oil industry back on its feet after years of sanctions, war and loss of expertise. But it will operate through "production-sharing agreements"[44], which are highly unusual in the Middle East; the oil industries of Saudi Arabia and Iran, the world's two largest producers, are state-controlled.

19   So far, major companies such as Shell, BP and ExxonMobil[45] have held back on[46] investing directly in the country while the violence continues—but the war has still contributed handsomely to their record-breaking profits because of sky-high oil prices. As the US prepared to march into Iraq, crude soared to what then seemed an impossibly high $37 a barrel. Last week it reached a record $110.

20   The Nobel prize-winning economist Joseph Stiglitz estimates that the war has added between $5 and $10 a barrel to the price of oil. The figure could be higher, if one believes that the rise also reflects a big additional premium for the threat of future supply disruptions that might be caused by geopolitical tensions or increased terrorist activity in oil-producing regions—any of which might be traced back to the passions inflamed by the war. (From *The Independent*, March 16, 2008)

New Words

Afghanistan /æfˈgænɪstæn/ *n.* a republic in W Asia(阿富汗)
Afghan /ˈæfgæn/ *adj.* of Afghanistan
arrogant /ˈærəgənt/ *adj.* feeling superior; acting in a haughty overbearing manner; exaggerating one's own importance in an overbearing manner(高傲自大的)
Baghdad /ˈbægdæd/ *n.* the capital city of Iraq(巴格达)
Basra /ˈbʌsrə/ *n.* a city in the S part of Iraq(巴士拉)
Bn (*abbrev.*) billion
bulwark /ˈbʊlwək/ *n.* a person or thing that supports, defends or protects(支持、防御或保护的人或事物)
bureaucracy /bjʊəˈrɒkrəsɪ/ *n.* government officials; officialdom(官僚,官僚机构)
cakewalk /ˈkeɪkwɔːk/ *n.* an easy accomplishment(易如反掌的事情)
coffer /ˈkɒfə/ *n.* (*pl.* ~s) treasury(资金库)
confirm /kənˈfɜːm/ *v.* to give approval to
contractor /kənˈtræktə/ *n.* a person, business, or firm that provides building materials or labor(承包人,承包商或公司)
convoy /kənˈvɒɪ/ *v.* to accompany and guard with armed force, esp. with armed ships(护航;护送)
courting /ˈkɔːtɪŋ/ *adj.* acting in such a way so as to provoke
crude /kruːd/ *n.* raw oil
demolish /dɪˈmɒlɪʃ/ *v.* to destroy; to tear down
displace *v.* to force to leave one's country or hometown because of war or oppression(被迫背井离乡)
draft /dræft/ *v.* to draw up the preliminary sketch, version, or plan of(起草)
embargo /emˈbɑːgəʊ/ *n.* an order of a government prohibiting the departure of commercial ships from its ports(禁运)
engender /ɪnˈdʒendə/ *v.* to produce; to cause to exist
escort /ˈeskɔːt/ *v.* to go with (someone) as a guard, or as a companion (护送;护卫;陪同)
expertise /ˌekspɛːˈtiːz/ *n.* the knowledge or skill of a person who is specialized or profound in a certain area(专业技术)
fare /fɛə/ *v.* to get along
fervour /ˈfɛːvə/ *n.* the quality of being fervent(热忱,热情)

Fijian /fiːˈdʒiːən/ *adj.* of Fiji, an independent state in the S W Pacific (斐济的)

Firdaus /fɪəˈdəʊs/ *n.* the name of the square in the center of Baghdad (菲尔杜斯)

foothold /ˈfʊthəʊld/ *n.* an established position or basis from which to progress

funnel /ˈfʌnəl/ *v.* to (cause to) pass through or as if through a funnel (从漏斗中通过；从通道中通过)

geopolitical /ˌdʒiːəʊpəˈlɪtɪkl/ *adj.* of the study of the influence of such factors as geography, economics and demography (人口统计学) on politics, esp. on international relations (地理政治学的，地缘政治政策的)

hamper /ˈhæmpə/ *v.* to hinder; to restrict the movement or operation of... by obstacles or bonds (阻碍)

hostage /ˈhɒstɪdʒ/ *n.* a precious thing or a person held by one party as a pledge that promise will be kept or terms met by the other party (抵押品，人质)

inflame /ɪnˈfleɪm/ *v.* to fill (sb) with strong feelings (使极度激动；使激怒)

infrastructure /ˈɪnfrəˈstrʌktʃə/ *n.* permanent installations (e.g. airfields) for military purposes; underlying foundations or basic framework (军事基地；基础设施)

instigator /ˈɪnstɪɡeɪtə/ *n.* a person who instigates (esp. sth bad) (发起者；教唆者，煽动者)

Iraqi /ɪˈrækiː/ *adj. & n.* 伊拉克的；伊拉克人

justification /ˌdʒʌstɪfɪˈkeɪʃən/ *n.* that which justifies (正当的理由，借口)

manipulation /məˌnɪpjʊˈleɪʃən/ *n.* operation or arrangement esp. by artful, unfair, or insidious means (操纵)

multiply /ˈmʌltɪplaɪ/ *v.* 乘，使相乘

muse /mjuːz/ *v.* to become absorbed in thought

prediction /prɪˈdɪkʃən/ *n.* sth that is declared in advance

premium /ˈpriːmɪəm/ *n.* the amount that sth in scarce supply is valued above its nominal value (加付款；加价，溢价)

preoccupy /priːˈɒkjʊpaɪ/ *v.* to engage the attention of to the exclusion of other things

projected /prəˈdʒektɪd/ *adj.* planned

promoter /prəˈməʊtə/ *n.* a substance that in very small amounts is able to increase the activity of a catalyst in a chemical reaction; (*fig.*) a

person who plays the role of a catalyst（催化剂；煽风点火之人）
resign /rɪˈzaɪn/ v. to give up one's office or position
retain /rɪˈteɪn/ v. to keep in mind
revenue /ˈrevɪnjuː/ n. the total income in a year
sanction /ˈsæŋkʃən/ n. an economic or military measure adopted to force a nation to change some policy or to comply with international law（国际制裁）
scepticism /ˈskeptɪsɪzəm/ n. an attitude of doubt
scrap /skræp/ n. material which cannot be used for its original purpose but which may still have some value（废品）
statue /ˈstætjuː/ n. a three-dimensional representation of a person（塑像）
surge /sɜːdʒ/ n. the motion of sweeping forwards like that of a wave or series of waves; sharp increase
Tehran /ˌtehəˈrɑːn/ n. the capital city of Iran（德黑兰）
tender /ˈtendə/ v. to offer for acceptance; to offer（正式提出；提供）
track /træk/ v. to follow the traces of
unprecedented /ʌnˈpresɪdəntɪd/ adj. having no earlier occurrence of sth similar
venture /ˈventʃə/ n. sth involving a risk which one decides to take（冒险行动；投机活动；企业）

Notes

1. "shock and awe" bombing campaign——北京时间 2003 年 3 月 20 日上午 10 点 34 分，美国以伊拉克拥有大规模杀伤性武器和生化武器为借口，开始对伊拉克发动军事进攻，第二次海湾战争爆发。战争爆发后，美军采取了一系列的军事进攻策略，其中之一就是为取得"震慑"效果而对敌方发动的重大轰炸和打击，即所谓的"震慑行动"（shock and awe）。
2. neocon——neoconservative（前自由派在政治上转向保守的）新保守主义者，新保守派。源自 neoconservatism（新保守主义）：出现于 20 世纪 70 年代，代表人物是美国前国会参议员及驻联合国大使 Patrick Moynihan 等民主党自由派。与传统的保守主义相同，重视资本主义自由经济，反对国家干预，但是不赞同传统的保守主义人人平等的平等主义以及政府对穷人实施补贴的扶贫计划等观念。可以说，新保守主义比较温和，愿意接受有限度的政府干预，但是小布什上台后，其政府里的新保守派副总统 Dick Cheney、国防部长 Donald Rumsfeld、副部长 Paul Wolfowitz 和总统安全事务助理 Condoleezza Rice 等抱成一团,在外交上更加强硬,要把美式的自由民主制度推向全球。但伊拉克战争的失败使他们遭受重大挫折。Donald 和 Paul 都被迫辞职。

3. George Bush —1946 — , U. S. President(2001－2009). In March 2003, Bush and the Congress asserted Iraq was in possession of weapons of mass destruction and ordered the invasion of Iraq.

4. Tony Blair—1953 — , Prime Minister of the United Kingdom (1997－2007). During his tenure, Blair strongly supported United States foreign policy and claimed Iraq was in possession of biochemical weapons, notably by participating in the invasion of Iraq in 2003.

5. Hussein—here referring to Saddam Hussein (1937 － 2006), President of Iraq (1979－2003). As president, he maintained power during the Iran-Iraq War (1980－1988) and the first Persian Gulf War (1991). In these conflicts, he repressed movements which threaten the stability and independence of Iraq. Thus, some Arabs look upon him as a hero for his aggressive stance against foreign intervention and for his support for the Palestinians, but United States leaders view him as militant tyrant who was a threat to the stability of the region. He was removed by the U. S. and its allies during the 2003 invasion of Iraq. On November 5, 2006, he was sentenced to death by hanging with guilty of crimes against humanity.

6. Kenneth Adelman—1946 — , an American diplomat, political writer, and policy analyst

7. Bush administration's hawks—布什政府里的"鹰派",它和"鸽派"(doves)是美国国内政坛存在的两种主要势力。主张强硬路线或用武力解决争端的一派被称为"鹰派",主张用和平手段解决问题的被称为"鸽派",两派之间的中间派为"dawk"。

8. weapons of mass destruction—(*abbrev*. WMD) weapons that can kill large numbers of humans and/or cause great damage to man-made structures (e. g. buildings), natural structures (e. g. mountains) or the biosphere in general. The term covers several weapon types, including nuclear, biological, chemical (NBC) and radiological weapons. 大规模杀伤性武器

9. the Pentagon—It is the headquarters of the United States Department

of Defense, located in Arlington, Virginia. As a symbol of the U.S. military, "the Pentagon" is often used metonymically (以借代的方式) to refer to the Department of Defense rather than the building itself.
10. Osama bin Laden's al-Qa'ida—Osama bin Laden is the founder of the jihadist organization Al-Qa'id / Al-Qaeda. He has been regarded as a terrorist by Interpol (国际刑警组织) and other law enforcement agencies. In conjunction (联系) with several other Islamic militant leaders, he issued that Muslims should force the United States and its allies to withdraw their military forces from the Arabian peninsula, by attacking American military and civilian targets. (See also Note 10 of Lesson Thirteen)
11. with no exit yet in sight—There is still no sign that can be seen that the U.S. troops are going to withdraw from Iraq.
12. Other studies have multiplied that figure by five or six—Other investigations have shown that the number of Iraqi civilian deaths must be five or six times the figure of 90,000.
13. troop surge—a sharp increase in military strength (兵力激增)。"surge"是 2006 年的新用法，2007 年 1 月因小布什总统发表电视演说中用了 troop surge 而一般成为时髦词(buzzword)，意思与越南战争中用的"escalation"相同。
14. Donald Rumsfeld —1932— , Secretary of Defense under President Gerald Ford (1975 — 1977), and under President George W. Bush (2001—2006).
15. Paul Wolfowitz—1943— , former US Ambassador to Indonesia, Deputy Secretary of Defense, and former President of the World Bank.
16. World Bank—Its full name being International Bank for Reconstruction and Development, it is an organiztion affiliated with the UN and designed to finance productive projects that further the economic development of member nations. Founded as a result of the negotiations that culminated in the UN Monetary and Financial Conference in July 1944, the bank officially began operations in June 1946. Although its first loans were made for post-World War II reconstruction, by 1949 the emphasis had shifted to loans for the purpose of economic development. World Bank

headquarters are in Washington, D. C.

17. John Bolton—1948 — , American statesman who has served in several Republican presidential administrations. He served as the interim（临时）Permanent US Representative to the UN from August 2005 until December 2006 on a recess appointment（临时任命）, and resigned in December 2006 when his recess appointment would have ended.

18. opinion poll—a canvassing（调查）of persons chosen at random or from a sample group in order to discover trends of public opinion

19. Tony Blair... has already gone—Tony Blair, as a partner of George Bush in this reckless Iraq war, has already been out of power.

20. those in a position to know—those with social or official rank or status who are in a situation that confers advantage or preference to know what ordinary people do not know（那些了解内幕的人,知情人士）

21. nuclear threats from the likes of North Korea—来自诸如朝鲜之类国家的核危险

    朝鲜核问题本来在克林顿政府时期取得重大进展,由美国、日本等国向朝提供重油等来换取朝去核。但是在小布什执政后宣布朝鲜为邪恶轴心国(axis of evil state),从而使朝核问题久拖未决。后来布什政府又回到克林顿政府的立场,但问题仍未解决。看来此事奥巴马政府也拍不了板。

22. the majority community in Iraq, the Shias/ Shiahs—伊拉克的什叶派是多数派。在伊斯兰教中,什叶派是除逊尼派外人数最多的一个教派。伊拉克、伊朗是什叶派占多数的国家,但伊拉克在萨达姆统治时代却是少数派逊尼派(the Sunnis)掌权。

23. The US insists that Tehran ... intelligence estimate that work on a weapon has stopped ... given Iran a hostage it could never have imagined having. —美国政府坚持认为,德黑兰有发展核武器的野心,诚然美国从自己掌握的情报评估报告认为,伊朗的核武器研制工作已经停止,然而,美国对伊拉克的占领却给了伊朗一个做梦都没有想到的可乘之机。

    a. Tehran—here referring to the government of Iran

    b. ... intelligence estimate that... —"that" introduces an appositive clause modifying "intelligence estimate"

    c. work on a weapon—to research on the production of a

nuclear weapon

    d. a hostage ... imagined having—Here "a hostage" is first used as the object of the verb "give" and then as the object of "having" in the modifying clause introduced by "which" (omitted in this sentence) rather than as the object of "imagine" and the verb "imagine" is generally followed by a v-ing if it is a verb. "hostage" 原意为"人质"，此处意为美国占领伊拉克而被捆住了手脚，从而给伊朗提供了可乘之机。

24. the Taliban—formed in 1994 in the southern Afghan province of Kandahar（坎大哈）by a group of graduates from Pakistani Islamic colleges on the border with Afghanistan, run by the Fundamentalist（原教旨主义者，此字常引申为"极端分子"或"极端保守派"）Jamiat-e-Ulema. The members of the Taliban Islamic Movement of Afghanistan（阿富汗伊斯兰学生运动组织，简称TIMA）were mostly Pushtus（普什图人）from Kandahar in southern Afghanistan and were led by a mullah (a village-level religious leader), Mohammad Omar. The Taliban advocated an Islamic Revolution in Afghanistan, proclaiming that the unity of Afghanistan should be re-established in the framework of Islamic law and without the mujahedin（穆斯林游击队员）. On 11 Sept. 1996, the Taliban captured Jalalabad, the eastern city bordering Pakistan, and on 27 the same month they captured Kabul, the capital city of Afghanistan, and ousted the government. At the beginning of June 1997, the Taliban effectively controlled two-thirds of the country. Under the reign of the Taliban in the following period, Afghan economy underwent collapse and the people suffered bitterly. At the end of 2001, they were toppled by the United States. 塔利班，意为"伊斯兰教学生"。
25. the Commons Defence Committee—(英国)平民院防务委员会
26. the private sector—economical section belonging to particular people or groups and not shared with others in any way(经济的私营部门)
27. money men—银行家，金融家，大亨，大老板。Here it refers to any one who has made great profit from the Iraq War, esp. the private contractors or companies working in Iran mentioned later in the text.
28. Blackwater—a private military company, founded in 1997 in US.

Sandline International and Aegis Defence Services (in the following paragraph) are also private military companies, founded in 1996 and 2002 in London respectively. 因其名声不佳，现已更名 Xe 公司

29. shine a spotlight on—to show clearly; to draw particular attention to
30. Sierra Leone—a republic and member of the British Commonwealth in W. Africa. It has been suffering from domestic turmoils and conflicts and thus some companies in western countries have taken the advantage to make money in spite of the UN embargo. 塞拉利昂
31. ArmorGroup—a British company founded in 1981, which provides private security such as protective security services, risk management consultancy, security training and mine action (排雷) services
32. Dick Cheney—1941— , Vice President (2001－2009). Out of office during the Clinton presidency, he was Chairman and Chief Executive Officer of Halliburton Company (1995－2000).
33. spin off the division—to derive, to establish a branch company from the head company
34. KBR—the name of the division operating in Iraq
35. 图中坦克上写着 HALLIBURTON(哈利伯顿)，炮管上的包袱写着 TAXPAYER(纳税人)；坐在坦克上的副总统切尼对山姆大叔说："YOUR WALLET. IN THE BAG. CHOP. CHOP."(快把你的钱放到钱袋里。)
36. Windfalls of War—"战争横财"(前文所说的 investigation 的代号)
37. DynCorp—a private military contractor and aircraft maintenance company in the United States
38. political donation—见"语言解说"
39. BearingPoint—As a global management and technology consulting company BearingPoint is traced back more than 100 years to Peat Marwick, which was founded in 1897. In 2001, BearingPoint completed its initial public offering and in 2002 changed its name from KPMG Consulting to BearingPoint. It provides strategic consulting, applications services, technology solutions and managed services to government organizations, Global 2000 companies and medium-sized businesses in the U.S. and around the world.
40. US Agency for International Development—an independent federal

government agency (abbrev. USAID), established on November 3, 1961 according to the U.S. Foreign Assistance Act, which became the first U.S. foreign assistance organization whose primary emphasis was on long-range economic and social development assistance efforts. Since its founding, USAID has been the principal U.S. agency to extend assistance to countries recovering from disaster, trying to escape poverty, and engaging in democratic reforms. 美国国际开发署

41. Coalition Provisional Authority—It was established as a transitional government following the invasion of Iraq by the United States, United Kingdom and the other members of the multinational coalition which was formed to topple the government of Saddam Hussein in 2003.

42. The IoS—a specialized web site serving the stationery and office supplies industry worldwide. It provides information of over 5,000 suppliers within the industry from different parts of the world.

43. hydrocarbon law—The Iraq hydrocarbon (碳氢化合物) law, also referred to as the Iraq oil law, is a proposed piece of legislation submitted to the Iraqi Council of Representatives in May 2007. As of June 2008, the law was still stalled in parliament. The Iraqi Oil Ministry announced plans to go ahead with small one or two year no-bid contracts to Exxon Mobil, Shell, Total and BP—once partners in the Iraq Petroleum Company—along with Chevron and smaller firms to service Iraq's largest fields.

44. production-sharing agreements—They are used primarily to determine the share a private company will receive of the natural resources (usually oil) extracted from a particular country. In PSAs, the national oil company awards the execution of exploration and production activities to the international oil company (contractor). The contractor bears the mineral and financial risk of the initiative and, when successful, it recovers capital expenditure and costs incurred in the year (cost oil) by means of a share of production. This production share varies along with international oil prices. 产品分成协议

45. Shell, BP and ExxonMobil—

    a. Shell—a global group of energy and petrochemical

companies. With 104,000 employees in more than 110 countries, Shell plays a key role in helping to meet the world's growing demand for energy. 壳牌公司

b. BP—British Petroleum, starting in 1908 with oil found in a rugged part of Persia, is one of the world's largest energy companies. 英国石油公司

c. ExxonMobil—founded in 1999 as the result of the merger Exxon and Mobil. 埃克森美孚是世界第一大石油公司。

46. hold back on—to restrain from; to stop the action of

Questions

1. On what pretext did the US and Britain launch the Iraq War?
2. Why do you think that the writer says "the international scepticism engendered by manipulation of the evidence on WMD has hampered efforts to deal with nuclear threats … North Korea"?
3. Why does the writer say that Iraqi people are not the winner?
4. Who really profits from the Iraq War? Can you just name a few?
5. Why do you think that oil price rose rapidly during the Iraq War and the US military occupation in Iraq?
6. What is the relationship between the biggest contract winners and the party in power?

语言解说

Political Donation/Contribution

本课第 16 段出现的 political donation 或下面例句中的 political contribution 值得探讨,因为其可作不同意义讲。如下例(1)出于本课课文。

(1) Many of the biggest contract winners have extensive lobbying budgets and funds for targeting **political donations.** Public records show that BearingPoint, the consulting firm appointed to advise on the economic reconstruction of Iraq, has paid hundreds of thousands of dollars into Republican Party coffers, including $117,000 to the two Bush presidential campaigns. The company is being paid $240m for its work in Iraq, winning an initial

contract from the US Agency for International Development (USAID) within weeks of the fall of Saddam. It was charged with supporting the then Coalition Provisional Authority to introduce policies "which are designed to create a competitive private sector".

本段难点都在课文后作了注释,关键在于"political donations"如何理解。下面不妨再看两例:
(2) The seven ruling and opposition politicians admitted to conceiving as much as $57,000 from Hanbo, but claimed the money was a proper **political contribution**. Prosecutors charged the money was a bribe, punishable by as many as 10 years in prison. (*The Asian Wall Street Journal*)
(3) Seven politicians acknowledged in court that they received money from Hanbo Steel Industry Co., but said it was in the form of legitimate **political donations**. (*The Asian Wall Street Journal*)

第(1)例报道的是 BearingPoint 这个咨询公司从美国开发署获得了 2.4 亿美元合同,其中几十万美元都入了共和党金库,单布什两次竞选总统就给了 11.7 万美元捐款。2002 年美国竞选改革法出台后,soft money(给政党的捐款)被取缔后,无限捐款就被视为非法(现在合法,最高法院裁定,公司和个人可以给候选人无限额限制的捐款,比 soft money 有过之而无不及,这真是金钱政治,富人游戏)。这就是说,political donations 在此处指的是正当"竞选捐款"。但上述官商勾结很难取证和被起诉。

(2)和(3)两例报道的是同一件事,有 7 名执政党和反对党政界人士承认从 Hanbo 钢铁公司收受了多达 5.7 万英镑的 political contribution/donations,自认为合法,但检察官可不这么看,指控他们是受贿,可判其长达 10 年徒刑。这里,在判决结果公布前我们在理解或翻译时就犯难了。如理解为"campaign contribution/donations"(竞选捐款),且数目没有超过法律规定的限额,那就是合法的。但如果译为"政治献金",那就是指像台湾前领导人陈水扁式受贿,或有的国家官员买官卖官的行为。当然,上述两例中检察官肯定认为是"政治献金",以使这些官员能在立法的兴废、政策规章的制定上为该公司谋利。

所以"竞选捐款"和"政治献金"是两个意义完全不同的概念,但都属"政治"这个范畴。

Unit Six
Britain

Lesson Seventeen

课 文 导 读

　　玛格丽特·撒切尔是英国保守党第一位女领袖,英国历史上第一位女首相,她创造了蝉联三届,雄踞政坛11年之久的记录,她始终不渝奉行强硬的保守派政策,被媒体喻为"铁娘子"。
　　在任英国首相期间,撒切尔大刀阔斧地进行改革。她主要采取四项措施:一是私有化,二是控制货币供应量,三是削减福利开支,四是打击工会力量。这一系列措施至今仍然影响着这个国家。
　　然而,读了此课,人们不觉感到这不但不像悼词,而是一篇声讨她的檄文。北爱尔兰新芬党党魁、工会和中右派都加入谴责她的队伍,而《卫报》此文也基本上支持他们的立场。客观地说,她从上台时把一个欧洲病夫的英国拯救出来是有功的,打击和压制工会也是有种种理由的。但她助富不济贫和极端自由派的经济政策是错误的。工党领袖布莱尔(Tony Blair)在1997年至2007年执政时基本上继承了她的经济政策,也执政达10年之久,所以我们要对她的功过加以分析,不被一人、一文的言论所左右。

Pre-reading Questions
1. Who is Margaret Thatcher, and what do you know about her?
2. Why is Mrs Thatcher called the "Iron Lady"?

Text

Little Sympathy for Margaret Thatcher[1] among Former Opponents
Anger and regret rekindled in those who still feel that Thatcherism[2] ruined their lives and wrecked their communities
By Michael White

1　　In death, as she had been in life, Margaret Thatcher proved to be a deeply divisive figure, with former opponents vocal in their criticism of her on Monday.

Margaret Thatcher at Selby coalfield in 1980. Photograph: PA

2   To no one's surprise, news of her death prompted expressions of satisfaction and even delight on social media. "May she burn in hell fires," tweeted George Galloway, who also quoted an Elvis Costello protest song, "Tramp the dirt down."[3]

3   The Sinn Fein president, Gerry Adams[4], was among the first to react, offering a scathing assessment of Thatcher's political legacy. He said she had done "great hurt to the Irish and British people during her time as British prime minister. Here in Ireland her espousal of old draconian militaristic policies prolonged the war[5] and caused great suffering."

4   No amount of genuine dismay at such sentiments within the rival family of Thatcher admirers—those new mobile classes of the skilled and the newly rich identified by the BBC's social survey only last week—or Fleet Street's synthetic finger-pointing could inhibit the toasts and cheers[6]. Some people claim to have kept champagne bottles in the fridge for the occasion for decades.

5   Any satisfaction that Britain's first female prime minister—and their personal enemy—is dead mingled with burning anger and regrets rekindled in those who still feel that Thatcherism ruined their lives and wrecked their communities. The further north, the more visible it was among people who felt she cared nothing for them, their skills or values or for a slower, gentler world. In Scotland her legacy has crippled the

Tory[7] vote and may contribute to the breakup of Britain, one of many ironies for her own declared values.

6   David Hopper, general secretary of the Durham Miners Association[8], now a shadow of its once mighty self, in part thanks to Thatcher's defeat of the miners union[9], spoke for millions—the white-collar teachers and clerical workers, nurses and bus drivers as well as former industrial workers—who blamed Thatcher for the loss of livelihoods that globalisation and technology might have taken anyway, but without her blunt coup de grace[10].

7   "It looks like one of the best birthdays I have ever had," said the ex-miner, 70 on Monday, who spent all of his working life at Wearmouth colliery[11]. "There's no sympathy from me for what she did to our community. She destroyed our community, our villages and our people. For the union this could not come soon enough and I'm pleased that I have outlived her."

8   Thatcher supporters will recoil from such sentiments as unfair and blind to economic realities and the selfish, sectional stranglehold then exercised by unions on behalf of their members. In 1979 it could take several months to obtain a phone—a landline installed by a state monopoly, the Post Office.

9   But such talk will not sway the likes of Hopper. "I imagine we will have a counter-demonstration when they have her funeral," he said.

10   "Our children have got no jobs and the community is full of problems. There's no work and no money and it's very sad the legacy she has left behind. She absolutely hated working people and I have got very bitter memories of what she did. She turned all the nation against us and the violence that was meted out[12] on us was terrible. I would say to those people who want to mourn her that they're lucky she did not treat them like she treated us."

11   It was Thatcher's misfortune that her insights were not tempered with much sympathetic imagination for people unlike herself—"is he one of us?" in the famous phrase—or by humour or emollient wit, by homely style or evident personal weakness.[13] She had tender feelings (her staff liked her), but rarely let them show in public until that last tear[14] after her party ejected her from power with a crude, male brutality she had not expected.

12 Even among the party faithful it made her more admired than loved. On holiday among friends the restless workaholic was not easy company. Among those she worsted in political battles it all made it much easier to hate her. Few prime ministers in Britain have been burned in effigy[15].

13 The gay rights campaigner Peter Tatchell[16] said Thatcher was "an extraordinary woman but she was extraordinary for mostly the wrong reasons. During her rule, arrests and convictions for consenting same-sex behaviour rocketed, as did queer-bashing[17] violence and murder. Gay men were widely demonised and scapegoated for the Aids pandemic and Thatcher did nothing to challenge this vilification."

14 Ken Livingstone[18] also offered a critical assessment. He blamed Thatcher for causing unemployment and leaving people dependent on welfare: "She decided when she wrote off[19] our manufacturing industry that she could live with two or three million unemployed," he said. (From *The Guardian*, April 8, 2013)

New Words

blunt /blʌnt/ adj. (of people, manner of speaking, etc.) lacking refinement or subtlety; straightforward and uncomplicated

colliery /ˈkɒliəri/ n. BrE a coal mine and the buildings around it 煤矿

consent /kənˈsent/ v. to give your permission for sth or agree to do sth

demonise /ˈdiːmənaɪz/ v. to convince sb that a person or thing is evil 将……妖魔化

dismay /dɪsˈmeɪ/ n. the worry, disappointment, or unhappiness you feel when sth unpleasant happens 哀伤

divisive /dɪˈvaɪsɪv/ adj. causing a lot of disagreement between people 引起分裂的,造成不和的

draconian /drəˈkəʊniən/ adj. very strict and cruel(法律等)严酷的,残酷的

effigy /ˈefɪdʒi/ n. a roughly made, usu. ugly, model of sb you dislike 肖像,画像

eject /ɪˈdʒekt/ v. to force sb to leave

emollient /ɪˈmɒliənt/ adj. making sb feel calmer when they have been angry 安抚的;抚慰的

espousal /ɪˈspaʊzl/ n. support for an idea, belief, etc., esp. a political one

finger-pointing *n.* the imputation of blame 相互指责
landline /ˈlændlaɪn/ *n.* telephone that is not a cell phone 固定电话，座机
militaristic /ˌmɪlɪtəˈrɪstɪk/ *adj.* (of groups, ideas, or policies) which support the strengthening of the armed forces of their country in order to make it more powerful 军国主义的
mingle /ˈmɪŋgl/ *v.* to bring or combine together or with sth else
monopoly /məˈnɒpəlɪ/ *n.* a large company that controls all or most of a business activity 垄断
outlive /ˌaʊtˈlɪv/ *v.* to remain alive after sb. else has died 比……长寿
pandemic /pænˈdemɪk/ *n.* a disease that affects people over a very large area or the whole world 传染病
recoil /rɪˈkɒɪl/ *v.* to move back suddenly and quickly from sth you dislike or are frightened of 退缩，畏缩
rekindle /ˌriːˈkɪndl/ *v.* to make someone have a particular feeling, thought etc. again 使重新激起
scathing /ˈskeɪðɪŋ/ *adj.* (of a remark) bitterly severe
stranglehold /ˈstræŋglhəʊld/ *n.* complete control over a situation, organization etc.
sway /sweɪ/ *v.* to influence sb so that they change their opinion 动摇
temper /ˈtempə(r)/ *v. fml* to make sth less severe or extreme 调和，使缓和
tweet /twiːt/ *v.* to post (a message) on Twitter for (people) to read
vilification /ˌvɪlɪfɪˈkeɪʃn/ *n.* a rude expression intended to offend or hurt 诋毁；诽谤；中伤
vocal /ˈvəʊkl/ *adj.* inclined to express oneself in words, esp. forcefully or insistently 直言不讳的
worst /wɜːst/ *v.* to defeat thoroughly

Notes

1. Margaret Thatcher—1925—2013, a British Prime Minister (1979—1990), Leader of the Conservative Party (1975—1990). She was the longest-serving British Prime Minister of the 20th century and the only woman to have held the office. 玛格丽特·撒切尔之所以在1990年被迫辞职是因为她在外交上对欧盟的前身欧共体(European Community)不合作和在国内执行的不分财富和收入一律按比例交人头税(poll tax)的问题上不得人心，党内不满而引起分裂，不得不将权

交给她不喜欢的梅杰(John Major)。

2. Thatcherism—the system of political thought attributed to the governments of Margaret Thatcher. It is characterized by decreased state intervention via the free market economy, monetarist(以货币为基础的) economic policy, privatisation of state-owned industries, lower direct taxation and higher indirect taxation, opposition to trade unions, and a reduction of the size of the Welfare State. 撒切尔主义是指撒切尔夫人上台后所推行的一套强硬的右翼政治、经济等政策，是当代西方"新自由主义"与"新保守主义"的混合物。如经济私有化，削减政府开支以减少赤字，控制货币供应量以降低通货膨胀率，大量限制工会权利等。她的这套政策使富人愈富，穷人愈穷，穷人的生活被毁掉了，各方面均无保障。此外，她与美国总统里根对经济不干预的极端自由派政策导致2008年后出现全球性经济危机和衰退。

3. "May she burn in hell fires"..."Tramp the dirt down"—George Galloway cursed Margaret Thatcher after her death that she would go to hell to be burned for her sins. And in Elvis Costello's song, "I'll stand on your (Thatcher's) grave and tramp the dirt down," he expressed his anger.

  a. George Galloway—1954— , a British politician, author, journalist, and broadcaster, and the Respect Party Member of Parliament (MP) for Bradford West. 乔治·加洛韦

  b. Elvis Costello—1954— , an English musician and singer-songwriter with Irish ancestry. 埃尔维斯·科斯特洛

  c. "Tramp the dirt down"—a fiery lament(哀悼词), depicting Costello's anger at the Thatcher government and its effect on Britain's society. In the song, Costello expresses his desire to live long enough to see Margaret Thatcher die and vows, "I'll stand on your grave and tramp the dirt down."

4. the Sinn Fein president, Gerry Adams—新芬党领袖格里·亚当斯

  a. the Sinn Fein—the second-largest political party and the largest nationalist party in Northern Ireland. 爱尔兰民族主义政党。成立于1905年，建党之初，党员成分复杂，政见也较温和。它反对与英国妥协，主张依靠自己的力量谋求独立。英政界认为，它实际是爱尔兰共和军(IRA)的政治组织。新芬(Sinn Fein)英文意为"we ourselfves"。

  b. Gerry Adams—an Irish Sinn Fein politician, the President of

Sinn Fein since 1983

5. the war—指英国政府与爱尔兰那时一直在谈判北爱尔兰的地位归属问题,爱尔兰主张与爱统一,英却坚持由北爱全民公决,因北爱支持留在英国的新教徒占多数。支持统一的武装组织北爱尔兰共和军(Irish Republican Army)代表天主教徒早在 20 世纪 50 年代就为统一而展开斗争,暴力不断。僵持不下时,英国就派军队镇压和维持秩序。IRA 的暴力行动一度渗透到英国,直至 1997 年 9 月 15 日它才最终宣布停火,采用政治手段达到目的。Adams 指的 war 外刊普遍用 troubles, violence, terrorist attack, terrorism 等字眼。

6. No amount of genuine dismay... or Fleet Street's synthetic finger-pointing... could inhibit the toasts and cheers. —no matter how sad people were, (such sadness) could not prevent some people from their celebration.

　　a. no amount of sth can/will do sth—used to say that sth has no effect on sth 再多……也不

　　b. Fleet Street—a street in the City of London named after the River Fleet. It was the home of British national newspapers until the 1980s. Even though the last major British news office, Reuters, left in 2005. The term Fleet Street continues to be used as a metonym for the British national press.

　　c. synthetic finger-pointing—insincere criticism or blame

7. Tory—*adj.* of the Conservative / Tory Party (*cf* the Tories)

8. the Durham Miners Association—a trade union in the U. K., founded in 1869 达拉谟矿工协会

9. Thatcher's defeat of the miners union—The Thatcher Government gradually reduced the power of the trades unions, and the greatest single confrontation with the unions was the NUM (National Union of Mineworkers) strike of 1984 to 1985, in which the union eventually had to concede(退让). Both Thatcher's approach to industrial relations(劳资关系) and the behaviour of the trades unions in the 1970s accelerated the departure from the British tradition of voluntarism (based on contract law, 唯意志论), bringing more and more aspects of labour relations into the sphere of government. 她打击和限制工会是因其好斗,动辄罢工,曾迫使过首相下台;是工党的坚定支柱。使它不得翻身,工党也因此在野 10 多年而不得掌权。

10. but without her blunt coup de grace—if she had not given a direct strike

coup de grace—a hit or shot that kills sb or sth 致命的一击, 决定性的一击

11. Wearmouth colliery—a major North Sea coal mine located on the north bank of the River Wear（威尔河）, located in Sunderland（巽得兰）. It was the largest mine in Sunderland and one of the most important in County Durham（达拉谟郡）in northeast England. 威尔茅斯煤矿

12. mete out—*fml* to give sb, esp. a punishment（给予[惩罚]）

13. It was Thatcher's misfortune... by homely style or evident personal weakness. —对于撒切尔来说, 不幸的是她的远见毫不温和, 不带有对与她不同的人的同情, ——比如, 她的口头禅"他是我们的人吗？"——不幽默、没有抚慰人心的智慧, 不亲切、没有表现出人性的软弱。

"is he one of us?"—a phrase derived from Thatcher's Conservative Party Conference speech（Thatcher brooked [容忍] little criticism. She sacked party members who questioned her divisive practices. "Is he one of us?" became a stock [常备的] Thatcher question, asked of impartial civil servants [公务员] and even would-be bishops [主教].）

14. She.... rarely let them show in public until that last tear—她几乎从不将她柔情的一面示之与众, 直到她辞职时, 她才潸然泪下。1990年11月22日, 撒切尔夫人发表声明决定退出党魁选举, 这个决定使她长达11年半的首相生涯步上终结。

15. burned in effigy—（Thatcher's）portrait is damaged or destroyed by fire.

16. Peter Tatchell—1952— , an Australian-born British political campaigner best known for his work with LGBT（lesbian, gay, bisexual and transgender 同性恋、双性恋及变性者）social movements. 彼得·泰切尔

17. queer-bashing—an offensive term for the practice or an instance of committing unprovoked acts of violence against gay and lesbian people 酷儿打压（即打压同性恋）。"酷儿"（queer）由英文音译而来, 原是西方主流文化对同性恋的贬称, 有"怪异"之意。

18. Ken Livingstone—1945— , a British Labour Party politician. Livingstone has positioned himself on the hard left of the Labour Party. 肯·利文斯通

19. write off—to cancel; regard as cancelled or useless

Questions

1. After hearing of Mrs Thatcher's death, how did the media react?
2. How did Gerry Adams comment on Mrs Thatcher's political legacy?
3. What did David Hopper think of Mrs Thatcher's policies?
4. How do the party faithful feel about Mrs Thatcher?
5. How did Ken Livingstone think of Mrs Thatcher?
6. What do you think about Mrs Thatcher?

读报知识

英国政党简介

翻开英国近代史，人们可以看到，政府都由保守党和工党轮流执掌或联合执掌。两党制根深蒂固，第三党受到选举等限制难以壮大。

1. 工党和新工党

工党(the Labour Party)成立于1900年，原名"劳工代表委员会"，1906年改用现名。第二次世界大战至2008年，工党已联合或单独组阁7次，是保守党的主要对手。它曾标榜"社会主义"，主张通过"议会斗争"和"议会民主"方式进行改革。虽然工党党员大部分是工人，但领导人的行动和政治策略也代表富裕资产阶级的利益。工党原先一贯主张扩大国有化，限制资本外流。对外政策强调"国家利益"。自1979年以来工党一直在野，已在4次大选中败给保守党。英报认为，该党政策正在向右转，与撒切尔夫人推行的一些做法相似。后来改革派领袖史密斯出任领袖，1994年5月，正值声望上升之时，史密斯猝然去世。这样，工党又陷入了内部权力斗争，保守党获得急需的喘息机会。直至1995年以改革家著称的布莱尔(Tony Blair)出任该党领袖，并在1997年的大选中击败保守党，改写了该党在野18年的历史。

工党的胜利靠的是布莱尔的"走第三条道路"(the third way)和改旧工党为"新工党"(New Labour)。与此同时，布莱尔改革党章，放弃了党章第四条国有化的条款(Clause Four)。

2007年，布莱尔因在伊拉克开战等问题上追随美国，结果吃了大亏，声誉扫地，国内问题也不如意，被迫将首相一职交给财政大臣布朗(Gordon Brown)。由于经济不振，该党在2010年大选中败北。为省略，报刊常用Labour(工党)，如Labour's plan。

2. 保守党

保守党(the Conservative Party)的前身为1679年成立的托利党(the Tory Party)，1833年改称保守党。1912年国家统一党并入保守党，称保守统一党(The Conservative and Unionist Party)，简称保守党。为省略，报刊常用 the Tories 或 the Conservatives(保守党)。在力量占优势的选区扎根深，自身又较能抑制内阁，屡次大选击败工党，从1951年至1964年和1979年至1997年曾长期执政。从不公布党员人数，据估计为180万左右，大多来自社会上层。保守党代表英国垄断资本家、大地主和贵族的利益。

1979年撒切尔夫人执政，大力推行"货币主义"经济政策(monetarist financial policies)，通过严格控制货币供应量和减少公共开支等手段控制通货膨胀。反对削减个人所得税，主张加强法律和社会治安，限制工会权力，加速私有化，将某些国有企业恢复为私营，有走极端市场经济倾向。对外主张加强防务，增加军费，加强与欧盟前身欧洲共同体各国的合作，协调外交政策和欧美立场，加强大西洋联盟，尤其强调英美的"特殊关系"。

撒一意孤行，推行不分财富和收入多寡，一律按比例交税的人头税(poll tax)失去民心而被迫下台。

1990年梅杰接班上台，内外政策均有所调整。但因爆发"疯牛病"(mad-cow disease)跟欧洲联盟的关系紧张，党内又纷争不断，不如当年一致对外，加之梅杰能力平庸，政绩乏善可陈。结果在1997年大选中被工党击败。2010年大选，该党在下院650个席位中获306席，稍多于工党的258席，未能过半，现任领袖卡梅伦(David Cameron)不得不与自民党组成联合内阁，出任首相。

3. 自由民主党

自由民主党(the Liberal Democrats 或 the Liberal Democrat Party)常简称 Lib Dems(自民党)，是自由派的政党，英国第三大党。1988年由自由党和社会民主党内多数派组成，正式名称为社会自由民主党(the Social and Liberal Democrats)。该党实力尚不如保守党和工党，但很有前途。Nick Clegg任该党领袖，现在联合政府中任副首相。在2010年大选中仅在国家议会(Parliament)中占有57席。(详见《导读》英国"政党")

Lesson Eighteen

> 课文导读

从常规衡量标准看,英国的报纸衰落了。自 20 世纪 80 年代中期起,英国出版的《每日快报》和《每日镜报》的发行量已锐减三分之二,年轻人因为电视和网络而摒弃了报纸,报纸衰亡似乎无可避免。事实真是如此吗?本文独特的分析告诉我们一个恰好相反的动态:四面楚歌的英国报纸正引领世界报业革新。其实纸质和电子报纸各有千秋。

Pre-reading Questions

1. Do you often read newspapers? If you do, do you prefer a printed paper or an electronic one?
2. What do you think is the key reason for young readers to abandon regular newspapers?

Text

Britain's Embattled Newspapers Are Leading the World in Innovation

1　　By most conventional measures, Britain's newspapers look doomed. Young readers are abandoning them for the Internet and television. The *Daily Express* and the *Daily Mirror*, both tabloids, have shed about two-thirds of their circulation since the mid-1980s. Yet Evgeny Lebedev[1], co-owner of the *Independent* and the *Evening Standard*, is optimistic. "People are hailing the death of newspapers," he says. "But if you go into the Tube[2], you'll see almost everybody is reading one."

2 Britain's newspaper market is the world's most savage. It is unusually competitive: there are nine national daily papers with a circulation of more than 200,000. And advertising has migrated online more quickly than elsewhere. Since 2009 more advertising money has been spent on the Internet than on newspapers, according to ZenithOptimedia[3], a marketer. British papers receive no government funding (as is the case in France, for example). Indeed, they face a fearsome state-sanctioned competitor in the BBC[4].

3 Fierce competition has created a scrappy, sometimes immoral trade. This week the *News of the World*, a tabloid that has been caught up in a celebrity phone-hacking scandal, revealed it had suspended an editor. But Britain's papers are also exceptionally innovative, busily testing new format sizes and prices. Paul Zwillenberg of Boston Consulting Group[5] says they are now experimenting in dramatically different directions. There are three main trends.

4 The first is being driven from Wapping, London home of News Corporation. Its four British titles—the *Times*, the *Sunday Times*, the *Sun* and the *News of the World*—are moving behind an exceptionally tough online paywall.[6] Unlike the *Wall Street Journal*, also owned by News Corporation, the *Times* does not allow people to read any articles free on the web. Its prices are steep: £2 ($3.10) per week after the first month.

Not worth the paper they aren't reading

5 As online commentators and rivals have gleefully pointed out, News Corporation's paywalls have led to a drastic drop in traffic. A survey by Mark Oliver, a consultant, finds that only 14% of regular *Times* readers and just 1% of non-regular ones subscribe to the website in some form: upon hitting the paywall, most head for the BBC's free website instead. That does not worry News Corporation. It sees online

advertising as an unreliable source of revenue. Online ad spending is growing, but the number of ad slots available is rising much faster; as a result, prices are so low that a reader who visits a website once or twice a month is hardly worth having. The firm would rather extract more money from dedicated readers directly.

6   Thus the pages of the *Times* and *Sunday Times* are thick with in-house ads offering entertainments to readers, from iPad applications to theatre tickets and Italian holidays. Some 250,000 people buy from the *Times* wine club. These things tend to make money, but the main goal is to hook readers on a bundle of services. Katie Vanneck-Smith, chief marketing officer for News Corporation's British papers, wants to get to the point where a newspaper subscription is like its pay-television or mobile-phone equivalents: something it hurts to cancel. Rivals fear the firm will bundle newspapers with BskyB[7], a hugely successful satellite broadcaster that it controls and wants to take over completely.

7   Britain's second great innovator takes the opposite view. The *Daily Mail* contends that online advertising works fine—if you are huge. The paper has been one of the most consistent sellers in print over the past few years, crushing its nearest competitor, the *Daily Express*. But it is even mightier online. With 35m unique visitors each month, it is now the world's second-biggest newspaper website, according to comScore[8], which measures online traffic[9]. It may take the top spot[10] when the *New York Times* goes behind a paywall this year.

8   In contrast to the paper, which is conservative and often alarmist, the *Daily Mail*'s website is a breezy read. It is big on celebrity news, particularly reports involving attractive women in swimsuits. Lots of online news aggregators link to it. Executives claim that the website is now so successful that it competes not with other newspaper websites but with portals such as Yahoo! and MSN.com. The *Mail* is now steering readers to its iPhone application.

9   Perhaps the most counter-intuitive strategy is being pursued by Mr Lebedev and his father, Alexander, a Russian tycoon. In the past two years they have acquired the *Independent* and the *Evening Standard*, a London paper that they have made a freebie. In October they launched *i*, a cut-down *Independent*, priced at 20p—one-fifth the price of most quality daily newspapers. It is the first new national paper since 1986.

10   Not one of the Lebedevs' British papers has a compelling website. They think young people do want to read newspapers—they just don't want to pay much, or anything, for them. The *Evening Standard*'s circulation has more than doubled since going free, to 700,000. Distribution costs have plunged. Papers are now handed out in central London and moved around the capital by Tube; because they are free, commuters often leave them on trains.

11   The *Independent* and *i* face a harder road. Because *i* is so cheap, newsagents make little money from sales. They often shelve it with bottom-feeding tabloids and the *Racing Post*. Yet *i* is an intriguing effort to prop up the *Independent*, which was nearing the point at which marketers were losing interest; now advertising often runs in both papers, which together offer a higher circulation. It costs little to assemble and may help keep alive the newspaper habit, by offering a halfway house[11] between free and premium papers.

12   The strategies being pursued by News Corporation, the Daily Mail and General Trust[12] and Lebedev Holdings rest on distinct assumptions about what readers want, what they will pay for, and the future of advertising. It is highly unlikely that all three experiments will work. It may well be that none of them does. But none can be faulted for lack of boldness.

13   The innovators also exude more confidence than others. The *Guardian*, which first championed a big, free online presence, has been overhauled by the *Mail*'s website.[13] It lacks News Corporation's expertise in bundling and is far more expensively staffed than the Lebedevs' outfits. It is a measure of how quickly things are moving that the newspaper closest to the cutting edge[14] a few years ago now seems most in need of a new strategy. (From *The Economist*, Jan 6, 2011)

New Words

aggregator /'ægrɪgeɪtə/ n. 聚合器（一种信息处理工具）
alarmist /ə'lɑːmɪst/ adj. making people feel worried about dangers that may or may not really exist
bottom-feeding /'bɒtəmˌfiːdɪŋ/ adj. sl. well-sold, widely required by readers
breezy /'briːzɪ/ adj. fresh and animated; lively 清新的，活泼的
bundle /'bʌndl/ n. a number of articles tied, fastened, or held together
v. to sell several products or services together, package

slae 捆绑销售

celebrity /sɪˈlebrəti/ *n.* a famous person, esp. in the entertainment sector 演艺界名人

circulation /ˌsɜːkjʊˈleɪʃən/ *n.* the average number of copies of a newspaper, magazine etc that are regularly sold(报刊等的)发行量

contend /kənˈtend/ *v.* to claim; say or state strongly 宣称

equivalent /ɪˈkwɪvələnt/ *n.* sth that has the same value, purpose, job etc as sth else 类似,同样

exude /ɪɡˈzjuːd/ *v.* if you exude a particular quality, it is easy to see that you have a lot of it 充满,洋溢,充分显露(某一品质)

format /ˈfɔːmæt/ *n.* the size, shape, design etc, in which sth. such as a book or magazine, is produced 格式,样式

freebie /ˈfriːbiː/ *n. infml* sth. that you are given free, usu. by a company 免费赠品

gleeful /ˈɡliːfəl/ *adj.* very excited and satisfied

in-house /ˈɪnˈhaʊs/ *adj. & adv.* working within a company or organization 内勤

outfit /ˈaʊtfɪt/ *n. infml* a group of people who work together as a team or organization 整体(形象)

overhaul /ˈəʊvəhɔːl/ *v.* to catch up with; overtake

paywall /ˈpeɪˌwɔːl/ *n.* a program that stops people who have not paid a subscription from using a website 网站的收费墙

plunge /plʌndʒ/ *v.* if a price, rate etc. plunges, it suddenly decreases by a large amount 下跌,颓市

portal /ˈpɔːtl/ *n.* a website that helps you find other websites 门户网站

premium /ˈpriːmiəm/ *adj.* of very high quality

scrappy /ˈskræpɪ/ *adj. BrE* untidy or badly organized; *AmE infml* having a determined character and always willing to compete, argue, or fight 不整,零乱;好斗

shed /ʃed/ *v.* to drop sth or allow it to fall; to lose by natural process 放手,让其倒,下

slot /slɒt/ *n.* a short period of time allowed for one particular event on a program or timetable(广告)位,时段

steep /stiːp/ *adj.* steep prices, charges etc are unusually expensive; involving a big increase or decrease 急剧升降的(价格)

subscribe /səbˈskraɪb/ *v.* to pay money, usu. once a year, to have copies of a newspaper or magazine delivered to you, or to purchase some other service 订阅

suspend /sə'spend/ v. to officially stop sth from continuing, esp. for a short time

tabloid /'tæblɔɪd/ n. a newspaper that has small pages, a lot of photographs, and stories mainly about sex, famous people etc., rather than serious news; tabloid newspaper 小报(cf. broadsheet)

traffic /'træfɪk/ n. number of people or amount of goods moved from one place to another by road, rail, sea or air(公路、铁路、海上或空中人员或货物的)流量

tycoon /taɪ'ku:n/ n. one who is successful in business or industry and has a lot of money and power 产业大亨

Notes

1. Evgeny Alexandrovich Lebedev—叶夫根尼·列别捷夫(1980—), the Russian-born British co-owner of the *Independent* and the *Evening Standard*. Under Lebedev's tenure (任期), the *Evening Standard* became the first large-circulation newspaper in Britain to be distributed free, its circulation tripling to 600,000 copies. Lebedev is a supporter of the Arts and chairman of the Evening Standard Theatre Awards. He is a sponsor of the Moscow Art Theatre (莫斯科艺术剧院) and the Anton ChekhovYalta Theatre (安东尼·契科夫雅尔塔剧院). He is also the founder and chairman of the Raisa Gorbachev Foundation(赖萨·戈尔巴乔夫基金会).

2. The Tube—The London Underground, a metro system in the UK, serving a large part of Greater London and some parts of Buckinghamshire (白金汉郡), Hertfordshire (赫特福德郡) and Essex (艾塞克斯郡).

3. ZenithOptimedia—a French multinational advertising and public relations company, headquartered in Paris, France. It is one of the world's three largest advertising holding companies (控股公司). Its current president is Maurice Lévy. The company owns several full-service advertising groups that undertake a range of media activities: mobile and interactive online communication, television, magazines & newspapers, cinema and radio, and outdoor ads. 实力媒体

4. a fearsome state-sanctioned competitor in the BBC—a competitor which is given official approval and so is very powerful and frightening. BBC is just such a competitor.

5. The Boston Consulting Group—a global management consulting firm with 78 offices in 43 countries. It is one of the largest private companies in the US. 波士顿咨询公司
6. The first is being driven from Wapping... an exceptionally tough online paywall. 第一种趋势源自新闻集团驻伦敦办事处——沃平，它旗下四份报纸——《泰晤士报》、《星期日泰晤士报》、《太阳报》和《世界新闻》，正移至特别强大的网站收费墙之后。

   News Corporation—a diversified multinational mass media corporation headquartered in New York City, the world's second-largest media group as of 2011 in terms of revenue, and the world's third largest in entertainment as of 2009, controlled by Rupert Murdoch and his family members. Its U.S. holdings include Fox News, *The Wall Street Journal* and Twentieth Century Fox. 新闻集团
7. BSkyB—British Sky Broadcasting Group, a British satellite broadcasting, broadband and telephone services company headquartered in London, with operations in the UK and Republic of Ireland, formed in 1990 by the equal merger of Sky Television and British Satellite Broadcasting, the largest pay-TV broadcaster in Britain and Ireland with over 10 million subscribers. It had a market capitalisation of approximately £11.47 billion (US $18 billion) as of 20 June 2012 on the London Stock Exchange. News Corporation owns a 39.14 per cent controlling stake in the company. 英国天空广播公司
8. comScore—an Internet analytics company providing marketing data and analytics to many of the world's largest enterprises, agencies, and publishers. ComScore Networks was founded in August 1999 in Reston, Virginia. 康姆斯克互联网公司
9. online traffic—the flow of data across the Internet 浏览量
10. top spot—top of the list 顶尖，第一
11. halfway house—Usually, it refers to a place where people with mental disorders, victims of child abuse, orphans or teenage runaways can stay. However, a halfway house more usually refers to something combining features of two other things, for example a solution to a problem based on two ideas. 收容所；折中的解决方法
12. The Daily Mail and General Trust—a British media conglomerate (传媒集团), one of the largest in Europe. In the UK, it has interests in national and regional newspapers, television and radio.

The company has extensive activities based outside the UK. Its biggest markets apart from the UK are in the US, Central Europe, the Middle East, India and Australia. The head office is located in the Northcliffe House in Kensington, London Borough of Kensington and Chelsea. 每日邮报集团

13. The *Guardian*, which first... by the *Mail*'s website.——The *Guardian* was the first to publish its free online edition, which was very popular, but now the *Daily Mail*'s website is more popular.
14. the cutting edge——the most recent stage of development in a particular type of work or activity 最前沿,先锋地位

Questions

1. Why is Britain's newspaper market considered the world's most savage?
2. Do online paywalls do good to Britain's embattled newspapers? Why or why not?
3. Why is News Corporation's main goal to hook readers by means of a bundle of services?
4. How could the *Daily Mail*'s website be successful?
5. What are the three main trends of innovation in Britain's newspapers?

学习方法

读懂标题（Ⅰ）

　　报刊标题（Headline）常用的有主题、副题、插题、引题、提要题等几种形式,不过现在趋向于只采用主标题。一般说来,英美报刊标题,突出"点",一语中的;中文报刊标题照顾"面",面面俱到。两者各有千秋,区别较大。标题是新闻也是报刊的"眼睛"。应该生动、炯炯有神,引人入胜;反之,索然无味,无人愿看。它是新闻内容的高度概括,犹如提纲挈领,画龙点睛。

　　标题读不懂,就看副标题或提要。有一篇文章标题是"The Greening of America"（1996/2/12 U. S. News & World Report）。乍一看,greening 费解,subheadline 是"This year, candidates will spend more money than ever buying your votes"。这样就明白了,"greening"此处指"dollar or money"。这两个标题对了解下面课文内容起到了纲举目张的作用。读懂标题须掌握其语言上的主要特点;了解背景知识;具有文学功底。

一、标题语言上的主要特点

1. 缩略词

标题要简短而不得不使用缩略词(Abbreviations and Acronyms),汉语标题也有此特点。

(1) 机构。报刊中常用政治、军事、经济、文化、教育等重要机构的简称,如:

a. **EU'S** Future: The Vision and the Slog
   EU = European Union(欧洲联盟)
b. World Bank, **IMF**—Do They Help Or Hurt Third World
   IMF = International Monetary Fund
c. **MIT**'s Leader Shape Program
   MIT = Massachusetts Institute of Technology(麻省理工学院)

为了快速读懂新闻标题,有必要熟悉一些"重要国际组织(Important International organizations)名称缩写"如 G8,ASEAN(东盟)等。

(2) 除机构的首字母缩略词外,标题也常用其他形式的缩短词(shortening word),如:

a. No Hope for 118 Crew of Russian **Sub**
   Sub = submarine
b. University Entry Hard for Would-be **Vets**
   Vet = Veteran(退伍老兵)
c. Put the **Sci** Back in **Sci-fi**
   sci = science;fi = fiction 必须注意,缩短词的拼法是固定的,不能随意乱造。

2. 短字

标题爱用常见的短字(short word),是报刊用语的一个特点。如:

a. The **Gems** of War
   用"gems"不用"jewels"
b. Dayton **Accord**, Reached
   用"accord"不用"agreements"
c. Carter Man in China
   用"man"不用"representative"

读者一定见过这些词汇,但用在标题上,或许不一定知道其中如 man 和 accord 的意思。编者建议,初学者应该读记 Terry Fredrickson & Paul Wedel 合写的 *English by Newspaper* 和 Janice Abbott 写的 *Meet the Press* 这两本书里的 The Vocabulary of Headlines(报刊标题词汇一览)里的标题词汇,这对看懂标题和正文大有裨益。(详见《导读》四章一节)

Lesson Nineteen

课文导读

2013年6月4日是英国女王伊丽莎白二世登基60周年纪念日。一方面,英国王室代表着英国的国家象征,是民族精神的图腾。但在另一方面,王室成员并非圣贤,以往绯闻不断。自20世纪初至第二次世界大战后,英国国力日趋衰弱,国际地位下降,曾经的"日不落帝国"——大英帝国已经瓦解而不复存在,但不少英国人的帝国情结依旧,而女王的存在确实给这些人提供了一种精神支柱。然而,质疑声也此起彼伏,君主制是否有存在的必要?其保留与废除究竟对英国意味着什么?女王还受到国民的爱戴吗?英国在17世纪曾实行过共和制,但并未能延续下去,这说明英国人并非不喜欢君主制,只是要求其进行改革而已。现在女王威望极高,主张共和的人压根儿没戏,请看本文是如何评论的。

这篇共和制与君主制之争的评论论古道今,以事实说话。通过此文,读者可以学到一些英国历史知识,了解英国人为何至今仍拥护君主制的部分缘由。当然,如果不看注释,也是难以读透。教师选教此课时,如能结合第四版"Why the Monarchy Must Stay"这一课和《导读》"英国"和"英美政治比较",教和学就容易多了。

Pre-reading Questions

1. What do you know about the British Royal family?
2. Do you think it better for Britain to keep the monarchy or abolish it?

Text

Mrs. Windsor[1], Anyone?

By Matthew Engel

For members of the anti-royalist group Republic, the queen's diamond jubilee[2] is a chance to get their views heard.

Members of the anti-monarchist group Republic with its campaign manager Graham Smith, standing second from left.

1   In keeping with the pattern across Britain this week, a small group of enthusiasts gathered in north London on Monday evening to complete their own arrangements for this weekend's celebration of the diamond jubilee.

2   There were eight of them, a pretty decent attendance on such an occasion, as any local event organiser would tell you. This group, however, was not dealing with last-minute crises about the bunting for the street party, or who was supplying the tea urn. They were putting finishing touches to the placards for their anti-jubilee demonstration. "Make monarchy history," one read; "Don't jubilee've it!"[3]; "9,500 nurses or 1 Queen?"[4].

3   These were the anti-monarchy campaigners of Republic. Like thousands of people, they will be spending Sunday afternoon by the Thames as the royal barge leads a flotilla of boats downstream to mark 60 years of Elizabeth II's[5] reign. Like many of the spectators, they will be hoping the Queen may just catch sight of them, and that maybe they might even be on telly. For this group, however, the TV coverage is particularly urgent.

Graceful: The late photographer Cecil Beaton shot this picture entitled: the Queen in Coronation Robes, in June 1953. It is now part of a 60-print show to mark the Diamond Jubilee at the V&A Museum in London

4   As a group Republic has slowly been gaining a little traction. Graham Smith says that when he joined in 2003, there were 300 people on the mailing list. Now, seven years after Smith was appointed full-time chief executive (funded by a supporter's legacy), he says the number has increased to 20,000. Major royal events constitute good news for Republic: both Prince William's wedding[6] last year, when they held their own anti-royal street party, and the jubilee have produced spikes in support.

5   However, it would be best not to exaggerate this, given that 99.9996 per cent of Britain is not on the mailing list. If you Google "Republic," a chain of clothes stores comes out first. And for the monarchy, an institution which has held firm—with one 11-year gap[7] since the start of the 9th century, the 21st century has marked a return to its customary popularity and dominance. The 1990s were disastrous for the royal family: three of the Queen's four children were divorced: Princess Anne discreetly; Prince Charles and Prince Andrew amid a global storm of horrendous publicity. The nightmare culminated in the death of Charles' ex-wife Diana[8] in the Paris car crash of August 1997, an event which the family mishandled—as they say—royally.

6   But the turnaround, widely perceived to have started with the initially rather apologetic golden jubilee of 2002[6], has been almost as spectacular.[9] The Queen is now 86, her husband Prince Philip almost 91; they appear to be enjoying the kind of active and mellow old age any of us might envy, just as their family life was once thought to represent an idealised version of domesticity. Last week a poll-commissioned by the leftish and republican-leaning Guardian[10]—asked 1,000 people whether Britain would be better or worse off without a royal family[11] and 69 per cent said worse off, a number in line with similar polls throughout the past 60 years.

7   Monday's gathering of republican activists took place in a borrowed office in Islington, the London borough renowned as the HQ of Guardianish opinions[12]. At the behest of the FT's photographer, they went down with their placards to pose in the quiet side street below. I only saw a couple of passers-by during this exercise. One emitted a distant cry of "Rubbish." The other was an elderly gent who came over, politely and firmly, to offer his opinion: "I hope to God you people

never get your way," he said.

8   Republic's supporters are equally polite and firm. "I think we need the best democracy we can get," said Jen Gingell, a banker. "We can do a lot better than having a monarch."

9   The mystery of British republicanism has long been its almost total non-

existence. The civil war that led to Charles I's execution in 1649 was (to oversimplify) a battle over the origin and extent of the king's authority rather than its existence. And since Oliver Cromwel, was briefly succeeded as "Lord Protector" by his own son before Charles II was invited back in 1660, the so-called interregnum might best be seen as a brief usurpation of the Stuarts by the House of Cromwell.[13]

Oliver Cromwell dissolves Parliament and establishes himself as Lord Protector of England, 1653.

10   In the 352 years since then there have been moments that might have been construed as republican opportunities. There was a bad run for the monarchy in the early 19th century: George III[14] (1760—1820) became demented; George IV[15] (1820 — 1830) was a licentious fat laughing-stock, and William IV[16] (1830—1837) a dimwit. But Britain's faith in its system had been cemented by the excesses of the French Revolution[17]: "there is a distinction between the unpopularity of the monarch and the unpopularity of the monarchy," says Professor Rodney Barker of the London School of Economics[18].

11   The institution recovered quickly after the accession of Victoria[19] in 1837. Then it wobbled again after the death of her husband Prince Albert in 1861, when Victoria retreated into seclusion and the Prince of Wales[20], the future Edward VII[21], began to exhibit signs of George IV-ishness: republican clubs spread across Britain, and the popular MP Sir Charles Dilke[22] led a campaign that appeared to have widespread support. And then the prince contracted typhoid and nearly died.

12   When he recovered, Victoria held a public thanksgiving service in Westminster Abbey[23]. "She insisted that 'the show,' as she called it, should be done properly," according to Peter Conradi[24] in his recent

account of modern monarchy, *The Great Survivors* (2012). "Dressed in black, but with a white feather in her bonnet, she travelled through London in an open landau drawn by six horses. The crowds went wild."

13   The Victorian constitutional scholar Walter Bagehot[25] described Britain as a "disguised republic"—a point echoed by Prochaska[26]. The Queen is there by consent, and she knows it. When countries choose to remove her as head of state—as Jamaica is about to do and Australia agonises about[27]—she yields with good grace. The process would be more traumatic in England or (what is far more plausible) Scotland, but there could be no question that the democratic would have to prevail.

14   Between the flag-wavers and the placard-wavers, there is a great deal of cynicism in Britain—people turned off by the flummery, the excesses, the expense and the sugar-coated coverage[28]. Outside the Conservative Party, there are also a lot of passive republicans among elected politicians who are getting closer to positions of power: Leanne Wood[29], the new leader of Plaid Cymru[30], once caused a storm in the Welsh Assembly[31] by calling the Queen "Mrs Windsor."

15   Several Republic supporters insisted that becoming head of state was a legitimate aspiration for any child of democracy, in the American log-cabin-to-president tradition[32]. I can't say I have ever felt this deprivation myself and I am not alone: the third option in the Charles or William[33] poll question was an election. It was backed by only 10 per cent.

16   Support for the monarchy is certainly full of contradictions but, the night after the Islington gathering, it was possible to sense the weaknesses in Republic's case. The Bishopsgate Institute in London[34] held a debate on the monarchy, and 50 people turned up to hear Smith (a cogent advocate) and the journalist Joan Smith take on the ex-Tory MP Jacques Arnold and Peter Conradi[35] (who was rather ambivalent himself).

17   The audience almost wholly comprised Republic supporters, not all of them as earnest and honest as the placard-makers. The speeches from

the floor brought forth bores, churls and obsessives, whingeing about the BBC (not normally criticised as a right-wing conspiracy) and the indoctrination of youngsters asked to wear red, white and blue to school this week.[36] Some thought the royal family (mainly Charles) interfered too much in politics; others thought the Queen's insistence on non-intervention[37] after the inconclusive 2010 election was a sign that she had no useful role to play.

18　　Eventually, a rare neutral spoke up. He had gone to the debate with some republican friends but could keep quiet no longer. "There are so many big problems in the world. Can't you put your energies into the big problems?" He didn't get a proper answer. "Make monarchy history," said the placard. What about making poverty history? Or global warming? Or terrorism? Or David Cameron[38] and Nick Clegg[39]?

19　　Republic's members insist they care about these things too. But I suspect that single questioner spoke for apathetic England. Unless you get stuck in a London traffic jam this weekend, the monarchy is not a nuisance. It probably does more good than harm and makes more money than it costs. It gives the country a sense of stability. The Queen seems a decent old stick[40]. There is an extra bank holiday[41] for her on Tuesday. Match that, President Blair.[42]

20　　Frank Prochaska sees little chance of this mood changing, even when the Queen dies. "After Edward VIII[43] abdicated in 1936, some of the Clydeside Labour MPs[44] thought the republican moment had come. Instead there was a lot of sympathy for the new King. Some of the republicans now see Charles as an opportunity but it's going to be very frustrating for them. There will be a wave of sympathy because of his mother's service."

Matthew Engel is an FT columnist. (From *The Financial Times*, June 2, 2012)

New Words

abdicate /ˈæbdɪkeɪt/ *v.* to give up, such as power, as of monarchs and emperors, or duties and obligations 退位

accession /ækˈseʃn/ *n.* the act of taking a high post or position, esp. after someone has left it 就职；继位

ambivalent /æmˈbɪvələnt/ *a.* uncertain or unable to decide about what

course to follow 矛盾的,有矛盾心理的;模棱两可的
apathetic /ˌæpə'θetɪk/ *adj.* lacking interest, strong feelings, or a desire to take action 冷漠的,无动于衷的
barge /bɑːdʒ/ *n.* a large rowing boat used chiefly on rivers for important people on ceremonial occasions
behest /bɪ'hest/ *n. fml* an urgent request or command
borough /'bʌrə/ *n.* a town, or a division of a large town, with some powers of local government 享有某些地方政府权力的市镇或区
bunting /'bʌntɪŋ/ *n.* small paper or cloth flags, tied together on a string and used as decorations for special occasions (用绳子穿成一连串的)小彩旗
cement /sɪ'ment/ *v.* to reinforce or consolidate 巩固,加强
churl /tʃɜːl/ *n.* a rude person
cogent /'kəʊdʒənt/ *adj. fml* (esp. of reasons or arguments) tending to persuade or to produce belief; convincing
commission /kə'mɪʃn/ *v.* to give a commission to 委派,委托
conspiracy /kən'spɪrəsɪ/ *n.* a group of conspirators banded together to achieve some harmful or illegal purpose 阴谋集团
construe /kən'struː/ *v.* to understand or explain in a particular way
cynicism /'sɪnɪsɪzəm/ *n.* the attitude or belief that people tend to act only in their own interests 愤世嫉俗,冷嘲热讽
demented /dɪ'mentɪd/ *adj.* mad; of unbalanced mind
deprivation /ˌdeprɪ'veɪʃn/ *n.* (usu. Plural) sth you need or usu. have that you are prevented from having 丧失;剥夺
dimwit /'dɪmˌwɪt/ *n. infml* a stupid person
domesticity /ˌdəʊme'stɪsətɪ/ *n.* (a liking for) home or family life 家庭生活;对家庭(生活)的喜爱
discreetly /dɪ'skriːtlɪ/ *adv.* with discretion; prudently and with wise self-restraint 谨慎地
flotilla /flə'tɪlə/ *n.* a group or fleet of small ships, esp. warships 小型船队
　　FT(*abbrev.*) Financial Times
Google /'guːgl/ *v.* to use the Google search engine to obtain information about (as sb) on the WWW
hereditary /hə'redɪtrɪ/ *a.* (of a position, title etc) which can be passed down from an older to a younger person, esp. In the same family (地位、称号等)世袭的
horrendous /hɒ'rendəs/ *adj.* really terrible; causing great fear;

extremely unpleasant

indoctrination /ɪnˌdɒktrɪˈneɪʃn/ *n.* teaching someone to accept doctrines uncritically 教化,教导

interregnum /ˌɪntəˈregnəm/ *n.* a period of time when a country has no king or queen, because the new ruler has not yet taken up his or her position (王位的)空位期;过渡时期

Islington /ˈɪzlɪŋtən/ a borough of northeast London, thought of as a place where many left-wing and middle class politicians and people who work in television, radio, and newspapers live 伊斯灵顿(伦敦东北部一区)

licentious /laɪˈsenʃəs/ *adj. fml* behaving in a sexually immoral or uncontrolled way 淫荡无度的,放荡的

mellow /ˈmeləʊ/ *adj.* (of people or behaviour) wise and gentle through age or experience 成熟的,老练的

monarch /ˈmɒnək/ *n.* a ruler of a state, such as a king, queen etc, who has a right to rule by birth and does not have to be elected 君主;国王或女王

monarchy /ˈmɒnəkɪ/ *n.* (the system of) rule by a king or queen 君主制;君主世袭(制)

objectionable /əbˈdʒekʃənəbl/ *a.* causing disapproval or protest 讨厌的,有异议的

obsessive /əbˈsesɪv/ *n.* a person who has a fixed and often unreasonable idea with which the mind is continually concerned

placard /ˈplækɑːd/ *n.* a sign posted in a public place as an advertisement 海报,标语牌

reign /reɪn/ *n.* a period of being the king or queen, esp. without holding real power 君主统治时期

seclusion /sɪˈkluːʒn/ *n.* the state or act of keeping (esp. oneself) away from other people 隐居

spike /spaɪk/ *n.* a sharp rise followed by a sharp decline 激增

telly /ˈtelɪ/ *n. BrE infml* television

traction /ˈtrækʃn/ *n.* the act of drawing or pulling 牵引力;吸引力

Thames /teɪmz/ *n.* the longest river in England, which flows from the west into the North Sea. In London, many well-known bridges across the Thames connect the north and south of the city, and many important buildings, including the Houses of Parliament and the Tower of London, are built nest to the river. 泰晤士河

traumatic /trɔːˈmætɪk/ *adj.* (of an experience) deeply and unforgettably shocking 痛苦难忘的

turnaround /'tɜːnəraʊnd/ *n.* an act of turning in a different or opposite direction; turnabout

typhoid /'taɪfɔɪd/ *n.* 伤寒(病)

urn /ɜːn/ *n.* a large pot for making coffee or tea (金属的)大茶水壶，咖啡壶

usurpation /ˌjuːzɜːˈpeɪʃn/ *n. fml* the act of taking power or position for oneself illegally or without having the right to do so 篡权

whinge /wɪndʒ/ *v. fml* to complain, esp. continually and in an annoying way 唠叨，发牢骚

wobble /'wɒbəl/ *v.* to move unsteadily from side to side

Notes

1. Mrs Windsor—"Windsor" is the family name of the British royal family from 1917. Some Republican activists call the Queen "Mrs Windsor" to show their position that monarchy should be abolished and that the Queen is just a common woman.

2. diamond jubilee—a celebration held to mark a 75th anniversary, but only the 60th anniversary in the case of a monarch (i.e. length of time a monarch has reigned). Traditionally, the diamond jubilee or anniversary of a person was on the 75th anniversary. This changed with the diamond jubilee of the British Queen Victoria's reign. There was considerable national unrest when Queen Victoria largely withdrew from public life after her husband's death in 1861. It was decided to bring the diamond jubilee forward to the 60th anniversary on 22 June 1897. The Diamond Jubilee of Queen Elizabeth II, celebrated on 2 June 2012, was only the second in the country's history. 通常指75周年纪念。用于指国王或女王登基等私人重要事件的60周年纪念庆典，钻石大庆。伊丽莎白女王在位60年仍不想让位给王储，大概想要超过维多利亚女王在位63年的记录。

3. "Don't jubilee've it"—这句标语运用了谐音和双关。一方面，把"jubilee"用作动词，"Don't jubilee"表达了"anti-jubilee"的态度；另一方面，"jubilee've"与"you believe"发音近似，整句读出来即"Don't you believe it"，表达了对君主制的怀疑。

4. 9,500 nurses or 1 Queen?—养活9,500个护士还是一位女王，哪个更重要和合算？拿护士说事儿或是她们工资低，又因英国医疗保健制

度弊端丛生，医务人员缺失严重。

5. Elizabeth II—1926— , Queen of UK since 1952, Head of the Commonwealth. Elizabeth was not born to be Queen. Her Uncle was King Edward VIII, but he was never crowned due to his abdication. Elizabeth's father was next in line to the throne and although he never expected to rule, he was declared King on 12 December 1936 and Elizabeth became his heir. In 1952, Elizabeth became Queen at the age of 25. In 2002, Elizabeth celebrated her Golden Jubilee (50 years on the throne), in 2012 her Diamond Jubilee (60 years on the throne) and in 2013 her 87th birthday. Queen Elizabeth II is currently the second longest reigning monarch of the United Kingdom, ranking behind Victoria, who reigned over the UK for 63 years. (见《导读》"英国国王")

6. Prince William's wedding—Prince William (Charles' son) and Kate Middleton's wedding took place on April 29, 2011.

7. with one 11-year gap—国王被迫召开了中间间隔了11年之久的国会，因为其间实行了共和制。

8. the death of Charles' ex-wife Diana—Charles' first wife Diana died On 31 August 1997 in a car crash in the Pont de l'Alma road tunnel in Paris. Millions of people watched her funeral. Diana was well known for her fund-raising work for international charities and as an eminent celebrity of the late 20th century.

9. But the turnaround... almost as spectacular.—但是转机来得同样惊人，人们普遍认为这个时刻源自于2002年一开始没人看好的登基50周年庆典。(In 2002, Elizabeth marked her Golden Jubilee as Queen. After the scandals of the previous years, people speculated as to whether the Jubilee would be a success. It proved to be the beginning of a turning point. There were street parties and commemorative events and monuments were named to honour the occasion. A million people attended each day of the three-day main Jubilee celebration in London and the enthusiasm shown by the public for the Queen was greater than many journalists had predicted.)

10. the leftish and republican-leaning Guardian—Founded by textile traders and merchants, *The Guardian* had a reputation as "an organ of the middle class." The paper's readership is generally on the mainstream left of British political opinion; according to a poll

taken in 2005, 48% of *Guardian* readers were Labour voters and 34% Liberal Democrat voters. (见"美英报刊简介")

11. a royal family—(英国王室) the British sovereign and his or her immediate family, regarded as representing the highest aristocratic presence in the land, with each member attracting much popular interest and the constant attention of the media. At present the royal family is headed by **Queen Elizabeth**, and directly includes the Duke of Edinburgh, Queen Elizabeth, the Prince and Princess of Wales, the Queen's other three children and the Queen's sister, Princess Margaret (born 1930). Outside this immediate circle, the royal family also includes the Queen's cousins, the Dukes of Gloucester and Kent, and the spouses and children of these and the other relations apart from those already mentioned. When members of the royal family attend an official ceremony the national anthem is played and the Union Jack (英国国旗) may be flown.

12. the **HQ** of Guardianish opinions—the centre or main source of liberal and left-wing opinions

    HQ—*abbrev.* headquarters

13. The mystery of British republicanism... by the House of Cromwell—A struggle between the Parliament and the Stuart Kings led to a bloody civil war 1642—1649, and the establishment of a republic under the Puritan Oliver Cromwell. The monarchy was restored in 1660, but the Glorious Revolution of 1668 confirmed the sovereignty (至高无上的权威或权力) of the Parliament: a Bill of Rights (权利法,美一直指人权法) was granted in 1689. 1649年,克伦威尔推翻了斯图亚特王朝建立了共和国,名叫 the Commonwealth。然而。他生前压制的各种社会矛盾在他死后又爆发了出来。于是,1660年又恢复了君主制,但君主的权力已受到宪法的限制,成了有名无实的国王。

    a. Republicanism—the ideology of governing a society or state as a republic, where the head of state is elected. 共和制或政体,其首脑由选举产生,君主制是世袭的。

    b. The civil war—英国内战是1642年至1651年在英国议会派与保皇派之间发生的一系列武装冲突及政治斗争,马克思主义史观称之为英国资产阶级革命(English Bourgeois Revolution)。建立君主专制制度的斯图亚特王朝国王查理一世在战后被处死,克伦威尔成立了共和国。

c. Charles I's execution in 1649—Charles I (1600 – 1649), king of England, Scotland, and Ireland from 1625 until his execution in 1649, second son of James I and Anne of Denmark. Charles engaged in a struggle for power with the Parliament of England, attempting to obtain royal revenue whilst Parliament sought to curb his royal prerogative (特权), which Charles believed was divinely ordained (神赐的). He was defeated in the civil war and was subsequently captured, tried, convicted, and executed for high treason (叛国罪).

d. Oliver Cromwell—1599－1658, was an English military and political leader and later Lord Protector of the Commonwealth of England, Scotland and Ireland (英伦三岛共同体共和国的护国公) (1653－1658). Cromwell is one of the most controversial figures in the history of the British Isles, considered a regicidal (弑君的) dictator by some historians, a military dictator by Winston Churchill (温斯顿·丘吉尔), but a hero of liberty by some others. In a 2002 BBC poll in Britain, Cromwell was selected as one of the ten greatest Britons of all time. 奥利弗·克伦威尔

e. Charles II—1630 – 1685, king of England, Scotland, and Ireland (1660 – 1685), eldest surviving son of Charles I and Henrietta Maria. He escaped into exile during the civil war and it was not until 1660 that he was invited back to England to reclaim his throne (恢复王位). Although those who had signed Charles I's death warrant (处决令) were punished, the new king pursued a policy of political tolerance and power-sharing.

f. the Stuarts—斯图亚特王朝(The House of Stuart), 1371 年至 1714 年间统治苏格兰、1603 年至 1714 年间统治英格兰和爱尔兰的王朝。

g. the House of Cromwell—克伦威尔公馆，喻其政权，犹如 Whitehall 常用来借喻英国政府。

14. George III—1738－1820, king of Great Britain and Ireland (1760－1820), son of Frederick Louis, prince of Wales, and grandson of George II, whom he succeeded.

15. George IV—1762－1830, king of Great Britain and Ireland (1820－1830), eldest son and successor of George III. George was hated for his extravagance and dissolute (放荡的) habits, and he aroused

particular hostility by an unsuccessful attempt, immediately after his accession (1820) to the throne, to divorce his long-estranged wife, Caroline.

16. William IV—1765—1837, king of Great Britain and Ireland (1830—1837), third son of George III. In 1830 he succeeded George IV as king.

17. But Britain's faith... of the French Revolution.—Because the French Revolution went too far in dealing with their monarch, the British people reinforced their faith in their system, i. e. monarchy.

    a. French Revolution—1789 年 7 月 14 日以巴黎人民攻占巴士底狱开始的一场法国大革命,四年后,国王路易十六和王后被送上断头台斩首,法国成立了共和国。这对欧洲历史有着重要影响。

    b. excess—the state or act of going beyond normal, sufficient, or permitted limits 过分;过头

18. the London School of Economics—The London School of Economics and Political Science (informally the London School of Economics or LSE) is a public research university specialised in the social sciences located in London, and a constituent college of the federal University of London. 伦敦政治经济学院,常简称为"伦敦政经学院",知名度高。

19. Victoria—1819—1901, queen of Great Britain and Ireland (1837—1901) and empress(女皇) of India (1876—1901). She was the daughter of Edward, duke of Kent (fourth son of George III), and Princess Mary Louise Victoria of Saxe-Coburg-Saalfeld. Her reign of 63 years and seven months, which is longer than that of any other British monarch and the longest of any female monarch in history, is known as the Victorian era. It was a period of industrial, cultural, political, scientific, and military change within the U. K. , and was marked by a great expansion of the British Empire. Her conscientiousness and strict morals helped to restore the prestige of the crown and to establish it as a symbol of public service and imperial unity.

20. Prince of Wales—a title traditionally granted to the heir apparent (法定继承人) to the reigning monarch of the U. K. The current Prince of Wales is Prince Charles, the eldest son of Queen Elizabeth II.

21. Edward VII—1841－1910, king of Great Britain and Ireland (1901—1910). The eldest son of Queen Victoria and Prince Albert, he was created Prince of Wales almost immediately after his birth.

22. the popular MP Sir Charles Dilke—2nd Baronet（男爵）(1843－1911), was an English Liberal and reformist politician. Paradoxically both an imperialist and a leading and determined radical, he helped to pass the 1884－85 parliamentary Reform Acts as well as supporting laws giving the municipal franchise（选举权）to women, legalizing labour unions, improving working conditions and limiting working hours, and being one of the earliest campaigners for universal schooling. Touted（吹捧）as a future prime minister, his political career was terminated in 1885, after a notorious and well-publicised divorce case.

    MP—Member of Parliament 国会议员（仅指平民院或下议院议员）

23. Westminster Abbey—a very large Gothic church in Westminster, London, first built in the 11th century. Almost all British kings and queens since William the Conqueror have been crowned in the Abbey and many famous people are buried there. 威斯敏斯特教堂/西敏寺是英王加冕和下葬之所,也是名人下葬之地。

24. Peter Conradi—an author and journalist. He works for the *Sunday Times* and is the author of *The King's Speech: How One Man Saved the British Monarchy*, *Hitler's Piano Player*, and several other books. His new book, *The Great Survivors: How Monarchy Made it into the Twenty-First Century*, was published in 2012. At a time when Western society appears to be demanding more equality and democracy, people's fascination with monarchies shows no signs of waning. Taking the reader on a journey between past and present, *The Great Survivors* analyses the reasons behind this anachronistic（时代错误的）paradox by looking at the history of the main European dynasties and providing a keyhole glimpse into their world, their lives and their secrets.

25. Walter Bagehot—1826－1877, economist, political analyst, and editor of *The Economist* who was one of the most influential journalists of the mid-Victorian period.

26. Prochaska, Frank—an historian of modern Britain with a special interest in philanthropy (慈善事业), the monarchy and nineteenth-century political thought. Currently based in Oxford, the author of a number of critically acclaimed books
27. as Jamaica is about to do and Australia agonises about—both Jamaica and Australia are members of the Commonwealth of Nations (英联邦), formerly (1931—49) British Commonwealth of Nations, which is a free association of 53 sovereign states comprising the United Kingdom and a number of its former dependencies (附属国) who have chosen to maintain ties of friendship and practical cooperation and who acknowledge the British monarch as symbolic head of their association.
28. people turned off... sugar-coated coverage.—people who have lost their interest or feel disgusted because the royal family are insincere, they don't behave well, they spend huge amounts of the taxpayers' money, and they are described in the press as much better than they are.
    a. flummery—complete nonsense; foolish humbug
    b. turn off—to cause (a person, etc) to feel dislike or distaste for (sth)
    c. sugar-coat—to make (sth difficult or distasteful) appear more pleasant or acceptable
29. Leanne Wood—1971— , a Welsh politician and the leader of Plaid Cymru.
30. Plaid Cymru—The Party of Wales; often referred to simply as Plaid. It is a political party in Wales and advocates the establishment of an independent Welsh state within the European Union.
31. the Welsh Assembly—The National Assembly for Wales. It is a devolved (委任的) assembly with power to make legislation in Wales. 威尔士国民议会是由1997年威尔士权力下放公民投票(Wales referendum 1997)后,英国国会通过《1998年威尔士地方政府法案》(Government of Wales Act 1998)时实现。除了英国保守党之外,威尔士各政党、社会各界全部赞成权力下放,兼成立威尔士国民议会及其行政机关。
32. the American log-cabin-to-president tradition—A log cabin is a

house built from logs. It is a fairly simple type of log house. The log cabin has been a symbol of humble origins in US politics since the early 19th century. Seven United States Presidents were born in log cabins, including Abraham Lincoln, Andrew Jackson, and James Buchanan. It has been used to show that a presidential candidate is a man of the people, making the idea of a log cabin—and, more generally, a non-wealthy background—a recurring theme in campaign biographies. If working hard, even a cowboy can be president, as the proverb goes. (见《导读》"总统选举")

33. the Charles or William poll—the poll to see who people think should be the next king, Prince Charles or Prince William. In the 2005 poll, Charles was favoured to be the successor to the Queen. But, shortly after William's engagement to Kate Middleton was announced (2011), two polls showed a majority of Britons thought he should succeed Queen Elizabeth and not heir-to-the-throne Charles. But after the Diamond Jubilee celebrations, Charles is now considered to be the best person to take over the throne. Charles 是王储,即女王长子,是理所当然的法定继承人,由于其与 Diana 离婚而与情人 Camilla(卡米拉)结婚,前途一度堪忧。

34. Bishopsgate Institute—a cultural institute, located on Bishopsgate, London. The institute was established in 1895, and describes itself as a "home for ideas and debate, learning and enquiry and as a place where independent thought is cherished." 主教门学院

35. ...50 people turned up to hear...and Peter Conradi—50 people were present to hear Smith and the journalist Joan Smith argue with the ex-Tory MP Jacques Arnold and Peter Conradi.

  a. turn up—to arrive or appear
  b. take on—to start to quarrel, compete, oppose, or fight with
  c. ex-Tory—a former member of the Conservative Party(前保守党人)(见《导读》"英国政党")

36. The speeches from the floor...to wear red, white and blue to school this week.—观众席里发言的人有一些枯燥无味的人、粗鄙的人和偏执的人,他们唠唠叨叨地抱怨 BBC(通常人们认为 BBC 并不是右翼的同谋)和灌输年轻人要求他们本周穿红、白、蓝色的衣服上学的做法。

  a. from the floor—from those listening

    b. bring forth—to give rise to; introduce
37. the Queen's insistence on non-intervention—指英女王不干预政治，对两党的争斗和选举等政事持超然态度。（见《导读》"英国"）
38. David Cameron—1966— ，the Prime Minister of the U. K. since 2010 and Leader of the Conservative Party. 戴维·卡梅伦，英国现任首相，保守党领袖。2010年举行的大选中，保守党未能取得过半数席位而不得不与自民党组成 coalition government。
39. Nick Clegg—1967— ，a British politician who has been Deputy Prime Minister of the U. K. since 2010. Clegg has been the Leader of the Liberal Democrats since 2007, and a member of parliament (MP) since 2005. 尼克·克莱格，英国现任副首相，自由民主党领袖。

    由于 Clegg 和 Cameron 相貌酷似，有人就杜撰了一个新词 Cleggeron
40. old stick—*idiomatic*, *colloquial*, *BrE* a man, chap, fellow, guy
41. bank holiday—public holiday. Banks close and the majority of the working population is granted time off work or extra pay for working on these days.
42. Match that, President Blair.—President Blair may be just as good as the Queen. Tony Blair is a British Labour Party politician who served as the Prime Minister of the U. K. from 1997 to 2007. He was criticised for his marginalisation（边缘化）of the Cabinet and the "presidential"（像美国总统那样，即大事不与内阁商量而一人定夺）handling of the war on terrorism. Here the author means that a republic is as good as or better than monarchy.
43. Edward VIII—1894－1972, Edward became king in early 1936. Only months into his reign, he caused a constitutional crisis by proposing marriage to the American socialite Wallis Simpson, who had divorced her first husband and was seeking a divorce from her second. Choosing not to end his relationship with Simpson, Edward abdicated. With a reign of 326 days, Edward was one of the shortest-reigning monarchs in British and Commonwealth history. 史称"不爱江山爱美人"之风流国王爱德华八世，其实另有隐情。
44. Clydeside Labour MPs—Clydeside refers to the Red Clydeside, the era of political radicalism and a significant part of the history of the labour movement. This period lasted from the 1910s until roughly

the early 1930s, although its legacy is still visible today.

Questions

1. Are there many Britons against monarchy according to the author?
2. What does the slogan "Don't jubilee've it!" on the placard mean?
3. How do you understand the slogan "9,500 nurses or 1 Queen"?
4. Why do you think the majority of Britons give their support to the royal family?
5. In your view, which is better for Britain, monarchy or Republicanism?

读报知识

英国人缘何拥护君主制?

据1988年的民意调查,多数英国人认为,女王的首要任务是英国国家形象的代表,其次是公民和家庭生活的楷模。伊丽莎白二世确实是英国人生活的典范,然而王室(royal family)成员却不争气,离婚、偷情丑闻不断,不免使英国人闻之而怒不可遏,他们所缴的税款居然供他们过着伤风败俗的腐朽生活。因而,英国一度要求废除君主制的呼声高涨。据民意测验,竟有高达三分之一的人主张废除或对其进行彻底改革。

1997年戴安娜王妃在巴黎丧身车祸,2005年查尔斯王子与情人卡米拉低调成婚。于是,查尔斯、戴安娜、卡米拉之间的三角关系,戴安娜王妃的死因,以及媒体盛传的她与一位马术教练,还有一位普通心脏外科医生之间的"真挚爱情故事",都成了人们茶余饭后的话题,并杜撰了一个不知是何君的"Squidgy"。小王子哈里对王室来说更是一个"麻烦的制造者":2001年偷偷酗酒和吸毒,2004年考试作弊并与记者大打出手,2005年在一个化装舞会上把自己打扮成了带着十字记号袖标的纳粹军官,背着女友去偷欢等等。这些丑闻在一定程度上打破了人们将王室看成是道德模范的神话。于是在英国社会又引起了一轮是否有必要保留君主的争论。现在,女王已在位60多年,王室窘事少见,形象提高。

2008年5月,尼泊尔废除了君主制。可仅在欧洲,就有英国、西班牙、荷兰、瑞典、挪威、丹麦和比利时仍保留着君王;在非洲有摩洛哥、莱索托;在亚洲,有沙特阿拉伯、约旦、泰国、日本。这些形形色色的君主,有名义的,有握有国家实权的。英国是最古老的资本主义国家,民主制在人们的头脑中已深深扎根,君主制显然不符合历史潮流。可时至今日,英国仍未实行共和制。那么英国缘何要保留君主制呢?总的来说,英国君主制

的存在顺应了英国民族、宗教和政治特点,是历史传统的产物。具体讲,大致有以下几个缘由:
1. 反对君主制会动摇民族意识的基础
2. 君主制与英国历史密不可分
3. 英国人不喜欢共和制
4. 国王比总统更能代表国家形象
5. 君主比总统更能凝聚人心
6. 伊丽莎白二世已成为民族精神和道德价值观的代表
7. "统而不治"成优点
8. 有助于维持大国地位和促进经济发展
9. 王室有严格的家规
10. 王权面临改革而非废止

政界要人如英国前首相丘吉尔认为:"议会民主制和君主立宪制并非十全十美,但这是人类迄今所创造的最好的政治体制。"另一位英国前首相梅杰也道出了最有说服力的理由:"没有人能设想除君主立宪制外,英国还能实行其他别的什么体制。"看来这两位英国政治家所说的话,基本上概括了大多数英国人对君主制的看法。当然,对于上述 10 个理由和丘吉尔等政要的说法也只能见仁见智。(详见《导读》五章二节十六"英国君主制的废留之争")

Lesson Twenty

课文导读

查戈斯群岛位于印度洋上毛里求斯东北面1200英里,由迪戈加西亚等五个岛屿组成,岛上的居民淳朴勤劳,过着自给自足的生活。上世纪六七十年代,美苏争霸,凸显出查戈斯群岛作为印度洋中心的战略地位。于是美国和英国合作在该岛建立海空军事基地,海军作补给港,空军作前哨基地。为此英国政府便在高度保密的情况下采取了坑蒙拐骗等种种等于集体绑架的手段,使岛上的居民失去了他们祖祖辈辈生于斯长于斯埋于斯的美丽祥和的家园,沦为流落异乡的难民。他们过着贫病交迫、无依无靠的生活,或为奴,或为娼,或自杀。一些正义之士挺身而出,为这些穷苦人请命,但英国政府能拖则拖,能赖则赖。美国政府更是讳莫如深,态度消极。一向以人权卫士自居的美英政府,居然用这种卑鄙的手段"霸占了一个国家。"由此可见,同宗同文的美英两国政府所谓的"人权外交"和"人道主义危机"无非是为了实施对外干涉,扩大自己的势力范围、争霸全球。

查戈斯群岛的居民为了回归自己的家园不断地提出诉讼,打了数十年的官司。2000年英国高等法院作出裁决,允许他们在该群岛的边远岛屿居住,但政府居然拒不执行。庆幸的是,2006年英国上诉法院做出终审裁决,认为英国政府驱逐居民并将这些岛屿出租给美国是"滥用权力"。这样被美英政府非法逐出家园的查戈斯群岛居民终于打赢了官司,结束40多年的流浪生活,回到自己可爱的故土迪戈加西亚。但此地现在仍是海空基地。

本课课文虽长,但语言简明易懂。通过这篇专题报道,不仅可以学到一些读报知识,同时也能更深认清西方国家的本质,这对今后从事外事工作的毕业生是大有裨益的。

Pre-reading Questions

1. Do you know something about Iraq and the Iraq Wars?
2. Do you think the U.S. will win the hearts and mind of the Iraq

people in the end?

Text

Stealing a Nation
A special report by John Puger

"This film is a shocking, almost incredible story. A government calling itself civilized tricked and expelled its most vulnerable citizens so that it could give their homeland to a foreign power ... Ministers and their officials then mounted a campaign of deception all the way up to the Prime Minister."

— John Pilger[1]

"In this part of the world, except if we go back to the days of slavery and to the days of indentured labour, I can't remember anything of the sort happening."

Cassam Uteem, former President of Mauritius

Introduction

1   Beginning in the late 1960s the British government removed the population of around 2,000 people from the Chagos islands[2] in the Indian Ocean. This policy was pursued as quietly as possible to ensure minimal international attention. Subsequently, successive British governments over nearly four decades have maintained this policy by not disclosing the fact that the Islanders were permanent Inhabitants.

2   The depopulation was done at the behest of the United States government to make way for a military base on the largest island in the Chagos group—Diego Garcia. Diego Garcia is now a large US military base used as a launch pad[3] for intervention in the Middle East, most recently in Afghanistan and Iraq.

3   All the while, the Chagossians, most of whom have been living in exile in poverty, have been campaigning for proper compensation and forthright to return to their homeland. Their nation has been stolen; but their plight has been little reported on in the media and little analysed by academics.

4   The British government of Tony Blair[4] delivered the latest blow to the hopes of the Chagossians in June 2004. After a long legal battle, the

Chagossians had won an historic High Court ruling in 2000 allowing their return to the outlying islands in the Chagos group, but later the same day the Government announced that they would not be allowing them to return to Diego Garcia. In 2004, the British government announced two "orders in council"[5] to bar the Chagossians from returning even to the outlying islands, in effect, overturning the High Court ruling. Foreign Office minister[6] Bill Rammell said that as a result of the new orders "no person has the right of abode[7] in the territory or has unrestricted access to any part of it".

5　　The Chagossians in exile now number around 4,500. Many are old and frail and want little more than to revisit their homeland to find their final resting place. For all of them, their struggle is for basic justice and for a redress to the wrongs done to them.

Creating a new colony

6　　During the 1960's, when many countries were undergoing a process of decolonization, Britain created a new colony—the British Indian Ocean Territory (BIOT)—in November 1965. This included the Chagos island group, which was detached from Mauritius, and other small islands detached from the Seychelles. As an inducement to Mauritius, and as part of the discussions with Britain on Independence, Britain offered £3 million as compensation for the loss of the Chagos islands.

7　　In December 1965, UN Resolution 2066XX passed by the General Assembly called on the UK "to take no action which would dismember the territory of Mauritius and to violate its territorial integrity". However, Britain defied this and the Mauritian government, whose politicians were divided over the British offer, eventually accepted it. The BIOT was created, while Mauritius proceeded to independence in 1968.

8　　In December 1966, the British government of Harold Wilson[8] signed a military agreement with the US leasing Diego Garcia to it for an initial 150 years for military purposes. This deal, which still stands today, was not debated in parliament and attracted virtually no publicity. The reason for US interest was that the Pentagon[9] had selected Diego Garcia as an ideal place to monitor the activities of the

Soviet[10] Navy and had ideas about turning it into a military facility. The US also made clear that it did not want people living on the island and therefore turned to[11] Britain to remove them.

9 Britain subsequently depopulated the Chagos islands. This was later described by the Chagossians' defence lawyers as:

10 "the compulsory and unlawful removal of a small and unique population, citizens of the UK and Colonies, from islands that had formed their home, and also the home of the parents, grand-parents and very possibly earlier ancestors".

11 The islanders were expelled, most to Mauritius but some to the Seychelles, without any workable resettlement scheme, left in poverty and given no compensation, and were otherwise[12] forgotten about by the British government.

12 Almost nothing was known of their plight until 1975, when some aspects of the affair surfaced in investigations by a US Congressional Committee, but by which time all of the inhabitants had been removed. Yet ever since, the Chagossians have refused to remain silent and have campaigned for the right to return and for adequate compensation.

13 Oliver Bancoult, the chair of the Chagos Refugees Group and leader of the Chagossians in exile, has said that:

14 "We believe that if the British public had known of these unlawful deportations at the time, we would probably still be living on the islands now. There is a lesson for our community[13], that we must learn to stand on our own feet and insist that we are consulted during the process leading to our return. We must never again rely on governments to tell us what we should have or not have."

The geography of the Chagos Islands

15 The Chagos islands are among the most remote in the world, situated in the Indian Ocean 1,200 miles northeast of Mauritius. They cover an area of ocean of 54,400 km^2 and comprise many atolls, Islands and submerged banks. Their land area is only 60 km^2 with the largest island, Diego Garcia, being horseshoe-shaped and 14 by 4 miles wide[14].

16 The outer islands consist of the atolls of Peros Banhos and Salomon, lying around 300 km north of Diego Garcia. These comprise 35 small islands with a total land area of 1,200 hectares; the largest of

these islands being 140 hectares in size. The Chagos Islands are noted for their great natural beauty, high species biodiversity and rich marine and terrestrial habitats. They have a benign maritime climate, with an average temperature of 27℃.

Depopulating the islands

17   When British foreign policy intervened, a variety of techniques were used to remove the inhabitants. It had long been the custom of the Chagossians to visit Mauritius to see relatives, to buy consumer goods or to obtain medical supplies and treatment that were unavailable on the Chagos islands. Some islanders, after visiting Mauritius, were simply—and suddenly—told by British officials they were not allowed back, meaning they were stranded, turned into exiles overnight. Many of the islanders later testified to having been tricked into leaving Diego Garcia by being offered a free trip. Some Chagossians claim they were deceived into believing what awaited them. Olivier Bancoult said that the islanders had been told they would have a house, a portion of land, animals and a sum of money, but when they arrived (in Mauritius) nothing had been done.

Children at a Chagos Island demonstration.

18   Most were moved first to the outlying islands of Peros Banhos and Salomen, where some 800 lived for two years. But in 1973 the British decided on a complete depopulation of the outlying islands as well, in

response to Pentagon insistence on a clean sweep[15] of the entire area. The BIOT arranged for its own ship, the Nordvaer, to take the last Chagossians to Mauritius. The Nordvaer provided harsh conditions for the deportees with limited sleeping accommodation and cramped conditions for the long journey. The Chagossians were forced to leave behind their furniture, brought with hard-earned money on the plantations, and were only able to take with them a minimum of personal possessions, packed into a small crate. Once in Mauritius, many of the Chagossians walked bewildered off the ship[16] and tramped through the slums of the capital, Port Louis, to try to find a relative or friend who would take them in.

The future

19   "The State Party (ie, the United Kingdom government) should, to the extent still possible, seek make exercise of the Illois' right to return to the territory practicable.[17] It should consider compensation for the denial of this right over an extended period."
  — United Nations, Human Rights Committee[18], Report on the UK, December 2001

20   Despite this position of the UN's Human Rights Committee, the future of the Chagossians is uncertain and somewhat bleak. It is clear that the UK government's use of legal mechanisms to block return to the islands, coupled with the US government's commitment to maintain the base, are the most significant factors affecting the fate of the Chagossians.

21   Given the importance of Diego Garcia to its military strategy, the US government is likely to continue to exert pressure on London to maintain the base. Although there is provision to review the original 1966 US/UK agreement in 2016, it is currently unlikely that either London or Washington will wish to do, at least without stronger international pressure. Chagossian hopes depend on whether governments at the United Nations will listen to current Chagossian lobbying and take up the issue more strongly. They also depend on the outcome of their current challenge to the government's June 2004 legal decision and a complaint for a breach of human rights to the European Court of Human Rights in Strasbourg.[19] The future of the Chagossians

also depends on citizens in the UK, and the degree to which they are able to communicate powerfully to the government that this is an issue of public concern. (Excerpt from *New African*[20], November, 2006)

New Words

abode /ə'bəʊd/ *n.* living or making a living in a certain place
academic /ˌækə'demɪk/ *n.* a member of a university or college who teaches or does research; a scholar 大学教师；研究人员；学者
accommodation /əˌkɒmə'deɪʃən/ *n.* space or capacity in vehicles that is available for certain people
atoll /'ætɒl/ *n.* an island consisting of a circular coral reef surrounding a lagoon 环状珊瑚岛，环礁
bank /bæŋk/ *n.* a large elevated area of a sea floor 沙洲
behest /bɪ'hest/ *n.* a command or urgent request
benign /bɪ'naɪn/ *adj.* mild; favourable
biodiversity /baɪəʊ daɪ'vɜːsəti/ *n.* the state of being different biologically 生物多样性
bleak /blɪk/ *adj.* without any reasons to feel happy or hopeful
Chagossian /'tʃɑːɡəsɪən/ *n.* inhabitant of Chagos 查戈斯岛民
commitment /kə'mɪtmənt/ *n.* a planned arrangement or activity that cannot be avoided; a strong will to do sth 难以放弃的既定方针；决意
cramped /kræmpt/ *adj.* restricted; without room to move 狭窄的；拥挤的
crate /kreɪt/ *n.* a large wooden box used for moving or storing goods 木板箱；板条箱
decolonization /diːˌkɒlənɪ'zeɪʃən/ *n.* the withdrawal of a state from its former colonies, leaving them independent; the acquisition of independence by a former colony 殖民地独立；去殖民化
defy /dɪ'faɪ/ *v.* If you defy sb or sth that is trying to make you behave in a particular way, you refuse to obey them and behave in that way. 抗命；违拗
depopulate /diː'pɒpjʊleɪt/ *v.* to reduce the number of inhabitants
depopulation /diːˌpɒpjʊ'leɪʃən/ *n.*
deportation /ˌdiːpɔː'teɪʃən/ *n.* a situation in which sb is deported from a country 驱逐出境
deportee /ˌdiːpɔː'tiː/ *n.* sb who has been deported or is going to be deported
detach /dɪ'tætʃ/ *v.* to separate, remove

dismember /dɪsˈmembə/ v. to divide (esp. a country)
diversity /daɪˈvɜːsɪtɪ/ n. the state or quality of being of different kinds 多样性
exile /ˈeksaɪl/ n. If sb is living in exile, he is living in a foreign country because he cannot live in his own country, usu. for political reasons.
forthright /ˈfɔːθraɪt/ adv. in a straight forward manner
given prep. taking ... into consideration
habitat /ˈhæbɪtæt/ n. the natural environment of an animal or plant in which it normally lives or grows 栖息地
hectare /ˈhektɑː/ n. a measurement of an area of land which is equal to 10,000 square metres, or 2.471 acres 公顷
indentured /ɪnˈdentʃəd/ adj. In the past, an indentured worker was one who was forced to work for sb for a period of time, because of an agreement made by people in authority. 受契约束缚的
inducement /ɪnˈdjuːsmənt/ n. the way to persuade sb to do sth by reasoning, coaxing, urging etc. 劝说；诱惑
initial /ɪˈnɪʃəl/ adj. of or occurring at the very beginning; designating the first period of
integrity /ɪnˈtegrɪtɪ/ n. wholeness, completeness
km (abbrev.) kilometer
km² (abbrev.) kilometer square 平方公里
lobbying /ˈlɒbɪɪŋ/ n. any attempt by a group or individual to influence the decisions of government 游说
marine /məˈriːn/ adj. relating to the sea or to the animals and plants that live in the sea 海洋的；沿海的
maritime /ˈmærɪtaɪm/ adj. relating to the sea and to ships 海洋的；海运的；船舶的
Mauritius /məˈrɪʃəs/ n. an island country in the Indian Ocean 毛里求斯
mechanism /ˈmekənɪzəm/ n. a device, system, process etc. by means of which some result is achieved
monitor /ˈmɒnɪtə/ v. to watch and check a situation carefully for a period of time in order to discover something about it 监测；监视
mount /maʊnt/ v. to organize a campaign or event and make it take place
outlying /ˈaʊtˌlaɪɪŋ/ adj. far from the central part of a place or region
plight /plaɪt/ n. being in a difficult or distressing situation that is full of problems

provision /prəˈvɪʒən/ n. an arrangement which is included in a law or an agreement 条款；规定

redress /rɪˈdres/ n. compensation for wrong or loss 赔偿；补救

resolution /ˌrezəˈluːʃən/ n. a formal decision taken at a meeting by means of a vote

Seychelles /seɪˈʃelz/ n. officially the Republic of Seychelles, a nation of 155 islands in the Indian Ocean 塞舌尔

species /ˈspiːʃiːz/ n. a group of individuals closely related in structure, capable of breeding within the group but not normally outside it 物种

stand /stænd/ v. to be valid

stranded /ˈstrændɪd/ adj. left somewhere with no way of going somewhere else 处于困境；进退两难

submerge /səbˈmɛːdʒ/ v. to go below the surface of some water or liquid 淹没

terrestrial /təˈrestrɪəl/ adj. existing on the Earth or happening on the Earth instead of in the sky or ocean 存在于陆地的；地球上的

territorial /ˌterɪˈtɔːrɪəl/ adj. of the area ruled by a sovereign or other authority 领土的

testify /ˈtestɪfaɪ/ v. to make a factual statement based on personal experience, or declare sth to be true from personal experience 以亲身经历作证

tramp /træmp/ v. to walk slowly and with regular, heavy steps, for a long time 跋涉

vulnerable /ˈvʌlnərəbl/ adj. weak and without protection; being easily hurt physically or emotionally 弱势的；易受伤害的

Notes

1. John Pilger—1939— , a multi-award-winning Australian-born journalist and documentary filmmaker. He acquired his first job in journalism as a copy boy with the *Sydney Sun* in 1958, later moving to *The Daily Telegraph*. Pilger left Australia to work for the *Daily Mirror* in Britain in the early 1960s and has since been based in that country.

   Pilger acted as a war correspondent during conflicts in Vietnam, Cambodia, Egypt, India, Bangladesh and Biafra. His reputation steadily emerged through both his documentary films and the books he has written. A number of his documentaries (纪录片) have focused upon what he alleges are human rights abuses perpetrated on civilian populations from the Israeli-occupied territories, to Indonesian East Timor and Iraq under UN sanctions.

Pilger has won many journalism and human rights awards, including Britain's prestigious Journalist of the Year award twice, and he has a number of honorary doctorates.

2. the Chagos islands—the Island group, in central Indian Ocean also known as "Chagos Archipelago". Acquired by Britain from France in 1814, it was originally administered by Britain as a dependency of Mauritius; since 1976 it has been the sole member of the British Indian Ocean Territory. Strategically situated at the centre of the Indian Ocean, its chief island, Diego Garcia, was developed as an air and naval refueling station by the U. S. and Great Britain in the mid 20th century, over the strong opposition from the region's coastal and island states.

3. a launch pad—the surface from which a space vehicle, missile, etc. is sent into the air or into space

4. Tony Blair—1953— , Prime Minister of the U. K (1997—2007), Leader of the Labour Party (1994—2007) and the Member of Parliament for Sedgefield (1983—2007). On the day he stood down as Prime Minister and MP, he was appointed official Envoy of the Quartet (四人小组) on the Middle East on behalf of the United Nations, the European Union, the United States and Russia.

He was the Labour Party's longest-serving Prime Minister and the only leader to have taken the party to three consecutive (连续的) general election victories.

Gordon Brown, Blair's Chancellor of the Exchequer (财政大臣) during all his ten years in office, succeeded him as party leader on 24 June 2007 and as Prime Minister on 27 June 2007.

5. Order in Council—an order issued by the British monarch on the advice of the Privy Council (枢密院) or an order issued by a government department under powers bestowed (授权) by Act of Parliament

6. Foreign Office minister—(英)外交大臣之简称。(见"读报知识")

7. right of abode—(law) the right to live in a country

8. Harold Wilson —1916－1995, Prime Minister of the UK (1964－1970) (1974－1976). He emerged as Prime Minister after more general elections than any other 20th century premier. He contested five general elections and won four of them, winning in 1964, 1966, February 1974 and October 1974. He is the most recent British Prime Minister to serve non-consecutive terms. Wilson managed a number of difficult political issues with considerable tactical skill, including such potentially divisive issues for his party as the role of public ownership, British membership of the European Community, and the Vietnam War. Nonetheless, his ambition of substantially improving Britain's long-term economic performance remained largely unfulfilled.
9. Pentagon—(fig.) the U.S. Department of Defense.
10. Soviet—connected with the former Soviet Union (1922－1991)
11. turn to—to apply to, call on, for help
12. otherwise—in another or different way. Here the word is used to emphasize the fact that the islanders were actually forgotten about in a different way by the British government though it moved the islanders to other places under the name of "resettlement".
13. community—here the public; people in general (见下册第 33 课"语言解说")
14. 14 by 4 miles wide—14 miles by length and 4 miles by width
15. in response to Pentagon insistence on a clean sweep—In response to the request of the US government, the British government depopulated the entire area to such an extent that not even one person was left on it. 应五角大楼的一再要求,彻底清除岛上的居民,一个不留。
16. many of the Chagossians walked bewildered off the ship—Many of the Chagossians walked off the ship in complete ignorance of what was happening.

  bewildered—mentally confused. The adjective is used to indicate an accompanying state of the subject of the sentence. And the sentence can be changed in to "many of the Chagossians, being bewildered, walked off the ship".
17. The State Party ... should, to the extent still possible, seek make exercise of the Illois' right to return to the territory practicable. —

The British government should seek whatever way that is still possible to fulfil the right of the islanders to return to their native place.

    a. to the extent still possible—to the extent that is still possible

    b. seek make—to seek to make

    c. the Illois—the former name for the Chagossians

    d. make ... practical—to fulfil; to make ... become true

18. Human Rights Committee—a UN body of 18 experts that meets three times a year to consider the five-yearly reports submitted by UN member states on their compliance with the International Covenant on Civil and Political Rights（公民权利和政治权利国际公约）.

    The Committee is one of seven UN-linked human rights treaty bodies.

    The Human Rights Committee should not be confused with the more high-profile（知名度）Commission on Human Rights, a Charter-based mechanism, or its replacement, the Human Rights Council(人权理事会). Whereas the Commission on Human Rights was a political forum where states debated all human rights concerns (since June 2006, replaced by the Council in that function), the Human Rights Committee is a treaty-based mechanism where a group of experts examines reports and rules on individual communications pertaining only to the International Covenant on Civil and Political Rights.

    联合国人权委员会（1946－2006）（简称人权委员会；英文：United Nations Commission on Human Rights, UNCHR)是联合国系统框架下的功能委员会。是一个政治论坛,属联合国经济社会理事会的职司委员会,也帮助联合国人权事务高级专员办事处（Office of the United Nations High Commissioner for Human Rights)开展工作。人权委员会是联合国系统审议人权问题的最主要机构之一,它的主要职责是:根据《联合国宪章》宗旨和原则,在人权领域进行专题研究、提出建议和起草国际人权文书并提交联合国大会。

19. They also depend on the outcome of ... a complaint for a breach of human rights to the European Court of Human Rights in Strasbourg. —Whether they can return to their native place depends

on the result of their present struggle against the British government's decision not to redress the mistreatment of the Chagossians and of their accusation of the British government for its violation of human rights to the European Court of Human Rights located in Strasbourg in France. 〔他们返回家园的愿望能否实现也取决于两点:(1)他们目前能否有效地抗争英国政府在 2004 年 6 月的法律判决;(2)他们向斯特拉斯堡的欧洲人权法庭控告英国违反人权能否成功。〕

  a. complaint——a formal allegation by the plaintiff（原告）in a civil action（控告）

  b. breach——the breaking of a legal or moral obligation

20. *New African*——《新非洲人》杂志,1966 年开始创刊发行,是一种在非洲大陆广受欢迎的英语月刊,杂志总的倾向是反对帝国主义和西方中心主义,它所发表的许多文章和评论都引起世界范围的关注,或呼吁整个非洲团结起来,或敦促非洲各国政府采取统一的方针,以便有助于非洲的发展。该杂志是最早的泛非英语月刊,也是销量最大的泛非杂志。

Questions

1. Why did the British government depopulate the Chagos islands secretly?
2. What is the US military base on the island used for?
3. How did the British government make the Chagos islands a new colony at the period of time when many colonized countries were winning their independence?
4. What methods did the British government take to depopulate the islands?
5. According to the writer, what were the major factors that affected the fate of the Chagossians?

读报知识

英国政府部门及官职

  英国政府各部名称和主管大臣官衔,英文原名也不一致。各部有叫 Ministry, Office 或 Department 的,而主管大臣或称 Secretary, 或称

President。从字面上看,似乎差别很大,其实不过有的是因袭旧名而已。如外交和联邦事务部、内政部、苏格兰事务部等都是由英王的秘书处扩大成部的,主管人本来都是英王秘书(King's Secretary of State),所以现在的部长沿用了旧的官衔,称为 Secretary of State。枢密大臣、掌玺大臣和大法官等职也是设立时间较长,一般由贵族担任,故称 Lord,如 Lord Chief Justice(高等法院王座庭庭长)。英王爱德华三世封其子为兰开夏郡的兰开斯特公爵,后来亨利四世将该郡财产和司法权收归王室,并设立 Chancellor of the Duchy of Lancaster(兰开斯特公爵郡大臣)一职,至今未变。贸易工业部现用 Department,先前称委员会(Board)。至于农业、渔业和粮食部、国防部、卫生和社会保险部等,则迟至 20 世纪才成立,故改用 Ministry。

在报刊中一般用非正式的简称,如"the Foreign and Commonwealth Office"(外交和联邦事务部)(报刊因随意性大也用 Ministry of...),一般简称"the Foreign Office"(外交部),而大臣也由全称"Secretary of State for Foreign and Commonwealth Affairs"(外交和联邦事务大臣)简化为"Foreign Secretary"(外交大臣)。

政府各部门中的官员分为两类:大臣、相当于副大臣的国务大臣(State Minister)(如 Minister of State for Foreign and Commonwealth Office——外交和联邦事务部国务大臣)和政务次官(Parliamentary Undersecretary 属于政务官员,即政治家)。其余的都是文官,各部首席文官称为常务次官(Permanent Undersecretary 或 Permanent Secretary)。文官是指常务次官及其以下的政府官员,又被称为职业官员,实行常任制,以其知识和技能为王国效力。政务官员必须随内阁进退,而文官则不然。

英国与美国的体制不同,官职繁杂,如财政部就有 First Lord of the Treasury(首席财政大臣)、Chancellor of Exchequer(财政大臣)和 Chief Secretary to the Treasury,对于后者有的工具书译为"财政部首席大臣",那么此职与首相兼任的"首席财政大臣"有何区别?是否高于财政大臣?事实上,他是财政大臣副手,但如译为常务副大臣也不合适,因为副大臣由政务次官担任,故不如将其试译为"财政部常务大臣"。再如 Permanent Secretary,有译"常务大臣"的,而将 Permanent Under Secretary 译为"常务次官"。实际上这两者是一个官职,各部文官之首,应都译为"常务次官"。再如 First Sea Lord 或 Sea Lord,有译"海务大臣"的,与 First Lord of the Admiralty(海军大臣)看成两个部门的官职了。事实上 First/Second/Second/Third/Fourth Sea Lord 都是海军部"副大臣"。前首相丘吉尔曾任海军大臣。见例句:

He [Winston Churchill] was home secretary (1910 — 1911), a dynamic **first lord of the admiralty** (1911—1915)...

(The *New American Desk Encyclopedia*)

Unit Seven
Prominent Figures of the U.S. and Britain

Lesson Twenty-one

课文导读

好莱坞硬汉、动作影星阿诺德·施瓦辛格在一系列电影中所扮演的"终结者"(Terminator)形象,早已经深入人心。那句经典台词"I'll be back!"是他扮演机器人战士在电影《魔鬼终结者I》中道出的,让观众对其下一个形象充满期待。2011年1月3日,63岁的施瓦辛格结束了长达7年的州长政治生涯。此后,人们不由自主地在猜想,施瓦辛格的下一个人生目标是什么?演电影,当教授,建智库……似乎,仅仅给他再加上学者、商人两个新头衔还远远不够。2012年9月,他又手持自传,全面回顾了他那令人难以置信的真实生活,再次引起世人的注目。

自传描写他从童年到成年的种种经历,既有传奇人生,也有失败和与常人不同之处。难怪书名叫"Total Recall"。青年读者应该学习他做事情的自信心和坚忍不拔、敢于闯荡、勇于创新的精神,但不要崇尚他那放荡不羁的性格和生活。

Pre-reading Questions

1. Have you ever seen any of the films starring Mr Arndd Schwarzenegger?
2. What is your impression of Mr Schwarzenegger?

Text

He's Back All Right, Now with a Memoir
"Total Recall," by Arnold Schwarzenegger with Peter Petre[1]
By Janet Maslin

1 When Arnold Schwarzenegger was governor of California, a reporter asked about the Cohiba[2] label on the cigar Mr. Schwarzenegger was smoking. "That's a Cuban cigar," the reporter said. "You're the governor. How can you flout the law?[3]"

2   The answer was as good a one-sentence encapsulation of the bodybuilder/entrepreneur/movie star/politician/braggart's philosophy as all of "Total Recall," his 646-page memoir, provides. "I smoke it because it's a great cigar," he said.

3   This is only one of countless ways Mr. Schwarzenegger has prized self-interest throughout his long, glory-stalking and (as he loves pointing out) extremely lucrative career. "Total Recall" contains nonstop illustrations of how he aims high, tramples on competitors, breaks barriers and savors every victory, be it large or small. Those who mistake "Total Recall" for a salacious tell-all may not 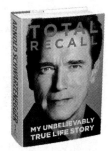 be that interested in how many Mr. Olympia[4] contests he won (seven) or who he beat for a Golden Globe[5] in 1977 (Truman Capote[6] and the kid who played Damien in "The Omen"[7]). Let's get the scandalous stuff out of the way, because Mr. Schwarzenegger certainly wants to.

4   About the son he conceived with the family housekeeper, Mildred Baena, in 1996, he says only this: that he had always promised himself not to fool around with the help[8]. That once, "all of a sudden," he and Ms. Baena "were alone in the guesthouse." And immediately after that: "When Mildred gave birth the following August. ..."

5   What "Total Recall" actually turns out to be is a puffy portrait of the author as master conniver. Nothing in his upward progress seems to have happened in an innocent way.

6   The book begins with the obligatory description of his Austrian childhood and says that he and his brother were forced to do situps to earn their breakfast. He also explains how the bodybuilder photos he pinned up in his room made his mother seek a doctor's advice. The doctor assured her that these were surrogate father figures, so there was nothing "wrong" with her red-blooded, heterosexual boy.

7   The book moves on to describe a hair-raising stint in an Austrian Army tank unit, where antics included driving one tank into water and trying to drag-race with another. This earned him an early release from service. He went on to win bodybuilding titles in Europe, move to America, garner the attention of the filmmakers who would feature him in "Pumping Iron"[9] and land the Hollywood acting role he coveted in

"Stay Hungry."[10]

8   When told by an acting coach to summon a sense memory of victory, he says, "I had to explain that actually I was not especially exhilarated when I won, because to me, winning was a given."

9   And so it goes, through progress from pedestal to pedestal, until "Conan the Barbarian"[11] makes him an action star. Mr. Schwarzenegger and his co-writer, Peter Petre, had to brush up on[12] the details of his acting career by reading biographies and movie journals; his memory for slights, triumphs and salaries seems more reliable than his memory for work. But one way or another we learn how raw meat was sewn into his Conan costume for a scene in which he is attacked by wolves. (Sadly, the audio version of "Total Recall" is not fully read by him. You would have to rewatch the film to hear him say: "Hither came I, Conan, a thief, a reaver, a slayer, to tread jeweled thrones of the earth beneath my feet." But it might be worth it.[13])

10 In 1977 he met Maria Shriver[14], who would become his wife and enthusiastic helpmate until the matter of Ms. Baena and her son came to light. Although Mr. Schwarzenegger says that others wrongly imagined that to "marry a Kennedy"[15] was one of his goals, he too speaks of their union as an accomplishment. Among many noxious references to his wife are a buddy's pre-wedding quip ("Oh boy, wait until she hits menopause") and his way of commissioning an Andy Warhol[16] portrait of her. "You know how you always do the paintings of stars?" he says he asked Mr. Warhol. "Well, when Maria marries me, she will be a star!" He does not appear to be joking.

11 When Mr. Schwarzenegger was at the height of his movie career, he thought of quip making as one of his strong suits[17]. (In "Commando,"[18] about a man whose neck he has just broken: "Don't disturb my friend, he's dead tired.") But he was personable enough to cultivate his Democratic Kennedy in-laws and also grow close to the Republican circle of President George H. W. Bush[19]. He claims to have been included in a decision-making meeting about the initial gulf war invasion of Iraq[20].

12 His account of his own political career is, of course, careful to accentuate the positive. He ran for governor of California in 2003's recall election[21] even after Karl Rove[22] told him that Condoleezza Rice[23]

was being groomed as a future candidate of choice. He emphasizes his centrist credentials as a Republican favoring a social safety net, solar energy and stem cell[24] research but also facing down his state's three most powerful public-employee unions[25]. He claims to have done his best to grapple with the state's dire budget woes. But he atypically keeps the crowing minimal: "I do not deny that being governor was more complex and challenging than I had imagined."

13 This book ends with a not-great list of "Arnold's Rules." They are basic ("Reps, reps, reps"), boorish ("No matter what you do in life, selling is part of it"), big on denial[26] ("When someone tells you no, you should hear yes") and only borderline helpful[27]. When he met Pope John Paul II[28] in 1983, they talked about workouts. The pope rose daily at 5 a.m. in order to stick to his regimen. If he could do it, this book says, you can do it, too. (From *The New York Times*, September 30, 2012)

New Words

accentuate /əkˈsentʃʊeɪt/ v. to stress or emphasize

antics /ˈæntɪks/ n. pl. behavior that seems strange, funny, silly or annoying 古怪可笑的举动

atypically /eɪˈtɪpɪkəl/ adv. not typically, different from what is usual 非典型地，非同寻常地

boorish /ˈbʊərɪʃ/ adj. rude 粗鲁的；粗鄙的

braggart /ˈbrægət/ n. one given to loud, empty boasting; a bragger 自夸者，大言不惭的人

California /ˌkælɪˈfɔːnjə, -ˈfɔːniːə/ n. a state in the western US on the Pacific Ocean

centrist /ˈsentrɪst/ n. a person who supports the centre in politics; a moderate 中立派；温和派; adj. marked by or adhering to a moderate political view 温和派的

conceive /kənˈsiːv/ v. to become pregnant with (offspring) (使)怀孕

conniver /kəˈnaɪvə/ n. one who works (together with sb) secretly to achieve sth, esp. sth wrong 阴谋家，串谋者

covet /ˈkʌvət/ v. to desire eagerly (esp. sth belonging to another person) 贪求；觊觎

credentials /krəˈdenʃlz/ n. pl. anything that proves a person's abilities, qualities, or suitability (任何证明人的能力，资格等的)证

明;资格

crow /krəʊ/ v. to express pride openly, esp. when taking pleasure from someone else's misfortune 洋洋得意,幸灾乐祸

Cuban /ˈkjuːbən/ adj. 古巴的;古巴人

Democratic /ˌdeməˈkrætɪk/ adj. (美国)民主党的

dire /ˈdaɪə(r)/ adj. extremely serious, bad or terrible

drag-race v. AmE to have a car race that is won by the car that can increase its speed fastest over a very short distance 参加短程汽车加速赛

encapsulation /ɪnˌkæpsjʊˈleɪʃən/ n. expression in a brief summary 概括

entrepreneur /ˌɒntrəprəˈnɜː(r)/ n. a person who organizes, operates, and assumes the risk for a business venture 企业家

exhilarated /ɪɡˈzɪləˌreɪtɪd/ adj. feeling extremely excited and happy 异常兴奋的

feature /ˈfiːtʃə(r)/ v. to include as a leading performer 由……主演

flout /flaʊt/ v. to show contempt for; scorn 轻视,蔑视

garner /ˈɡɑːnə(r)/ v. to acquire, to get by one's own efforts 取得,获得

given /ˈɡɪvn/ n. sth taken for granted 理所当然的

glory-stalking adj. 风光无限的,伴随荣耀的

grapple /ˈɡræpl/ v. (with) to work hard to deal with sth difficult 努力设法解决

groom /ɡruːm/ v. to prepare (someone) as for a specific position or purpose 培养(某人),使做好准备

hair-raising /ˈheəˌreɪzɪŋ/ adj. causing excitement, terror, or thrills 令人兴奋、恐惧或刺激的

heterosexual /ˌhetərəˈsekʃʊəl/ adj. sexually oriented to persons of the opposite sex 异性恋的,异性性取向的

hither /ˈhɪðə(r)/ adv. here 这里

in-laws /ˈɪnlɔːz/ n. one's relative by marriage, esp. the father and mother of one's husband and wife 姻亲,亲家

lucrative /ˈluːkrətɪv/ adj. producing wealth; profitable 可赚大钱的,利润丰厚的;能获利的

memoir /ˈmemwɑː(r)/ n. an account of the personal experiences of an author 自传,回忆录

menopause /ˈmenəpɔːz/ n. 【医】停经;更年期;绝经期

noxious /ˈnɒkʃəs/ adj. harmful or poisonous 有害的,有毒的

obligatory /əˈblɪɡətrɪ/ adj. sth must be done because of a rule or a law 必须做的

pedestal /ˈpedɪstl/ *n.* a base on which a pillar or statue stands(柱子或雕像的)基座;基础

personable /ˈpɜːsənəbəl/ *adj.* pleasing in personality or appearance; attractive 风度翩翩的;招人喜爱的

puffy /ˈpʌfɪ/ *adj.* 爱炫耀的,自夸的

quip /kwɪp/ *n.* a clever amusing remark made without planning it in advance (即兴的)俏皮话,嘲讽,妙语

reaver *n.* one who robs 抢劫者

recall /rɪˈkɔːl/ *n.* the procedure by which a public official may be removed from office by popular vote 罢免

regimen /ˈredʒɪmən/ *n.* a regulated system, as of diet, therapy, or exercise, intended to promote health or achieve another beneficial effect 养生法

reps /reps/ *n.* = repeats 重复

Republican /rɪˈpʌblɪkən/ *adj.* (美国)共和党的

salacious /səˈleɪʃəs/ *adj. fml* expressing or causing strong sexual feelings, usu. in an unpleasant or shocking way 好色的,淫秽的

scandalous /ˈskændələs/ *adj.* containing material damaging to reputation; defamatory 诽谤的,丑闻的

situp /sɪtˈʌp/ *n.* an exercise in which you sit up from a lying position while keeping your legs straight on the floor 仰卧起坐

slayer /ˈsleɪə/ *n.* killer, murderer

slight /slaɪt/ *n.* the act or an instance of slighting, insult 冷落,轻蔑,怠慢

stalk /stɔːk/ *v.* to walk in a proud or angry way, with long steps

stint /stɪnt/ *n.* a limited or fixed period of work or effort 规定期限,任期

surrogate /ˈsʌrəgət/ *adj.* substitute 替代的,作为代用品的

trample /ˈtræmpl/ *v.* to deliberately ignore 践踏;无视(*cf.* tread)

tread /tred/ *v.* to press beneath the feet; trample 践踏,踩(*cf.* trample)

woe /wəʊ/ *n.* a cause of trouble; problem

workout /ˈwɜːkaʊt/ *n.* a period of physical exercise (尤指体育的)训练,赛前集训

Notes

1. "Total Recall," by Arnold Schwarzenegger with Peter Petre—the book is written by the two.

a. Total Recall—"Total Recall: My Unbelievably True Life Story"(《全面回忆：我那难以置信的真实生活》), Arnold Schwarzenegger's memoir, a New York Times bestseller published in October 2012, by Arnold Schwarzenegger and his co-writer Peter Petre. The name of the memoir is borrowed from a 1990 American dystopian(反乌托邦的) science fiction action film directed by Paul Verhoeven and starring Arnold Schwarzenegger, which is referred to as the audio version of "Total Recall" in Para 9.

b. Arnold Schwarzenegger—1947 — , an Austrian and American former professional bodybuilder, actor, businessman, investor, and Governor of California (2003—2011).

c. Peter Petre—an American writer

2. Cohiba—a brand for two kinds of cigar, one produced in Cuba for Habanos S. A., the Cuban state-owned tobacco company, and the other produced in the Dominican Republic for US-based General Cigar Company. （高希霸）

3. "That's a Cuban cigar ... How can you flout the law?"—Following the Cuban Revolution of 1959, Cuba-US relations deteriorated substantially and have been marked by tension and confrontation since. The US does not have formal diplomatic relations with Cuba and has maintained an embargo （禁运） which makes it illegal for U. S. corporations to do business with Cuba.

4. Mr. Olympia—the title awarded to the winner of the professional men's bodybuilding contest held annually by the International Federation of BodyBuilding & Fitness （IFBB）. The first Mr. Olympia was held on September 18, 1965 at the Brooklyn Academy of Music, New York City. There is also a female bodybuilder crowned, the Ms. Olympia, as are winners of Fitness Olympia and Figure Olympia for fitness and figure competitors. 奥林匹亚先生：奥林匹亚健美大赛男子专业健美最终冠军的荣誉称号。

5. Golden Globe—The Golden Globe Award is an honor bestowed by the 93 members of the Hollywood Foreign Press Association （HFPA） recognizing excellence in film and television, both domestic and foreign. The annual formal ceremony and dinner at which the awards are presented is a major part of the film industry's awards season. The 1st Golden Globe Awards were held in January 1944 at

the 20th Century-Fox studios in Los Angeles. The 70th Golden Globe Awards, honoring the best in film and television for 2012, were presented on January 13, 2013, at the Beverly Hilton Hotel in Beverly Hills, California, where they have been held annually since 1961. 美国影视金球奖

6. Truman Capote—1924－1984, an American author, many of whose short stories, novels, plays, and nonfiction are recognized literary classics, including the novella *Breakfast at Tiffany's*《蒂凡尼早餐》(1958) and the true crime novel *In Cold Blood*《冷血》(1966), which he labeled a "nonfiction novel". At least 20 films and television dramas have been produced from Capote novels, stories and screenplays. 杜鲁门·卡波特,美国著名作家、编剧,1977年因出演电影《怪宴》(*Murder by Death*)获金球奖最佳新人奖(Best Acting Debut in a Motion Picture-Male)提名。

7. "The Omen"—a 1976 American/British suspense horror film directed by Richard Donner. The film received numerous accolades (奖励) for its acting, writing, music and technical achievements.《凶兆》。1977年,该剧中饰演小男孩达米恩(Damien)的演员哈维·史蒂芬斯(Harvey Stephens)获金球奖最佳新人奖提名。

8. to fool around with the help—to involve in a sexual relationship with the house servant (口) 与佣人搞不正当的男女关系
　　fool around—to spend time idly or aimlessly

9. "Pumping Iron"—a 1977 docudrama(文献记录片) about the world of bodybuilding, focusing on the 1975 International Federation of Bodybuilding (IFBB) Mr. Universe and Mr. Olympia competitions. Inspired by a book of the same name by Charles Gaines and George Butler, the film nominally focuses on the competition between Arnold Schwarzenegger and one of his primary competitors for the title of Mr. Olympia, Lou Ferrigno. The film helped launch the acting careers of Arnold Schwarzenegger. 电影纪录片《健美之路》,另译为《铁金刚》或《泵铁》。

10. "Stay Hungry"—an American dramatic comedy film in 1976, for which Arnold Schwarzenegger was awarded a Golden Globe for New Male Star of the Year.《饥饿生存》,施瓦辛格凭借该片中的出色表现荣获1977年金球奖"最佳新人奖"。

11. "Conan the Barbarian"—a 1982 American sword and sorcery (魔

法)/adventure film directed and co-written by John Milius. It is about the adventures of the eponymous character in a fictional prehistoric world of dark magic and savagery. The film stars Arnold Schwarzenegger and James Earl Jones, and tells the story of a young barbarian (Schwarzenegger) who seeks vengeance for the death of his parents at the hands of Thulsa Doom (Jones), the leader of a snake cult. This was Schwarzenegger's breakthrough film, which was a box-office hit (十分卖座的电影).《野蛮人柯南》，又译《王者之剑》，乃施瓦辛格在银幕上名副其实的成名之作。

12. brush up on—to refresh one's memory of, review one's knowledge of
13. But it might be worth it—But it might be worth rewatching the film to hear what he says.
14. Maria Shriver—1955— , an American journalist and author of six best-selling books. She has received a Peabody Award, and was co-anchor (共同主持) for NBC's Emmy-winning coverage of the 1988 Summer Olympics. She was formerly First Lady of California as the wife of actor and then-California Governor Arnold Schwarzenegger, from whom she is now separated. She is a member of the Kennedy family (her mother, Eunice Kennedy Shriver was a sister of John F. Kennedy, Robert F. Kennedy, and Edward Kennedy).
15. marry a Kennedy—On April 26, 1986, Schwarzenegger married television journalist Maria Shriver, who is the niece of the former President John F. Kennedy. On May 9, 2011, Shriver and Schwarzenegger separated after 25 years of marriage. 肯尼迪家族是美国的名门望族，无论是在金钱财富上，还是在政治权力上，都曾经达到登峰造极的程度。所以，与肯尼迪家族联姻，即意味着高攀。本句中的 a Kennedy 指肯尼迪名门家族的一员。
16. Andy Warhol—1928—1987, an American artist who was a leading figure in the visual art movement known as pop art. 安迪•沃霍尔，美国艺术家、印刷家、电影摄影师，是视觉艺术运动波普艺术最有名的开创者之一。
17. he thought of quip making as one of his strong suits—he thought of telling witticism as one of what he is good at

    one's strong(est) suit—one's best quality or what one is good at
18. "Commando"—a 1985 American action-comedy film starred by

Arnold Schwarzenegger. The film was a commercial success. It was also the 7th top-grossing film of 1985 worldwide《魔鬼司令》，又译《独闯龙潭》，是施瓦辛格第一次以现代战士角色出镜，并且奠定了他的这一现实人物形象，是他的代表作之一。commando 本义为"突击队员"。

19. George H. W. Bush—1924— , the 41st President (1989—1993), Vice President of the US (1981—1989), and Director of Central Intelligence. He is often referred to as "George H. W. Bush," "Bush 41," "Bush the Elder," and "George Bush, Sr." to distinguish him from his son, 43rd President George W. Bush. 乔治·赫伯特·沃克·布什，第 41 任总统。常被称为"老布什"，以区别于其长子、担任过第 43 任总统的乔治·沃克·布什。

20. gulf war invasion of Iraq—a war waged by a U. N-authorized coalition force from 34 nations led by the US, against Iraq in response to Iraq's invasion and annexation（吞并）of Kuwait. 指的是第一次海湾战争或伊拉克战争。由小布什领导打的是第二次战争

21. recall election—a procedure by which voters can remove an elected official from office through a direct vote before his or her term has ended. The 2003 California gubernatorial recall election（州长罢免选举）was a special election permitted under California state law. Governor Gray Davis of California was recalled over the state budget. The voters replaced incumbent（在职的）Democratic Governor Gray Davis with Republican Arnold Schwarzenegger. 罢免选举

22. Karl Rove—1950 — , American Republican political consultant and policy advisor. He was Senior Advisor and Deputy Chief of Staff（白宫办公厅副主任）during the George W. Bush administration until Rove's resignation on August 31, 2007. 卡尔·罗夫是小布什的恩师，助选高手

23. Condoleezza Rice—1954 — , an American political scientist and diplomat, Secretary of State (2005 — 2009), and the first female African-American secretary of state, as well as the second African American (after Colin Powell), and the second woman (after Madeleine Albright). Rice was President Bush's National Security Advisor during his first term, making her the first woman to serve

in that position. 康多莉扎·赖斯,曾任国务卿,是小布什的亲信
24. stem cell—Stem cells are biological cells found in all multicellular organisms（多细胞生物）, that can divide through mitosis（细胞有丝分裂）and differentiate into diverse specialized cell types and can self-renew to produce more stem cells. Adult stem cell treatments have been successfully used for many years to treat leukemia（白血病）and related bone/blood cancers through bone marrow transplants. 干细胞
25. facing down his state's three most powerful public-employee unions—defeating and showing confidence before the three most powerful public-employee unions in California

　　face down—to appear strong and confident when someone is threatening or criticizing you 压倒,降服

　　three most powerful public-employee unions-probably refers to the three National trade union organizations: American Federation of Labor and Congress of Industrial Organizations（AFL-CIO 美国劳工联合会－产业工会联合会）, Change to Win Federation（CtW 改变以获胜联盟）, Industrial Workers of the World（IWW,世界产业工人联盟）
26. be big on sth—to like sth very much
27. and only borderline helpful—and almost helpful but not enough

　　borderline—*adj.* almost reaching a particular level 勉强可以的,刚刚够格的
30. Pope John Paul II—1920－2005, born in Poland, reigned as Pope of the Catholic Church from 1978 until his death in 2005. He was the second-longest serving Pope in history and the first non-Italian since 1523. 约翰·保罗二世,罗马天主教第 264 任教皇,梵蒂冈城国国家元首。

Questions

1. What is "Total Recall"?
2. What does "Total Recall" contain?
3. What happened to Mr Schwarzenegger with his housekeeper Mildred Baena?
4. What information can you get from the book about Arnold Schwarzenegger's childhood?

5. Can you name some films starring Arnold Schwarzenegger?
6. How did Mr Schwarzenegger start his political career?
7. What is Peter Petre's attitude towards Schwarzenegger and his book?

学习方法

读懂标题（Ⅱ）

3. 省略

（1）标题往往只标实义词，略去虚词。省略最多的是冠词和动词"to be"，其次是介词、连词、助动词和代词，有时连实义词甚至主句也省略掉。这是新闻多、节省版面的缘故，但以不影响理解为前提。例如：

a. Italian Ex-Mayor Murdered
= (An) Italian Ex-mayor (Is) Murdered

b. Rail Chaos Getting Worse
= (The) Rail Chaos (Is) Getting Worse

c. No Survivors in Gulf Air Crash
= (There Are) No Survivors in (the) Gulf Air Crash

d. Alaskan Oil for Japan?
= (Will There Be) Alaskan Oil for Japan?

e. Have Dollars, Will Sell
= (If You) Have Dollars, (They) Will Sell

f. Ballots, Not Bullets
= (The Algerians Want) Ballots, (Do) Not (Want) Bullets

（2）并非所有的冠词都能省略。如：

a. West Point Makes a Comeback
"西点军校东山再起"。"make a comeback"是成语，"a"不能省。

b. How America Sees the World
"美国怎样看待世界？" "the World"冠词不能省，如省了，词义不同。

c. Killing in the Name of God
"邪教教主以上帝之名大开杀戒。" "of God"作定语修饰"Name"，所以这个"the"也不能省。还有因排行需要或从美观原则出发而保留冠词的。

(3)"And"常被逗号所取代。如：
a. Thailand, Malaysia Ink Sea Treaty
   = Thailand (and) Malaysia Ink (a) Sea Treaty
b. Woman Kills Husband, Self
   = (A) Woman Kills (Her) Husband (and) (Her)self
c. Volunteer, Terrorist Killed in an Ambush
   = (A) Volunteer (and) (a) Terrorist (Are) Killed in an Ambush
(4)动词"to be"有时由冒号取代，如：
a. Chinese Cooks: Masters at Turning a Turnip into a Flower
   = Chinese Cooks (Are) Masters at Turning a Turnip into a Flower
b. Kaka: Brazil's Mr. Perfect
   =Kaka(Is) Brazil's Mr. Perfect
(5)动词"say,said"用冒号或引号代替。如：
Mao: We Should Support Third World Countries
= Mao (Says) (That) We Should Support (the) Third World Countries
(6)以名词作定语组成的标题，既无动词，也无连词。如：
a. Channel Tunnel Halt
   （[英吉利海峡]隧道工程[暂]停[施]工）
b. Shotgun Death Riddle Drama
   （枪杀事件，扑朔迷离）
c. Zoo Escape Drama
   （动物园猛兽出逃，虚惊一场）

4．时态
动词时态用法大大简化。如：
(1)几乎都用一般现在时，这是标题的另一个重要特点。新闻所述的事件多半是刚刚发生、正在发生或将会发生，按英语语法规则应用动词的相应时态。但为了使读者感到是"新闻"而不是"旧闻"，常用一般现在时来表示：
A. 过去发生的事，如：
   a. 13 **Die** as crowded Van Crosses M4
   b. Jeweler **Is** Slain
B. 正在发生之事，如：
   Schools **Ask** Parents for Money Toward Books
(2)用动词不定式表示将来时态，如：
   a. Peking **to Fire** Test Rocket to South Pacific

(3) 过去分词表示：
A. 现在时态，如：
   a. U. S. Car Makers **Viewed** as Threat by Europeans
   b. Case **Probed**
B. 过去时态，如：
   Colombian **Sent** to U. S. for Drug Trial
C. 正在进行时态，如：
   Brazil Elite **Forced** to Make Loans
D. 现在完成时态，如：
   Petrol Bomb **Found** outside Cardiff Conservative Club

这些标题中用动词不定式和过去分词所表示的时态与日常英语并无不同，只要语言基础打好了，一看就明白。动词现在式、不定式及过去分词在标题中所表示上述时态如何确定呢？一是主要看导语(lead)。二是根据常识。如：

Brazil Elite **Forced** to Make Loans

RIO DE JANEIRO，May 6（AP）—The economic elite of Brazil **is being forced** to lend money to the Treasury at 6-percent annual interest over two years...

(4) 应该说明，引语和设问式标题中，除现在时外，还可能有其他时态，如：
a. "I **Was** Not His Mistress"
b. Jones **Planned** to Kill Carter?
c. "We **Won't** Quit"

这些时态的应用，主要是为了强调动作的时间性，否则会产生误解。

Lesson Twenty-two

课文导读

盖茨1977年1月辍学，提前离开哈佛大学，在美国建立微软公司。自此，带着他的微软帝国走过了36个辉煌的春秋。2008年6月，他正式宣布辞去在微软的全职工作，只保留其董事长一职。这令很多人感到惊奇。然而这就是盖茨。众所周知，他辞去日常工作并不是享清福，而是去从事回报社会的慈善工作，因为是社会给了他创新的机遇。

盖茨是全球首富的代名词，然而从本课的"Internet Computing"，"network effects"，"Microsoft Basic/DOS"等方面来看，他为今天因特网的普及、应用、推广及自动化等等一系新技术作出了何等巨大的贡献，为世界创造了何等巨大的财富，因而说他是他这一代一位最伟大的创新企业家，其成功事例(success story)值得人们研究探讨。

Pre-reading Questions

1. What do you know about Bill Gates?
2. What does Gates' retirement mean to Microsoft and to the IT world?

Text

Bill Gates is retiring, sort of

By Steve Lohr

1 NEW YORK: Bill Gates is retiring, sort of.[1] He is still only 52, and he is going off to spend more time guiding the world's richest philanthropy, the Bill and Melinda Gates Foundation[2]. He will still be Microsoft's chairman and largest shareholder, but Friday is his last day as a full-time worker at the software giant, marking the unofficial end of his career as a business leader.

2 Sure, there are the blockbuster Microsoft products, like Windows and Office, used in offices and homes, everywhere, every day. But

Bill Gates speaking at the Consumer Electronics Show in January 2008. (Rick Wilking/Reuters)

beyond that, Gates, and his company, founded 33 years ago, have fundamentally shaped how people think about competition in many industries where technology plays a central role, the behavior of modern markets, and even antitrust.

3 In a sense, Bill Gates can be seen as the foremost applied economist of the second half of the 20th century.

4 Yet the old rules of competition, so lucratively mastered by Microsoft, are being altered by the current wave of Internet computing[3]—and Google is the company at the forefront. So far, Microsoft is struggling to adjust, and it will be up to Gates's successors to overcome the challenge or watch Microsoft's wealth and leadership in the industry steadily erode.

5 Whatever the future for Microsoft, the Gates legacy is impressive. The main reason that there are more than a billion copies of the Windows operating system on personal computers around the world, according to industry experts and economists, is that Gates grasped and deployed two related concepts on a scale no one ever did in the past—"network effects[4]" and the creation of a technology "platform."

6 Put simply, a network effect is that the value of a product goes up as more people use it. A technology platform is a set of tools or services that others can use to build their own products or services. So building the workbench-like platform encourages more people to join the network, which attracts more interest in the platform, enlarging the

network and so on.

7   For Gates, the strategy started with its first product, Microsoft Basic[5], a programming language, but really took off with its operating systems, first Microsoft DOS[6] and then the many versions of Windows. Today, there are many thousands of software applications that run on the Windows platform, not just word processing and spreadsheets but the specialized programs in doctors' offices, factory floors and retail stores mainly run on Windows—a very broad network, on a technology platform.

8   "Gates saw software as a separate market from hardware before anyone else, but his great insight was recognizing the power of the network effects surrounding the software," said Michael Cusumano, a professor at the Sloan School of Management at the Massachusetts Institute of Technology[7].

9   That, Cusumano added, was the essential difference in the paths of Microsoft and Apple[8], the early leader in personal computing. Apple, he said, focused on making outstanding products alone, while Microsoft nurtured a growing business ecosystem[9] of outside software developers who use, and are dependent upon, Microsoft's technology.

10 "Apple has always been a product company, and Microsoft is a platform company," Cusumano said.

11 The result, he adds, is that Apple today does make outstanding products, though its market share is small, while more than 90 percent of personal computers run Microsoft software.

12 Hindsight tends to bring clarity. In the early years, it is unclear how much Gates was pursuing each opportunity as it came as opposed to a grand strategy. He had large ambitions. When he was a Harvard undergraduate, Gates lamented that so many of his fellow students pursued a "narrow track for success[10]," diligent strivers in safe professions, instead of being willing to "take big risks to do big things," recalled Michael Katz, who was a Harvard student at the time.

13 While Gates dropped out of college to found Microsoft, with Paul Allen, Katz went on to become an economist. In fact, he was the co-author of a seminal paper in 1985 on network effects and the use of technology standards as weapons of competition, a paper that would eventually be cited prominently in the landmark U. S. government

antitrust suit against Microsoft[11].

14   In the early 1980s, when Katz and a fellow economist, Carl Shapiro, were doing the research for the paper, they looked at technology standards like the rivals in videocassette recording, Sony's Betamax versus VHS[12], backed by other Japanese companies. They looked at personal computers, mainly in terms of the competition between Apple and IBM-compatible personal computers. They were aware of Microsoft's role, as an operating system supplier, Katz said, but had no inkling how things would play out[13].

15   "At the time, we weren't thinking that Microsoft would rise to dominate the computer world," said Katz, a professor at the Stern School of Business at New York University[14].

16   By the early 1990s, Gates spoke fluently in the economic language of network effects, network externalities, increasing returns and technology standards. In a Harvard business school case study, Gates explained, "We look for opportunities with network externalities—where there are advantages to the vast majority of consumers to share a common standard. We look for businesses where we can garner large market shares, not just 30 or 35 percent."

17   Microsoft's market share in Internet search in the United States is less than 10 percent, while Google holds more than 60 percent and Yahoo has about 20 percent. And the rise of Internet services and social networks, like Facebook and MySpace[15], but also Web-based alternatives to traditional desktop software including e-mail, word processors and spreadsheets poses a fresh challenge to Microsoft.

18   Traditional desktop software—and the technology standards Microsoft controls there—matter far less when more software is accessed with a Web browser and delivered over the Internet from vast data centers run by Google and others. The new technology is widely known as "cloud computing[16]" and the business model behind it is typically to sell online advertising.

19   "The threat to any technology company is to miss one of the big shifts in technology, and Microsoft missed the transition to cloud computing and advertising as the revenue source for the Internet," said David Yoffie, a professor at the Harvard business school.[17]

20   "The Web is now the platform," Yoffie added. "People are writing

Web applications for everything from Facebook to business programs inside corporations. The business ecosystem is migrating to the Web and away from Microsoft."

21   At Microsoft, there is scant sign of panic, despite its trailing position and its failed bid to buy Yahoo as a catch-up strategy. Microsoft sees an evolution in computing instead of any disruptive revolution that would imperil the company, said Craig Mundie, Microsoft's chief research and strategy officer.

22   Microsoft, Mundie said, is preparing for a widening world of both cloud computing and "client" machines, not only PCs but also cellphones, cars, game consoles and televisions, all running Microsoft software.

23   "Our conclusion is no, you're not really looking at some tectonic shift," Mundie said. "The next big platform is the union of the clients and the cloud." (From *International Herald Tribune*, June 27, 2008)

New Words

antitrust /ˌænti'trʌst/ *adj.* opposing or intended to regulate business monopolies, such as trusts or cartels（反托拉斯的，反垄断的）

blockbuster /'blɒkˌbʌstə/ *n. infml* sth very effective or remarkable, esp. a very successful film or book（轰动一时的事物）

compatible /kəm'pætəbl/ *adj.* able to exist together（兼容的）

console /kən'səʊl/ *n.* a flat surface containing the controls for a machine, piece of electrical equipment etc（控制台，操纵台）

deploy /dɪ'plɔɪ/ *v.* to spread out or arrange for effective action; to put (a software system) available for use（展开；运用）

disruptive /dɪs'rʌptɪv/ *adj.* causing disorder

erode /i'rəʊd/ *v.* (of sb's power, authority, rights etc) to be gradually reduced, destroyed, or removed

externality /ˌekstɜː'næləti/ *n.* the condition or quality of being external or externalized（外形；外化，表面化）

forefront /'fɔːfrʌnt/ *n.* the leading position

garner /'gɑːnə/ *v.* to collect or store

hindsight /'haɪndsaɪt/ *n.* understanding the reasons for an event after it has actually happened

imperil /ɪm'perɪl/ *v.* to put into danger

inkling /'ɪŋklɪŋ/ *n.* (*usu. in questions or negatives*) a slight idea or suggestion

lament /ləˈment/ *v.* to feel or express deep sorrow (for or because of)（为……痛惜）

landmark /ˈlændmɑːk/ *n.* an important point in a person's life, in the development of knowledge etc

lucratively /ˌluːkrəˈtɪvlɪ/ *adv.* (of a business) bringing in plenty of money（获利多地，赚钱地）

nurture /ˈnɜːtʃə/ *v.* to cause or encourage to develop

prominently /ˈprɒmɪnəntlɪ/ *adv.* famously

scant /skænt/ *adj.* hardly enough（缺乏的）

seminal /ˈsemɪnəl/ *adj.* influencing future development in a new way（启发新观念的；对未来发展有重大影响的）

shareholder /ˈʃeəˌhəʊldə/ *n.* an owner of shares in a business

spreadsheet /ˈspredˌʃiːt/ *n.* a type of computer program that allows figures to be shown in groups so that quick calculation can be made（电子数据表）

striver /ˈstraɪvə/ *n.* a person who makes a great effort, esp. to gain sth

successor /səkˈsesə/ *n.* a person who takes position formerly held by sb else

tectonic /tekˈtɒnɪk/ *adj.* relating to construction（构造的）

trail /treɪl/ *v.* to fall behind

workbench /ˈwɜːkbentʃ/ *n.* (a table with) a hard surface for working on with tools（工作台）

Notes

1. Bill Gates is retiring, sort of.—比尔·盖茨即将退休，似乎是这样。(On June 16, 2006, Gates announced that he would move to a part-time role within Microsoft, leaving day-to-day operations management in July 2008 to begin a full-time career in philanthropy, but would remain as chairman.)

  a. Bill Gates—1955— , American computer entrepreneur（企业家）. He co-founded the computer software company Microsoft and became the youngest multi-billionaire in American history.

  b. sort of—(*Infml*) in a way; somewhat; rather（好像，似乎）(The phrase suggests that the author is uncertain about what he is saying or wondering if he is using the right word.)

2. Bill and Melinda Gates Foundation—founded in 1994 by Bill Gates

and his wife, Melinda, to improve the lives of the poor throughout the world. Known as the William H. Gates Foundation until 1999, it was merged in 2000 with the Gates Learning Foundation. As the world's wealthiest charitable foundation, it had assets of more than ＄30 billion in 2006, when investor Warren Buffet donated an additional ＄31 billion. 比尔与梅琳达·盖茨基金会

3. Internet computing——因特网应用。"Computing" means "the use of computers, esp. as a job, or in business, industry, or administration（计算机应用）"。

4. network effects——网络效应。根据以色列经济学家奥兹·夏伊（Oz Shy）在《网络产业经济学》（*The Economics of Network Industries*）中提出的定义，"当一种产品对用户的价值随着采用相同的产品、或可兼容产品的用户增加而增大时，就出现了网络效应。"受"网络效应"影响的最常见的例子是电话。如果不能打电话给别人，或者你想要交谈的那个人没有购买电话的迹象，就根本不会有人去买电话。此种情况同样适用于传真机、电子邮件、手机、信用卡、借记卡以及其他同类事物。这样一组用户就形成了某种网络。缺乏网络的支持会阻碍一些特定技术的发展，那些没能成功组建网络的企业经常会在这种类型的市场中遭遇失败。

5. Microsoft Basic——the foundation product of the Microsoft company. It first appeared in 1975. It became the basis for a lucrative software licensing business, being used in the majority of the numerous home and personal computers in the 1970s and especially the 1980s. 微软BASIC语言，是一种人机交互式语言。

6. Microsoft DOS——MS-DOS (short for Microsoft Disk Operating System) is an operating system commercialized by Microsoft. It was the most commonly used member of the DOS family of operating systems and was the dominant operating system for computers during the 1980s. It was gradually replaced by operating systems offering a graphical user interface (GUI), in particular by various generations of the Microsoft Windows operating system. MS-DOS操作系统

7. Sloan School of Management at the Massachusetts Institute of Technology——麻省理工学院史隆管理学院 Based in Cambridge, Massachusetts, it is one of the world's leading business schools, conducting cutting-edge（前沿的） research and providing

management education to top students from more than 60 countries.
8. Apple—an American multinational corporation with a focus on designing and manufacturing consumer electronics and closely related software products. The company's best-known hardware products include the Macintosh line of personal computers(Mac 系列个人电脑), the iPod line of portable media players(iPod 系列个人影音随身听), the iPhone, and Ipad. Apple's software products include the Mac OS X operating system(Mac OS X 操作系统), iTunes media browser(iTunes 媒体浏览器), the suite(iLife 系列)of multimedia and creativity software, and Final Cut Studio, a suite of professional audio, and film-industry software products.
9. business ecosystem—商业生态系统,一种新型的企业网络。它是由组织和个人所组成的经济联合体,其成员包括核心企业、消费者、市场中介、供应商、风险承担者等,在一定程度上还包括竞争者,这些成员之间构成了价值链,不同的链之间相互交织形成了价值网,物质、能量和信息等通过价值网在联合体成员间流动和循环。不过,与自然生态系统的食物链不同的是,价值链上各环节之间不是吃与被吃的关系,而是价值或利益交换的关系,也就是说,他们更像是共生关系,多个共生关系形成了商业生态系统的价值网。
10. a "narrow track for success"—a narrow way to success, which means so many people pursue the same conventional path to success that it is difficult for them to attain their goal
11. U. S. government antitrust suit against Microsoft—*United States v. Microsoft* was a set of consolidated civil actions filed against Microsoft Corporation on May 18, 1998 by the United States Department of Justice (DOJ) and twenty U. S. states. The plaintiffs(原告) alleged that Microsoft abused monopoly power in its handling of operating system sales and web browser sales. 美国政府诉微软垄断案,被称为是美国历史上最为重大的反垄断官司之一。1998年5月美国司法部及19个州和华盛顿哥伦比亚特区起诉微软垄断,控辩双方在法庭上唇枪舌剑,斗红了眼。一方是权大势重的政府,一方是财大气粗的世界最大的软件制造商,案情的一起一落牵动着美国人的心。2000年4月,华盛顿哥伦比亚特区地区法院法官杰克逊认定,微软的营销行为造成了垄断。随后,杰克逊进一步判决,将微软一拆为二,分为主要经营操作系统和应用软件的两家公司。然而,微软并不服,决心到上诉法院再战。2001年9月6日,美国司法部宣布不再要求分拆微软,也不再坚持针对微软将互联网浏览器与视窗操作系统捆绑销售的行为进行反垄断的诉求。

  suit—a lawsuit

12. Sony's Betamax versus VHS—Sony 力挺的小型盒带录像系统与 VHS 格式之争。Sony's Betamax is the 1/2 inch (12.7 mm) home videocassette tape recording format introduced on April 16,1975 and derived from the earlier, professional 3/4 inch (19.05 mm) U-matic video cassette format. Like the video home recording system VHS (Video Home System) introduced by JVC in 1976, it had no guard band, and used azimuth recording to reduce cross-talk. Betamax and VHS competed in a fierce format war which saw VHS come out on top in most markets. 盒式录像机系统是使用0.5英寸(12.7mm)磁带的盒式录像机(VCR)技术。它由日本 Sony 公司研制开发。盒式录像机系统大多用于某些专业电视节目的制作,一般消费者用得很少。几乎所有的家用 VCR 都是基于另外一种视频录像技术——家用12英寸录像系统(VHS,家用录像系统)。它是由日本 JVC 公司在1976年开发的一种家用录像机录制和播放标准。70年代索尼对 JVC 录像机大战以索尼的失败告终。

13. but had no inkling how things would play out—(they) didn't have the slightest idea what would be the result in the end.

  play out—continue (a game or struggle) until a result is gained 进行到分出胜负

14. Stern School of Business at New York University—The Leonard N. Stern School of Business is New York University's (NYU) business school. Established in 1900, it is considered to be one of the top business schools in the United States. (纽约大学斯特恩商学院)

15. Facebook and MySpace—Founded in February 2004, Facebook is a social utility that helps people communicate more efficiently with their friends, family and coworkers. The company develops technologies that facilitate the sharing of information through the social graph, the digital mapping of people's real-world social connections. MySpace is an online community that lets people meet their friends' friends.

16. cloud computing—It refers to computing resources being accessed which are typically owned and operated by a third-party provider on

a consolidated basis in Data Center locations. Consumers of cloud computing services purchase computing capacity on-demand and are not generally concerned with the underlying technologies used to achieve the increase in server capability. 云计算，是通过使计算分布在大量的分布式计算机上，而非本地计算机或远程服务器中，企业数据中心的运行将更与互联网相似。这使得企业能够将资源切换到需要的应用上，根据需求访问计算机和存储系统。在未来，我们只需要一台笔记本或者一部手机，就可以通过网络服务来实现我们需要的一切，甚至包括超级计算这样的任务。

17. "The threat to any technology company... a professor at the Harvard business school. —"对任何一个技术公司的威胁就是错过一次重要的技术转移，而微软就错过了向云计算和广告的转移，没有能够将其转化为因特网收入的来源。"哈佛商学院教授 David Yoffie 说。

Harvard business school—Hbs, a renowned business school, founded in 1908, also known as HBS. It is one of the graduate schools of Harvard University. The school offers a full-time MBA program, doctoral programs, as well as many executive education programs. 哈佛商学院。哈佛商学院只是一个研究生院，而不设大学本科。招生标准之一是学生必须具备学士学位。哈佛商学院是美国培养企业人才的最著名的学府，被美国人称为商人、主管、总经理的西点军校，美国许多大企业家和政治家都在这里学习过。哈佛工商管理硕士学位成了权力与金钱的象征，成了许多美国青年梦寐以求的学位。

Questions

1. How does the blockbuster Microsoft products affect people's life?
2. Why is the Gates legacy so impressive?
3. What is the disadvantage to Microsoft when it missed the web services?
4. What does Mundie mean by saying "you're not really looking at some tectonic shift"?
5. Why does the author say Bill Gates is sort of retiring?

> 学 习 方 法

读懂标题（Ⅲ）

二、情况与知识

对初学者而言，要读懂标题，还必须要具备各种文化知识，了解全球动态。否则，若不看消息体的导语和特写体的全文，单凭标题就望文生义，肯定会闹出笑话。见例句：

1. Bush's Monica Problem

乍一看，以为小布什总统也出现了克林顿与 Monica Lewinsky 那样的绯闻（Monicagate）。此标题是在揭发布逼几个联邦检察官（U. S. Attorney）辞职，任用亲信。Monica Goodling 由此揭开了他借反恐大搞窃听的内幕。

2. **Venus** Rising

Venus（Williams）是网坛美国黑人女明星，此处并非是"金星"。

三、具有文学功底

1. 引经据典型，或直接引用、套用、改用文学名著之名、《圣经》典故，或运用名言、谚语、习语等。如：

(1) A Farewell to Arms

前苏联共产党总书记戈尔巴乔夫向前美国总统里根建议彻底销毁核武，引用了海明威所著小说的书名《永别了，武器》。

(2) Liberty is the true mother of invention

强调自由对发明的重要性，套用谚语 "Necessity is the mother of invention"（需要是发明之母）。

(3) Refugees in Dire Straits

"in dire straits"是习语，意思是 "in a difficult or dangerous situation"。

2. 艺术加工型，运用各种修辞手段，如使用比喻、押韵、反语、夸张、双关语等手段以求得生动、形象、幽默、讽刺等效果。因此，读者往往难以一目了然，有的需读完全文才知道其主题思想。例如：

(1) Ballots, Not Bullets

"Ballots"和"Bullets"这两个发音近似的词来达到某种语言上的效果。

(2) Soldiers Salary Soars

每个单词的第一个字母都是"S"，使用的押头韵手法。

(3) Bovver Boy's Hover Ploy

这个标题的四个字为间隔押（尾）韵（alternate rhyme）。

(4) Thatcher's Style Wars

style wars 是 star wars 的谐音,为讽刺性俏皮语。
(5) African Statesman Still Sowing Seeds for Future
因此标题中的"Sowing Seeds"是个双关语。

从以上两种类型的标题可以看出,标题体现编者和记者语言素养和文字技巧等综合水平,有的标题寥寥数字,有的拖沓冗长,有的平铺直叙,有的引经据典,有的极具艺术技巧,讲究修辞手段。日报天天出,不能过夜。期刊编者有时间推敲,标题比报纸精炼优美。

Lesson Twenty-three

课文导读

2006年,巴菲特宣布他将捐出总值达370亿美元的私人财富给慈善事业,一时间引起全球的关注。谁是巴菲特?这位被称为"股神"和誉为"世界上最伟大的投资者"的传奇人物是怎样拥有如此巨大财富的?他又是如何游戏于危机四伏的股票和外汇市场而立于不败之地呢?2007年,巴菲特被《时代》周刊列为全世界最具影响力的人物之一。2008年,他更以620亿美元的身家超过了蝉联13年首富桂冠的微软主席盖茨跃居全球首富。而出乎意料的是,巴菲特却是一个生活非常节俭的人。他给自己的年薪只相当于一个普通白领,而且至今仍然住在他于1958年在家乡内布拉斯加州的奥马哈购买的一所普通房子里。他从小就学习从小事做起,从祖父那里批发口香糖卖,从一分一角积累做起,取得经验和锻炼自己。他也进大学深造过,理论与实践相结合,使他一步步成为当今家喻户晓的人物。其阅历是值得人们借鉴和学习的。

Pre-reading Questions

1. Do you know anything about Warren Buffett?
2. What would you like to do if you want to make big money?

Text

He's Just Like You and Me, Except for the £31bn Fortune

PROFILE: Warren Buffett[1]

1 When F Scott Fitzgerald[2] observed that "the very rich are different from you and me", the novelist was clearly not thinking of people like Warren Buffett. Proclaimed the world's richest man last week, the American investment strategist eats at his local grill and drives to work from the modest home that he bought in unfashionable Omaha,

Nebraska, in 1958, which is today valued at about £350,000.

2   Such is the frugality of the 77-year-old "sage of Omaha", whose wealth increased by £5 billion last year to £31 billion, that when he married in 2006 he bought a discount ring from his own jewellery company. He has vowed to pass on only a small chunk of his fortune to his children, Susie, Howard and Peter. He wants them to have "enough to do anything but not to do nothing".

3   His advice has enriched more investors than anyone else in history, but Buffett pays himself a mere £50,000 a year and prefers such ordinary fare as steaks and hamburgers, washed down with Cherry Coke[3]. Not for him the bright lights of New York[4], even though he owns a private jet, his one extravagance: "I have everything I need and am very comfortable right here at home in Omaha. I feel sorry for people who are consumed by possessions[5]."

4   Known for his wry homilies, Buffett has bet his house in jest against that of his friend and bridge partner Bill Gates, the Microsoft co-founder now relegated from first to third place in the zillionaire stakes, according to *Forbes* magazine.[6] They used to meet for games at a Holiday Inn[7] near Buffett's home, but of late they play online—Buffett's only concession to newfangled technology—under the user names "T-bone" (Buffett) and "Challenger X"[8].

5   Buffett's ranking may seem puzzling, given that in 2006 he announced he was donating his fortune to charity, with about £15 billion going to the Bill and Melinda Gates Foundation[9], dedicated to combating Aids, tuberculosis and malaria. The donations are in instalments[10]—the latest for £880 m—but Buffett just gets richer.

6   This act of philanthropy was an indirect consequence of Buffett's unorthodox role as a husband and lover. In 1952 he married Susan Thompson, a former cabaret singer who, after raising their children, announced in 1977 that she was leaving Omaha to pursue her singing career in San Francisco. They remained married and on good terms, holidaying together and helping charitable groups.

Buffett Donates Billions to Gates Foundation.

7 Buffett had always expected that Susan would inherit his wealth and pass it to charitable causes, he explained later: "When we got married, I told Susie I was going to be rich ... [not] because of any special virtues of mine, but simply because I was wired at birth to allocate capital[11]." Susie was less than thrilled by this prospect: "But we were totally in sync about what to do with it—and that was to give it back to society."

8 In 1978 Susan introduced her husband to Astrid Menks, a Latvian working as a waitress in a restaurant, who soon moved in with him. Buffett sent out Christmas cards signed "Warren, Susie and Astrid".

9 Two years after Susan died from a stroke in 2004, Buffett married Astrid, then 60. "Astrid loves him and takes care of him," his daughter Susie said. "If Warren didn't have a cent she'd still be with him."

10 Just before their wedding, he revealed his plan to release his ever-growing riches to charitable causes for decades to come.

11 Buffett likes to make wealth-generation sound simple. [12] He once summed it up thus: "Rule No 1: never lose money. Rule No 2: never forget rule No 1." His prescience is world-renowned: he refused to buy stocks in the booming 1960s, only to strike gold[13] in the plummeting 1970s. He walked away from the dotcom boom in the 1990s, sticking with boring blue-chips such as Gillette, Coca-Cola and American Express[14]. He always came up smelling of greenbacks. [15]

12 He is one of the most respected voices in financial America[16], embodying Midwest virtues of probity, modesty and common sense, so his recent warning that America was in recession stirred panic.

13   He was born in 1930 in a house in Omaha on the banks of the Missouri River, the son of Leila and Howard, a Republican stockbroker elected to Congress on a platform described as "to the right of God"[17]. His grandfather ran the family's grocery store dating from 1869, where Buffett's fortune began.

14   "My grandfather would sell me Wrigley's chewing gum[18] and I would go door to door around my neighbourhood selling it," he recalled. "He also sold me a six-pack of Coca-Cola for a quarter [25c] and I would sell it for a nickel [5c] each, so I made a small profit." He supplemented his earnings by selling lost golf balls. When the family moved to Washington, the 12-year-old Warren took on five paper rounds, using his access to customers to sell them magazine subscriptions.[19]

15   By the following year he was making £80 a month, an incredible sum in the 1940s. Through shrewd investment, at the age of 14 he saved the £400 needed to buy 40 acres of local farmland, which he rented out. His first dabble in the stock market earned him a $2 profit before the shares shot up, teaching him that patience pays off.[20]

16   After a first degree at the University of Nebraska Lincoln, he went to Columbia Business School in New York, where he fell under the spell of Benjamin Graham[21], an investment guru who awarded Buffett the only A$^+$ grade he ever bestowed.

17   Buffett worked for his mentor[22] after graduation but outgrew him, according to Roger Lowenstein, Buffett's biographer: "Graham would amaze the staff with his ability to scan a page with columns of figures and pick out an error. But Buffett was faster at it."

18   His strategy was to search for "cigar butt" companies, no longer of interest to the market and thus undervalued, but which still had "a few puffs" left in them.[23]

19   In 1962 he spotted a run-down Massachusetts textile firm, Berkshire Hathaway[24], which he bought and transformed into an insurance company. His empire now extends to sweet shops and Fruit of the Loom clothing.[25] He has shares in The Washington Post, Tesco[26] and a controlling stake in CE Electric[27], which supplies energy to 3.7m English homes.

20   He denounced the "outright crookedness" of Enron[28], the collapsed

American conglomerate, and the dubious methods used by corporations to calculate pension charges[29] and stock option[30] costs: "CEOs will be respected and believed ... only when they deserve to be. They should quit talking about some bad apples and reflect instead on their own behaviour."

21   This rigor extends to his family dealings[31], notably his past stinginess with his children. On one occasion his daughter Susie needed $20 to get her car out of an airport car park, but Buffett made her write a cheque to him first. He doesn't spare himself either: "Only my clothes are more expensive now, but they look cheap when I put them on."

22   To most Americans, however, Buffett is a national treasure. But as he put it: "You only learn who has been swimming naked when the tide goes out." (From *The Sunday Times*, March 9, 2008)

New Words

bad apple a discontented, troublemaking, or dishonest person
bestow /bi'stəʊ/ v. to give
blue-chip /'bluː-tʃɪp/ n. an industrial share that is expensive and in which people have confidence（蓝筹股）
bond /bɒnd/ n. an official paper promising to pay a sum of money to the person who holds it, esp. one by which a government or company borrows money from the public with the promise of paying it back with interest at a fixed time（债券，证券）
butt /bʌt/ n. the last unsmoked end (of a cigar)（烟蒂）
cabaret /'kæbəreɪ/ n. a performance of popular music and dancing while guests in a restaurant have a meal, usu. at night（餐馆夜间的歌舞表演）
conglomerate /kən'glɒmərɪt/ n. a large corporation formed by merging several different firms
crookedness /'krʊkɪdnɪs/ n. dishonesty（不诚实；狡诈）
dabble /'dæbl/ n. working at or studying sth without serious intentions（涉足，浅尝）
denounce /dɪ'naʊns/ v. to express strong disapproval of, esp. publicly; to condemn[（公开）指责；谴责]
dubious /'djuːbɪəs/ adj. causing doubt; of uncertain value or meaning or possibly dishonest

extravagance /ɪksˈtrævɪgəns/ *n.* excessive spending; sth extravagant（奢侈行为；奢侈品）
frugality /fruːˈgælɪtɪ/ *n.* thrifty（节俭）
greenback /ˈgriːnbæk/ *n.* a U.S. banknote
guru /ˈguruː/ *n.* a greatly respected person whose ideas are followed（权威；大师）
homily /ˈhɒmɪlɪ/ *n.* a talk, esp. a long one, which gives advice on how to behave
instalment /ɪnˈstɔːlmənt/ *n.* a single payment of a set which, in time, will complete full payment of a debt[（分期付款中）每一期摊付的款项]
jest /dʒest/ *n.* the act of speaking without serious intention; joke
Latvian /ˈlætvɪən/ *n.* 拉脱维亚人
mentor /ˈmentə/ *n.* a person who gives advice to another over a period of time, esp. to help sb in their working life
Missouri River /mɪˈzʊərɪ ˈrɪvə/ a long river in the U.S., flowing from the Rocky Mountains to join the Mississippi at St Louis（密苏里河，源自落基山脉，在圣路易斯汇入密西西比河）
Nebraska /nɪˈbræskə/ a state in central U.S.（内布拉斯加州）
newfangled /ˈnjuːˌfæŋgld/ *adj.* (of ideas or things) modern or fashionable in a way that many people dislike or refuse to accept（新潮的，新花样的）
Omaha /ˈəʊməˌhɑː/ the largest city in the state of Nebraska of U.S.（奥马哈）
philanthropy /fɪˈlænθrəpɪ/ *n.* a feeling of kindness and love for all people, esp. as shown in an active way by giving help or money to people who are poor or in trouble; benevolence [慈善（事业），仁慈]
plummet /ˈplʌmɪt/ *v.* to fall steeply or suddenly
prescience /ˈpresɪəns/ *n.* the ability to foresee sth
probity /ˈprəʊbɪtɪ/ *n.* the quality of being honest and trustworthy; integrity（正直；诚实）
proclaim /prəˈkleɪm/ *v.* to make (sth) known officially or publicly; to announce
profile /ˈprəʊfaɪl/ *n.* a brief biography of sb or description of sth in a newspaper article, broadcast programme, etc.[（报刊文章、广播节目等中的）人物或事物之简介，概况，传略]
puff /pʌf/ *n.* the action of taking the smoke from a cigarette into your lungs

recession /rɪ'seʃən/ *n.* a period of reduced trade and business activity 经济衰退期

relegate /'relɪgeɪt/ *v.* to dismiss sb or sth to a lower or less important rank, task or state

sage /seɪdʒ/ *n.* sb, esp. an old man or historical person, well known for their wisdom and long experience

stake /steɪk/ *n.* ranking (esp. in a horse race); a share in a business, that gives one an interest in whether it succeeds or fails(名次;股份)

stinginess /'stɪndʒɪnɪs/ *n.* meanness 小气,吝啬

stroke /strəʊk/ *n.* an occasion when a blood tube in the brain suddenly bursts or is blocked, which damages the brain and can cause loss of the ability to move some part of the body 中风

subscription /səb'skrɪpʃən/ *n.* an arrangement to pay regularly for sth 订购;订阅

supplement /'sʌplɪmənt/ *v.* to add to; to provide an additional amount to

sync /sɪŋk/ *n.* synchronization; agreement 同步;一致

thrill /θrɪl/ *v.* to cause to feel a sudden very strong feeling of excitement, joy, or sometimes fear, that seems to flow round the body like a wave

unorthodox /ʌn'ɔːθədɒks/ *adj.* different from usual or ordinary beliefs, methods etc.; not conventional or traditional 非正统的;非常规的

wry /raɪ/ *adj.* (esp. of an expression on the face) showing a mixture of amusement and displeasure, dislike, or disbelief 苦笑的,嘲讽的

zillionaire /ˌzɪljə'neə/ *n.* a person having an immense, incalculable amount of wealth 亿万富翁,大富翁

Notes

1. Warren Buffett—1930— , American investor, businessman and philanthropist. He is regarded as one of the world's greatest stock market investors, and is the largest shareholder and CEO of Berkshire Hathaway. With an estimated net worth of around US $62 billion, he was ranked by *Forbes* as the richest person in the world in March, 2008.

2. F Scott Fitzgerald—1896—1940, an American writer of novels and short stories. He has been widely regarded as the literary spokesman of the Jazz age and one of the twentieth century's great writers.

Fitzgerald is considered a member of the "Lost Generation". 菲茨杰拉德的代表作是 1925 年出版的《了不起的盖茨比》(*The Great Gatsby*),小说入木三分地刻画了财富和成功掩盖下的未被满足的欲望,反映了 20 世纪 20 年代"美国梦"的破灭。

3. washed down with Cherry Coke—swallowed down together with Cherry Coke

   Cherry Coke—a brand of Coke produced by Coca-Cola Company

4. Not for him the bright lights of New York—The bright lights of New York are not for him.

   the bright lights—灯红酒绿的娱乐场所

5. who are consumed by possessions—who are so preoccupied with making money and obtaining possessions that they could not live a true life

   consume—fill the thoughts or feelings of sb continuously, esp. in a damaging way 使某人为某种思想或感情而不断受折磨

6. Known for his wry homilies... according to Forbes magazine.—巴菲特以嘲讽式说教闻名,他曾开玩笑用他的房子与他的朋友、桥牌搭档并且与人共同建立微软的比尔·盖茨打赌。据《福布斯杂志》报道,盖茨已经从亿万富翁排行榜的第一名降到第三名。(After 13 years on top of the Forbes' List of Billionaires, Bill Gates is no longer the richest man in the world. That honor now belongs to Warren Buffett.)

   Forbes magazine—Forbes is an American publishing and media company. Its flagship publication, Forbes magazine, is published bi-weekly. Its primary competitors in the national business magazine category are *Fortune*, which is also published bi-weekly, and *BusinessWeek*. The magazine is well-known for its lists, including its lists of the richest Americans (the Forbes 400) and its list of billionaires. The motto of *Forbes* magazine is "The Capitalist Tool." 《福布斯》杂志是福布斯集团[Forbes Inc.]的旗舰刊物,美国最早的大型商业杂志,全球最为著名的财经出版物之一。《福布斯》杂志着重于描写企业精英的思维方式,倡导"企业家精神"。其报道不是停留在新闻事实的层面,而是着力于洞悉新闻背景,把握动态信息和行业趋势,深入探讨和研究企业运作的经济环境。该杂志的前瞻性报道为企业高层决策者引导投资方向,提供商业机会,被誉为"美国经济的晴雨表"。现任福布斯公司 CEO 斯蒂夫·福布斯先生(Steve Forbes)也是

杂志的总编辑。
7. Holiday Inn—a brand name applied to hotels within the InterContinental Hotels Group (IHG). 假日酒店是洲际酒店集团的酒店品牌。假日酒店及度假村于1952年在美国成立，目前在全世界拥有超过40万间客房(3,125家酒店)，是全球最具知名度的国际酒店品牌之一。
8. but of late they play online ... under the user names "T-bone" (Buffett) and "Challenger X"—but recently, naming themselves "T-bone" (Buffett) and "Challenger X", they play bridge on the Internet, which is the only new thing that Buffet makes use of.
9. Bill and Melinda Gates Foundation—比尔与梅琳达·盖茨基金会 (See Note 2 of Lesson Twenty)
10. The donations are in instalments—他的慈善款是分期捐赠的

    in instalments—paying small sums of money at regular intervals over a period of time, rather than paying the whole amount at once 分期付款；分期交付
11. I was wired at birth to allocate capital.—I was born with the ability to control large sums of money.

    wire—(*infml*) to prepare, equip, fix, or arrange to suit needs or goals 使准备好；使具备达到某种需求或目标的能力
12. Buffet likes to make wealth-generation sound simple.—Buffet likes to make the process of making money seem simple.

    generation—the process of producing sth or making sth happen
13. strike gold—to make money; to lay one's hand on wealth or success
14. boring blue-chips such as Gillette, Coca-Cola and American Express—诸如吉列、可口可乐、美国运通这样不活跃的蓝筹股

    a. blue-chip—指Blue Chip Stock蓝筹股，即在所属行业内占有重要支配性地位、业绩优良、成交活跃、红利优厚的大公司的股票。"蓝筹"一词源于西方赌场，在西方赌场中，有三种颜色的筹码，其中蓝色筹码最为值钱。

    b. Gillette—The Gillette Company, which was founded by King C. Gillette in 1901 as a safety razor manufacturer. It was based in Boston, Massachusetts, United States. In July 2007, Gillette was dissolved and incorporated into Procter & Gamble. 吉列公司，主要生产剃须产品、电池和口腔清洁卫生产品。公司的创始人金克·吉列曾经是一名瓶盖公司的推销员。2007年被世界上

最大的日用消费品公司之一的宝洁公司收购。

15. He always came up smelling of greenbacks. —He always makes a lot of money. 字面义为：他走过来时身上总是散发着钱的味道。

16. He is one of the most respected voices in financial America—He is one of the most respected persons in the financial sector of America, whose opinions are highly valued. (Here "voices" refers to people, esp. people who say sth. The figure of speech used here is metonymy[借喻].)

17. a Republican stockbroker elected to Congress on a platform described as "to the right of God"—a republican stockbroker who was elected a member of Congress because of his right-wing view of politics

    a. platform—position; view of politics 候选人或政党的政纲

    b. to the right of God—extremely right (Here "God" symbolizes the Republican point of view because the Republicans often appeal to God when expressing their ideas.)

18. Wrigley's chewing gum—The William Wrigley Jr. Company was founded in 1891 originally selling products such as soap and baking powder. In 1892, William Wrigley, Jr., the company's founder, began offering chewing gum with each can of baking powder. The chewing gum eventually became more popular than the baking powder itself and Wrigley's reoriented the company to produce the popular chewing gum. 美国箭牌糖果有限公司是全球最大的口香糖生产及销售商。箭牌公司在中国的品牌组合包括"绿箭"(Doublemint)、"黄箭"(Juicy Fruit)、"白箭"(Wrigley's Spearmint)、"箭牌咖啡口香糖"(Wrigley's coffee gum)、"益达"(Extra)无糖口香糖、"劲浪"(Cool Air)超凉口香糖、"大大"(Ta Ta)泡泡糖和"真知棒"(Pim Pom)棒棒糖等。

19. the 12-year-old Warren took on five paper rounds ... to sell them magazine subscriptions.—Warren made five regular journeys to deliver newspapers and at the same time, he made use of the opportunity to urge customers to subscribe to magazines.

    a. take on—to accept (work, responsibility etc.)

    b. paper round—a regular journey to deliver newspapers to a number of houses, offices etc

20. His first dabble ... before the shares shot up, teaching him that

patience pays off.—他第一次涉足股市赚了两美元,可是在他卖出之后股市便大涨,这件事教会他有耐心才会有好的收益。

  a. shoot up—to go upwards, increase, or grow quickly 迅速升起;猛增

  b. pay off—to yield a profit or result; result in success 有好的结果;获利;成功

21. he fell under the spell of Benjamin Graham—he was strongly fascinated by Benjamin Graham

  a. spell—a condition caused by magical power; enchantment 着魔,着迷

  b. Benjamin Graham—1894 – 1976, an influential economist and professional investor. Graham is considered the first proponent of Value Investing, an investment approach he began teaching at Columbia Business School in 1928 and subsequently refined with David Dodd through various editions of their famous book *Security Analysis*. Buffett, who credits Graham as grounding him with a sound intellectual investment framework, described him as the second most influential person in his life after his own father. 本杰明·格雷厄姆被誉为"证券分析之父"。

22. mentor—见"语言解说"

23. His strategy was to search for "cigar butt" companies ... still had "a few puffs" left in them.—Buffett's strategy in business was to search for those undervalued companies that had been thrown away by other investors because they thought that such companies were of no interest to the market. However, Buffett thought that these companies still had the potential to develop to a certain extent, and he thus would invest and put new energy in them. 〔The phrases "cigar butt"（烟蒂）and "a few puffs"（抽上几口）are vividly used to indicate that such companies, though considered to be worthless by some people, have development potentials.〕

24. Berkshire Hathaway—a conglomerate holding company(联合控股公司) headquartered in Omaha, Nebraska, U.S., that oversees and manages a number of subsidiary companies. Its core business is insurance. Warren Buffett is the company's chairman and CEO. 巴菲特接手之后,一度濒临破产的伯克希尔-哈撒韦公司不仅很快起死回生,而且已成长为资产达1,350亿美元的"巨无霸"。如今,伯克希

尔-哈撒韦公司旗下已拥有各类企业约50家,其中最主要的产业是以财产保险为主的保险业务。此外,伯-哈公司还生产从油漆、毛毯到冰激凌等一系列产品,该公司同时持有诸如沃尔玛和宝洁等许多大型企业的股票。

25. His empire now extends to sweet shops and Fruit of the Loom clothing. —Now, the range of his business has reached sweet shops and Fruit of the Loom clothing.

  Fruit of the Loom clothing——一种服装品牌

26. Tesco—a British-based international grocery and general merchandising retail chain. It is the largest British retailer by both global sales and domestic market share with profits exceeding ￡2 billion. In 2008, the company overtook German retail giant Metro AG to become the world's fourth largest retailer.

27. CE Electric—CE Electric UK Funding Company is an electrical distribution company.

28. Enron—a U.S. company that in 2001 became the largest bankruptcy and stock collapse in U.S. history up to that time. The company was formed in 1985 when InterNorth purchased Houston Natural Gas to create the country's longest natural-gas pipeline network. Renamed Enron in 1986, the company transformed itself in the 1990s from a gas-pipeline business into a natural-gas and electricity trading giant. By 2000 it was the seventh largest U.S. corporation. Enron employed shoddy(卑劣的) and deceptive accounting practices to hide its financial losses (and occasionally its gains). 安然公司原是世界上最大的综合性天然气和电力公司之一,在北美地区是头号天然气和电力批发销售商。这个拥有上千亿资产的公司2002年因为财务造假丑闻在几周内破产。安然欧洲分公司于2001年11月30日申请破产,美国本部于12月2日后同样申请破产保护。从那时起,"安然"已经成为公司"欺骗"的同义词。

29. pension charges——养老金费用

30. stock option—an option giving the holder, usually an officer or employee, the right to buy stock of the issuing corporation at a specific price within a stated period 优先认股权,股票期权。一般是指企业在与经理人签订合同时,授予经理人将来以签订合同时约定的价格购买一定数量公司普通股的选择权,经理人有权在一定时期

后出售这些股票,获得股票市价和行权价之间的差价,但在合同期内,期权不可转让,也不能得到股息。
31. family dealings—family relations
    dealings—personal or business relations

Questions

1. Does Warren Buffett live an extravagant life?
2. How does Buffett educate his children?
3. How did Buffett deal with his big fortune?
4. What are Buffett's rules of making money?
5. What is the most valuable quality in Buffett?
6. How do you understand the last sentence in this article?

语言解说

Mentor 和 Guru 等

本课第17段中"mentor"的意思是"a wise and trusted counselor or teacher"或"an influential senior sponsor or supporter",即"有智慧且可以信赖的导师"、"有影响的资深赞助者或支持者",常用来指在某一领域有影响的人物。如用于政治常指总统等高官"受信赖的顾问"(a trusted counselor),如候选人的竞选顾问,总统的政治、法律顾问等。在小布什总统作 buzzword(时髦词)时,它已被 guru 所代替。为避免重复,两词也交替使用。

guru 的原意指"印度教或锡克教的宗教领袖或宗教教师",后转喻到政治领域,指"有权势或影响的政治保护人或支持者",后来词义进一步变化,用来指"任一领域所公认的领军人物(a recognized leader in a field)"或"受人信赖的顾问、师爷或导师(a trusted counselor and adviser; a mentor)"。例如:
   a. The elder senator was her political **guru**.
   b. the city's cultural **gurus**.

现在最时髦的词已不是小布什执政后期的"troop surge",指布什政府为今后撤军反而要在伊拉克加速"兵力的激增"。Barack Obama 上台后的"smart power"是一般最时髦的词,即使硬实力和软实力相结合而使用"巧实力"。还有本书节课出现的"entitlements"曾是20世纪80年代初出现的时髦词,当时美国有所大学的英文系教授都不知何意,让学生问政治系或社会学系教授。

　　应该指出,报刊为赶时髦和创新,有的时髦词用得不如旧词意思准确,不拟随意模仿使用。虽然这类词语不再时髦,但大多数都保留了下来,且还常诸报端。